THE CANADIAN ROCKIES
Bicycling Guide

by
Gail Helgason
and
John Dodd

Also by John Dodd and Gail Helgason

BICYCLE ALBERTA
THE CANADIAN ROCKIES ACCESS GUIDE

THE CANADIAN ROCKIES
Bicycling Guide

by
Gail Helgason
and
John Dodd

LONE
PINE

The Publishers:
Lone Pine Publishing

Typesetting by Pièce de Résistance Typographers, Edmonton

Printed by D.W. Friesen and Sons Ltd., Altona, Manitoba

Canadian Cataloguing in Publication Data

Helgason, Gail,
    The Canadian Rockies bicycling guide

    Includes index.
    ISBN 0-919433-09-X

    1. Cycling - Rocky Mountains, Canadian -
Guide-books.* 2. Rocky Mountains, Canadian
- Description and travel - Tours.* I.
Dodd, John,   II. Title.
GV1046.C3H44 1986   917.11'044   C86-091181-0

Cover Photo Jon Murray

Contents

Acknowledgements

Our thanks to Parks Canada staff in Banff, Jasper, Yoho, Kootenay, Glacier, Mount Revelstoke and Waterton Lakes, who patiently answered our many queries and provided slides. Our appreciation goes as well to the staff at Travel Alberta, especially photo librarian Shirley Hauck for her invaluable assistance, and to staff at Kananaskis Country and Tourism British Columbia.

Jon Murray of Vancouver provided a selection of fine cycling photos, including the cover photo. Denise Ashby, director of recreation and transportation with the Canadian Cycling Association, answered many queries. The Canadian Hostelling Association, the British Columbia Museum Association and chambers of commerce in Banff, Jasper, Kimberley, Nelson, Creston and Revelstoke also contributed.

We are grateful to all the cyclists along the road who have enriched our travels and encouraged us in this project.

May the roads ride with you and the winds be always at your back.

Bow Summit, Icefields Parkway   TRAVEL ALBERTA

1

Bicycle Touring in the Mountains

Welcome to the best cycling in North America. With their staggering scale, smooth highways and impressive national and provincial parks, the Canadian Rockies form a backdrop of grandeur for the visitor to experience with all five senses — on a bicycle.

Some of the 60 tours in this book follow wild rivers or traverse subalpine passes, travelling from dry grasslands to interior rain forests of huge skunk cabbage and thorny Devil's Club. Others wind beside clear, tranquil mountain lakes. Some challenge the energetic; others are casual tours of an hour or two, suitable for anyone with a bike.

We do not commend the Canadian Rockies to the cyclist for beauty or challenge alone. The Colorado Rockies are stunning, so too Wyoming's Grand Tetons, British Columbia's Gulf Islands and New England's autumn colors.

What the Canadian Rockies offer the cyclist are beauty, challenge — and relaxation. Some might call it safety.

Most of the highways in other scenic parts of Canada, the United States and Europe require unrelenting vigilance by the touring cyclist. You can't allow yourself to be overwhelmed by the unfolding spectacle. Not when you have to watch out for cars, trucks and meandering RVs all the time. You have to concentrate to remain far enough over to the right — where the pavement may be cracked and rough — for safety.

In the Canadian Rockies and most of the scenic areas to the east and west of them, wide paved shoulders (sometimes as wide as the driving lane) tend to be the rule, not the exception. The cyclist is separated from motor vehicles much of the time, free to meditate upon glaciers and forests — or simply on lunch.

As much as this may engender a dreamy, meditative state, cyclists still need to plan their tours. They need specific information about the best cycling routes, degrees of difficulty, grades, times, facilities, groceries, phone numbers and more. Unlike the motorist, the cyclist needs to know, and to know in advance.

"Perhaps more than most forms of recreation, long-distance cycling requires some thoughtful preparation if it is to be enjoyed to its fullest," writes Gary Ferguson in *Freewheeling: Bicycling the Open Road.*

Even those who have motored many of the cycling routes described in the book may gain inspiration by reading about them from a cyclist's point of view. The countryside changes when seen over the handlebars of a bike as you sweat up mountain passes and whizz down the other side. You feel part of it; not a visitor behind glass. Those who frequently travel a highway in an automobile report that they experience it anew on a bicycle.

Too many long-distance cyclists, after completing the famed Icefields Parkway, mistakenly feel they have "done" the Canadians Rockies — when in fact they have only started.

Yet this book is for day cyclists as well as long-distance pedallers. So many bicycles brought into the Rockies are not used much, except for perhaps a loop or two around the campground.

The reason must partly be lack of information; it cannot be lack of opportunity or displeasure with cycling. North Americans love to cycle — one of every two Canadian adults owns a bicycle and cycling is the second most popular recreation in Canada, second only to walking.

Although the main focus is the Canadian Rockies, the tours extend into the Selkirk Range to the west, down through the East and West Kootenays in southeastern British Columbia and even across the border into northern Montana.

To do less would cheat the cyclist of natural loops, of opportunities to link tours together for long mountain trips. There's so much glorious cycling country adjoining the Rockies, we couldn't resist describing it.

TRANSPORTATION

Sometimes the hardest part of cycling is getting your bicycle to the mountains. Even when you drive to the mountains, you must still face the hassle of getting bikes back to the starting point at the end of a trip.

Buses operated by Greyhound and other companies run almost everywhere in Alberta and British Columbia. While bicycles are carried at no extra charge, they must be boxed, meaning partial disassembly.

If planning a round trip, you can probably arrange to leave your bicycle box under shelter in back of a store, gas station or hostel. People in the small towns tend to be very helpful. If travelling from A to B, you should find out in advance whether you can obtain or buy a bicycle box at a bicycle or sporting goods store (see Appendix) at your destination.

If travelling to the Rockies by car from distant points and planning an A-to-B cycling tour, consider this option: Box your bike at home. Drive with boxed bike to your destination point. Leave your car and take a bus to the starting point. Then set up your bike and trash the bike box. When you finish the trip, your vehicle awaits and there is no hassle about boxing your bike on the road. (The disadvantage of this system is that you probably travel your cycling route in advance by bus. When you go back along it by bike, there's less feeling of exploration.)

Another possibility is to debox the bike at point A, then ship the empty box to point B on the bus while you ride the route.

Cyclists travelling to Banff, Jasper, Lake Louise, Field, Golden, Hinton or Revelstoke can take their bicycles unboxed on the train, a great convenience.

Similarly in the U.S., there is daily Amtrak train service to such convenient jumping-off places for Glacier National Park (U.S.) and points north as East Glacier and Whitefish in Montana.

The most convenient starting place for cyclists arriving by air (again, bicycles must be boxed on most airplanes) is Calgary International Airport. Brewster Transport offers bus service between the airport and Banff, as well as between Banff and Jasper. Call toll free to 1-800-332-1419.

Or you can take the daily train from downtown Calgary to Banff. The energetic alternative is to simply cycle the 141 kilometres on Highway 1A which is fairly quiet and scenic. See Tour 33. Scheduled air service can also take you to Edmonton (although it is 362 kilometres from Jasper) or to Cranbrook, which is right on Tours 56, 57 and 60. Lethbridge is a fairly convenient arrival point for Waterton and Glacier (U.S.), 130 kilometres away.

CYCLING ROUTES INTO THE ROCKIES

Some will prefer to cycle from east or west into the Rockies. In Canada, the natural inclination is to travel on Highway 1, the Trans-Canada. This is usually the most direct route, the best highway. That's where we'd drive and that's where most of us would cycle.

The Trans-Canada in most parts of the country is the antithesis of everything that cycle-touring should stand for. Cyclists tour to get a feel of the country, to hear the birds and mountain streams, to explore small towns and winding rural routes off the beaten track, to make contact with people and gain a sense of exploration. And that's only part of it.

But the Trans-Canada, with the exception of the stretches in the national parks and a few others, is wide, noisy and usually straight, filled with exhaust fumes, high-speed traffic, strips of fast-food joints and towns hardened to visitors. It has a wide shoulder in most places, to be sure. Yet with such a heavy volume of mixed traffic, the shoulder is scant protection. Indeed, the Trans-Canada has seen too many fatalities involving cyclists.

The alternatives below have their drawbacks. They are invariably longer than the Trans-Canada. Some of the roads, especially on the Prairies, have few services and long stretches between towns. And, at least in B.C., even the alternate roads can sometimes be very busy. Yet virtually every experienced cyclist we've talked to has preferred this kind of road to Canada's main drag.

West Coast to the Rockies

The Trans-Canada is off limits to cyclists, for the most part, between Vancouver and Chilliwack so you can forget it. A better alternative anyway, although very busy in places, is the North Shore route. Follow East Hastings St. from downtown Vancouver and onto the Barnet Highway, which turns into the Lougheed Highway, No. 7, in Port Coquitlam. The route has a paved shoulder (and better scenery than the Trans-Canada) all the way to Hope.

At Hope, resist the temptation to head up the dangerous Fraser Canyon and instead take the stiff climb up 1,352-metre Allison Pass on quieter Highway 3 through scenic Manning Provincial Park.

From there, the road decends into dry ranching country. At Princeton, you could take Highway 5 north for a beautiful cycle through Canada's drylands up to Merritt and Kamloops. From Kamloops, the going is relatively easy, traffic moderate and scenery good up to Tete Jaune Cache and Mt.

Robson. See Tour 20. From there, it's a short cycle down to Jasper and the Icefields Parkway.

Cyclists heading for Banff and points south might stay on Highway 3 at Princeton and parallel the U.S. boundary into Osoyoos.

One good route from Osoyoos is north up the beautiful Okanagan (which can be very hot in summer) to Vernon, then east on Highway 6 to Lower Arrow Lake, across the lake on the ferry and north to Revelstoke at the entrance to Mount Revelstoke and Glacier national parks. See Tours 19 and 52.

We have to admit that some of our tours do follow parts of the Trans-Canada, despite all the nasty things we say about it. However, these sections through Mount Revelstoke, Glacier and Yoho national parks are perhaps the most pleasant, most interesting and least crowded stretches of Highway No. 1 in Western Canada. And they help cyclists make fine loops.

Cyclists heading for Waterton or seeking a southern route to Banff that avoids the Trans-Canada altogether could continue east from Osoyoos on Highway 3, through mining towns, over high passes to Creston. See Tour 56. Then follow Tours 60 and 16 up to Radium and along the gorgeous Banff-Windermere Highway, ending at Banff townsite.

A good route into Waterton and Glacier (U.S.) national parks is through Cranbrook and Fernie, over the Crowsnest Pass and then south from Pincher Creek on Alberta's eastern slopes. See Tours 59, 58, 37 and 36, in that order.

Through the Prairies to the Rockies

Long-distance cyclists from Eastern Canada usually come through Winnipeg. West of Winnipeg, we suggest leaving the Trans-Canada, or coming north from Highway 6, just east of Portage la Prairie and taking Highway 16, the Yellowhead.

Cyclists bound for Edmonton and Jasper could just stay on the Yellowhead which, though busy, is still generally quieter than the Trans-Canada. Those who really want quiet roads might take Highway 15 east from Yorkton. The towns are really tiny and far apart on this road — and that's the route's charm. Highway 15 will take you to Rosetown, south of Saskatoon. Those heading for Edmonton and Jasper should head up to Biggar and North Battleford, then west again on surprisingly hilly and scenic Highway 40 and Highway 14 which leads to Edmonton, then the busy, (but unavoidable) Highway 16 to Jasper.

Cyclists heading for Banff could keep straight at Rosetown on Highways 7 and 9 through mostly flat, open prairie (subject to strong headwinds) past Drumheller (a cycle by the Badlands will be a highlight) and then down to Calgary and scenic Highway 1A (Tour 33) to Banff.

CYCLING WEATHER

All you can really count on is change. Weather conditions in the Rockies vary hour to hour more rapidly than most places. You can get rain, snow and sunshine all in the same day. Over the Rockies, warm, moist air from the Pacific often collides with cool, dry air from the plains. This can cause heavy rain or snow, depending on elevation and the locations or peaks and valleys. The mountains mix up the air flow.

Sometimes, the cyclist must cope with cold, heat, rain and snow and perhaps strong winds, all on the same trip, if not on the same day.

CLIMATE
MEAN SUMMER RAINFALL (millimeters), MEAN ANNUAL SNOW-FALL (centimeters) AND MEAN ANNUAL TOTAL PRECIPITATION (millimeters)

	May	June	July	Aug.	Sept.	Mean Annual Snowfall	Mean Annual Total Precipitation
Banff	39.2	59.3	42.4	48.8	36.2	250.9	470.0
Jasper	30.3	54.8	49.7	48.4	36.8	152.4	409.5

Cold

Cold weather means that head protection is essential, at any time of year in the mountains. Thirty per cent of the body's heat is lost through the head, so a wool cap should be kept handy. In addition, we always carry gloves, even in July and August, to supplement our fingerless cycling gloves.

In spring and fall, we add a compact down parka to the list, although it's usually only needed at night. For cycling, use several layers, perhaps starting with polypropylene long underweather, top and bottoms, and ending with a wool sweater and a windproof/rainproof jacket. Silk sock liners under light wool socks help keep feet warm.

CLIMATE/AVERAGE DAILY MINIMUM (L), MAXIMUM (H), AND MEAN MONTHLY (M) TEMPERATURE DEGREES CELCIUS (°C)

	Banff			Jasper		
	L	**H**	**M**	**L**	**H**	**M**
Jan.	-16	-7	-12	-18	-8	-13
Feb.	-12	-1	-6	-12	-1	-7
Mar.	-9	3	-3	-9	3	-3
Apr.	-4	8	2	-3	10	3
May	1	14	8	2	16	9
June	5	18	12	6	19	12
July	7	22	15	8	23	15
Aug.	6	21	14	7	21	14
Sept.	3	16	9	3	16	10
Oct.	-1	10	4	-1	10	5
Nov.	-8	1	-4	-9	1	-4
Dec.	-13	-5	-9	-14	-5	-9

TRAVEL ALBERTA

Heat

Heat, sad to say, is seldom much of a problem in the Canadian Rockies and we always feel fortunate when we can strip down to cycling shorts and T-shirt.

Rain

The new Gore-Tex or other "breathable" fabrics are ideal for rain, although they're expensive. They let some, but by no means all, of your sweat escape while keeping rain out. However, many of the rain jackets aren't cut long enough for cyclists and allow the backside to get wet when you're crouched over the handlebars.

Coated nylon rain jackets and possibly rain pants are adequate for most conditions, although they should be well-vented to let moisture out. Hard rain tends to get into a backvent when you're crouched over the handlebars.

The fact of the matter, is that rain isn't as much of a problem as you might expect, once you're cycling. Probably the most distressing aspects of rainy days are the lowered clouds and reduced visibility which make the mountain scenery less interesting.

National parks are good places for rainy-day cycling because virtually every campground and most of the larger picnic areas have rain shelters or cook shelters. On the Icefields Parkway, there are hostels every 50 km or so, although these aren't usually open during the day.

Watch that you don't get too cold when you stop on a rainy day. If you start shivering, climb into a sleeping bag promptly, change into dry clothes or build a fire. Do something to preserve body heat. Don't let a chill develop into hypothermia.

Winds

The windiest areas are not in the middle of the Canadian Rockies, they are on its eastern slopes. The prevailing westerlies drop their moisture over the mountains of British Columbia and the high peaks of the Continental Divide, then descend over the eastern slopes, blasting the entrance passes, the foothills and plains with their full force.

Winds, which may be far more unpleasant than rain, can often be a significant hazard in tours on the eastern slopes of the Rockies, especially in the south around Waterton and Glacier (U.S.) where they are strongest. Some days are better spent in a sheltered campsite than grinding along in low gear against the wind, even on flat ground. Encounters with the winds can often be minimized by travelling early in the morning or in the evening.

SNOW AND THE CYCLING SEASON

Sudden snowstorms can blow in, even during July and August. Summer storms are unlikely to cause serious problems, however. The snow should quickly melt and the roads won't stay slippery for long.

June and September can bring heavier snowstorms, although cycling weather is often ideal through these months. The roads should be good, except the high passes which might remain slippery. Snow at this time of year is usually more of an inconvenience for camping. Hostels or motels can look very inviting.

In May or October, cyclists are taking a chance. Sudden storms can leave considerable snow on the ground and roads may stay slippery for some time. On the other hand, the weather can often be good for cyclists, although most of the park facilities are closed. Traffic is wonderfully light and there's an exhilaration in having the mountains almost to yourself.

Cyclists can often have a whole campground to themselves in spring and fall. While the closed campgrounds are barricaded against vehicles, cyclists can just wheel their bikes around the gates and pick a site. Most park authorities have been tolerant of this practice because they realize that cyclists can't just zip 50 km more down the road to the next campground. But it's best to check with them in advance at the information centres to avoid trouble.

By May, much of the snow has gone from the lower valley forest and some of the south-facing slopes. The roads are bare. But you'll still find snow in more shaded areas in campgrounds. The passes and higher campgrounds, such as Columbia Icefield and Mosquito Creek on the Icefields Parkway will probably remain snow-covered into June.

June is our favorite month for mountain cycling. The evenings remain light until 9:30 p.m. or later, making camping a joy. While September is a drier month, darkness comes much earlier. By mid-September, it may or may not be too cold for really enjoyable cycling.

July and August are the warmest, of course. Yet the roads are crowded with an amazing daily armada of cars and recreational vehicles. Campgrounds and other park facilities are strained.

CAMPING

Cyclists have an advantage over motorists at campgrounds. While national park campgrounds are on a first-come, first-served basis with no reservations, cyclists are unlikely to be turned away from a campground (at least in the national parks) because it is officially full. Park authorities will often try to squeeze you in somewhere.

In other cases, you may be able to camp between two occupied sites. Or you can cycle around the campsite and find somebody who looks sympathetic (likely somebody with bicycles in their party) and ask if you could share their site.

Although it is not possible to reserve sites in advance in the national parks, you can show up early in the day and pick a site to your liking. At the larger campgrounds, you are assigned a campsite at the gate (although you can always request a specific site, if it's vacant) and it will be held for you. Most smaller campgrounds have a self-registration system and an "Occupied" card to post beside the site number.

There is a limited reservation system in Kananaskis Country and Peter Lougheed Provincial Park. Phone numbers are provided in Chapter Seven.

Private campgrounds and some in the provincial parks may turn cyclists away if full. You can reserve at most of the private ones. Phone numbers, when available, are in the road logs for each tour.

Cyclists can also "rough camp," although this isn't permitted in the parks. Try to find a clearing close to a stream, well out of sight of the highway.

If you carry a collapsible plastic water container holding a couple of gallons or more, you don't even need to camp close to a stream. Find a good spot, unload your panniers, and then cycle back to a stream or campground to fill the container. With care, that should be enough water for the night and possibly for breakfast. In more inhabited terrain, we just knock on the door of the nearest farmhouse and ask if they would mind filling our water container. Farmers will usually grant you permission to camp overnight on their land, especially if you are able to tell them you have a cookstove and won't be making a fire.

HOSTELS

For the cyclist, the advantages of hostelling are obvious: economy, a chance to meet other travellers and to avoid carrying camping gear, a not-insignificant consideration. Disadvantages include crowding, dozens of people trying to cook dinner at the same time and for some, a sense of regimentation, not to mention separation of the sexes at bedtime. Many feel cut off from the mountains in a hostel; they prefer a quiet tent. You either like hostels or you don't.

Fifteen hostels are situated in the Canadian Rockies. They range in amenities from primitive to superior. The hostels are open to all; members simply pay less than non-members. It is usually necessary to provide your own sleeping gear.

Eight hostels are conveniently spaced along the Icefields Parkway between Banff and Jasper, making it an ideal trip for hostelling.

Except for the Icefields Parkway, however, the long-distance cyclist in the Rockies cannot depend on finding a hostel every night. There are none in Kootenay or Waterton Lakes national parks and only one in Yoho — and it's up a long steep climb at Takakkaw Falls.

Note also that the hostels are popular. It is advisable to make reservations, especially in summer and for groups and families at any time. Some of the hostels are reserved through Edmonton, some through Calgary and some through the actual hostels. Phone numbers are in the road logs.

The large modern international hostel on Tunnel Mountain Road three kilometres from Banff townsite is recommended. It has a few family rooms. Also recommended is Ribbon Creek Hostel in Kananaskis Country, which has family rooms.

Calgary, Edmonton and Jasper townsite have hostels as well. See appendix for addresses and closing nights.

MOTELS, HOTELS AND LUXURY ACCOMMODATION

Those choosing the hotel-motel route enjoy the luxury of travelling without heavy tents, sleeping bags or stoves in their panniers. There's nothing like a hot shower and a soft bed after a day slogging up the passes. But there's a price, a high price.

Accommodation is expensive in Canada's mountain parks, especially in summer. June and September are easier on budgets. Rates are somewhat lower just outside the parks, in Canmore near Banff townsite for example, or in small towns along the eastern slopes of the Rockies. Lodging in the East and West Kootenays also tends to be less pricey.

Banff and Jasper townsite have many cozy chalets, located away from crowds and complete with fireplaces and cooking facilities. These make ideal bases for day cycling, and are enjoyable at the end of long tours.

For those staying in Banff townsite, we recommend chalets situated along Tunnel Mountain Road above the townsite. While they involve a climb, the peace and quiet should be worth it. In Jasper, there are a number of chalets just south of the townsite.

Accommodation is also limited (and mostly expensive) along the Icefields Parkway between Banff and Lake Louise. The Columbia Icefield Chalet is magnificently situated across from the Athabasca Glacier; Num-Ti-Jah Lodge is beside lovely Bow Lake near Bow Pass. Sunwatpa Bungalows is a friendly place with home baking near the falls.

In Waterton, lodging is restricted to the village. There are a few lodges and cabins in Kootenay and Yoho, which are listed in the road logs.

Splurging? If you crave luxury and elegance — and money is no object — you can relax in the baronial splendour of Banff Springs Hotel, situated at the confluence of the Spray and Bow rivers beneath Mt. Rundle. The hotel is even said to have a ghost or two.

Chateau Lake Louise, Jasper Park Lodge, newly-renovated Emerald Lodge in Yoho, the stately Prince of Wales Hotel in Waterton or Glacier Park Lodge in Montana also offer deluxe accommodation in exquisite settings. See appendix for addresses and phone numbers.

Travel Alberta and Tourism British Columbia publish excellent free booklets listing accommodation and campgrounds. See appendix.

GROUP TOURING AND GUIDED TOURS

Several organizations offer group cycling tours in the Rockies and the Kootenays. These vary in comfort and price.

The best known is the Golden Triangle, a 313-km tour held on the Victoria Day long week each May and organized by Calgary's Elbow Valley Cycle Club. Sagwagons and food are provided.

The tour is open to non-members. Reservations should be made well in advance as it is highly popular. See Tour 16 for details.

The Alberta Hostelling Association has a reasonably-priced five-day tour of the Icefields Parkway each summer. Cyclists spend nights in hostels and a support vehicle is provided. Another 1,050-km tour begins in Calgary, goes through interior British Columbia and across the lush Fraser Valley to Vancouver.

Bikecentennial, an American non-profit bicycle touring organization, offers tours through the Rockies beginning in Missoula, Montana. Some tours end in Jasper, others continue on to Alaska.

Rocky Mountain Cycle Tours of Banff organizes cycle tours of the Icefields Parkway, the Kananaskis and the British Columbia Lake district among others, with accommodation ranging from campgrounds to lodges.

Bicycle touring clubs in both Calgary and Edmonton organize numerous tours most summer weekends. Itineraries can include the Icefields Parkway, Logan Pass, and some off-road cycling. This is no doubt the most economical group way to go — and camaraderie is great.

For all-terrain bike enthusiasts, Kootenay Mountain Bike Tours has off-road tours in British Columbia's Kootenay country. A combination of camping and hotel accommodation is provided, plus full meal service. A recent brochure offered a trip through Nakusp, Kaslo and Trout Lake.

See appendix for above addresses and phone numbers.

MOUNTAIN BIKES

The mountain bike opens up all kinds of terrain to the cyclist. Gravel roads — which would be murder on skinny tires — become easy; fireroads become a joy. The cyclist can reach the backcountry and escape motorists with ease.

Mountain bikes, also known as ATBs (all-terrain bikes), can be used to quickly reach the base of mountains that previously required a day's backpacking to attain. All the cyclist needs is a good map showing fireroads and trails and a willingness to explore.

The status of the mountain bike remains uncertain in national and provincial parks, however. Regulations are changing fast. In 1986, Jasper National Park seemed generally open to the mountain bike whereas Glacier National Park (a wetter spot, to be sure) in British Columbia had banned them completely.

General rules everywhere focus on the environmental impact of bicycles — and make sense.

These rules include staying on trails and roadways and generally avoiding fragile alpine areas where a wheelprint can become a channel for water, causing erosion.

Cyclists on the trails should dismount and move off the path when horses approach, preferably on the lower side of the trail. Cyclists should maintain good relations with hikers — who could probably have mountain bikes banned from the trails if they complain enough. Stop and let hikers by on narrow trails. Don't pedal up close behind somebody without calling out a warning ("Hello" is considered better form than "Track!").

Give wildlife time to move off the trail. Pack your litter out. Where possible, check trail conditions and potential hazards at park offices. They may be able to tell you which trails are muddy and therefore less suitable for cycling and which trails might have a bear nearby.

MOUNTAIN BIKE ROUTES

Here is a list of the permitted trail cycling areas in the national parks, effective in 1986. Check with the park offices for changes. See phone numbers in appendix.

Banff National Park

Sundance Road
Spray Fireroad to Spray Reservoir
Goat Creek Trail
Redearth Creek to Egypt Lake via Pharaoh Creek
Bryant Creek Trail to Assiniboine Pass
Brewster Creek to Bryant Creek
Lake Minnewanka Trail to Devil's Gap
Cascade Fireroad to Stoney Creek
Skoki, Red Deer Lakes and Pipestone
Forty Mile Creek, Elk Lake summit to Stoney Creek
Trails in the immediate townsite vicinity

Jasper National Park

All trails open to mountain bikes except Skyline Trail, Tonquin Trail and Lake Annette Trail.

Kootenay National Park

East Kootenay Fireroad from the Concorps Camp to Hector Gorge on Highway 93

West Kootenay Fireroad from Crook's Meadows to the Kootenay Crossing Warden Station (Dolly Varden Fireroad) to the park boundary

Yoho National Park
Kicking Horse/Van Horne Fireroad
Amiskwi Fireroad to Amiskwi III campsite
Ottertail Trail
Ice River Trail

Waterton Lakes National Park
Snowshoe Trail from Red Rock Canyon to Snowshoe Cabin
Akamina Pass Trail
Park Line Trail from Bison Paddock along the park boundary to the
Oil Basin Warden Cabin

Glacier National Park (Canada), Glacier National Park (U.S.) and Mount Revelstoke National Park
Bicycles not allowed on trails

MOUNTAIN BIKING IN KANANASKIS COUNTRY

Kananaskis Country is a paradise for mountain biking with its network of logging roads and long, easy trails that follow lakes and rivers. The terrain tends to be less steep than in the national parks and authorities seem receptive to mountain bikes. (Outside Peter Lougheed Provincial Park mountain bike traffic will sometimes be mixed with motorized trail bikes.)

Nonetheless, bicycles are not welcome in alpine areas or near treeline where delicate plants — that may take decades to grow — can easily be destroyed under the wheel. Nor are bicycles welcome on interpretive trails or heavily-used hiking and equestrian routes.

Approved mountain bike routes in and around Peter Lougheed Provincial Park, in 1986:

— From Boulton parking area, along Whiskey Jack Trail to Pocaterra Trail to Pocaterra Hut parking area.

— From Elk Pass parking area along Elk Pass Trail to Elk Lakes Provincial Park in British Columbia.

— From North Interlakes parking area, as described in Tour 27.

— From Elbow Pass day-use area along Elbow Pass Trail to Elbow Lake and on into Elbow Recreation area.

— From Sawmill day-use parking area along the system of old logging roads that make up the Smith-Dorrien cross-country ski area.

— From Burstall day-use parking area along Burstall Lake trail to Robertson Flats area or from Chester day-use parking along the old logging road to its end.

— Any of the logging roads in the Highwood and Cataract Creek areas.

— Any hydro-line areas.

WATER

The clear tumbling mountain streams look inviting. In the mountains, we used to dip our cup or water bottle into them — and drink deeply. Alas, no more. These days, Giardia Lamblia has reared its tiny, ugly head, and taken the fun right out of drinking.

Giardia is a bacterial parasite which contaminates water, causing stomach upsets and cramps in humans. It is widespread in Western Canada and the U.S. Parks Canada recommends that drinking water taken from lakes, streams and rivers be boiled for five minutes before use.

This is virtually impossible for cyclists to carry out during the day. So we try to fill up water bottles — we always carry at least two each — at pumps, restaurants and filling stations. And we often carry containers of fruit juice as well. Water treatment tablets — which we always bring — are effective against most pollutants, including bacteria in water but are not 100 per cent effective against Giardia. You can buy portable water filters that are said to increase effectiveness.

TRAVEL ALBERTA

WILDLIFE WATCHING

The cyclist has an advantage.

One of the great joys of cycling in the Rockies is the opportunity to see mountain goats, bighorn sheep, deer, wapiti, coyotes and other wildlife, unfettered and in their own setting. The cyclist travels slowly enough to spot what motorists miss.

The best times for wildlife watching are early in the morning and at dusk. Autumn, when game move into the protected valleys, and spring, before the migration to high country, are the recommended times of year.

Even in summer, the visitor is unlikely to cycle Highway 16 in Jasper, the Icefields Parkway, the Banff-Windermere Highway or the Bow Valley Parkway without spotting bighorn sheep, mountain goats, mule deer or elk.

Sheep are frequently encountered on the cycle to Upper Hot Springs in Banff or at Disaster Point on Highway 16 east of Jasper townsite.

Goats haunt the flanks of Mt. Wardle in Kootenay National Park and are often seen on the climb to Yoho's Takakkaw Falls, as well as along the Icefields Parkway between Sunwapta Falls and Athabasca Falls.

Many visitors confuse sheep and goats: if it's brown, it's a sheep, if it's white, even a dirty white, it's a goat.

Watch too for wapiti — the name given to elk of this area. They are grazers who usually migrate to higher areas in summer. In early September Jasper's forests ring with the sound of the bugling males.

We've cycled by moose, the largest of the deer family, on Highway 16 to Mt. Robson, along the marshes of Vermilion and Emerald lakes and at Upper Kananaskis Lake.

Mule deer are also commonly seen in the parks. Rarely seen — but out there somewhere — are wolves, woodland caribou, mountain lions, lynx, and wolverines.

BEARS

Yes, the Rockies and the Kootenays are home to both grizzlies and black bears. This fact should be interesting and perhaps humbling, not terrifying.

In summer, the grizzly tends to stay on avalanche slopes and alpine meadows, feeding on succulent plants and Columbian ground squirrels. The black bear spends the summer near valley floors. Both hibernate in winter.

The cyclist's chances of encountering a grizzly are slight. In 10 years of backpacking, hiking and cycling in the Rockies, we've seen only one — on an avalanche slope, several kilometres away from the road.

Black bears are a more common sight. They're occasionally seen feeding by the roadside along the Icefields Parkway and other mountain roads, usually in more remote portions. Sometimes a bear that has learned to associate humans with food will stand by the roadside, creating a bear-jam of stopped traffic. The cyclist is not protected by a vehicle and should give the bear a wide berth.

Prudent cyclists should take the normal precautions associated with bear country. Parks Canada has an excellent brochure detailing these. Don't leave food lying around and don't take it into your tent. Hoist food overnight onto a line suspended between two trees well over your head and away from tents. Keep a clean camp. Should you come across a bear, it goes without saying that you shouldn't try to approach it or feed it.

Remember that the greatest danger seems to come from a sudden encounter with a grizzly, particularly a threatened mother with cubs. Such meetings are unlikely along paved park roads.

Speedy mountain bikes, however, now take cyclists deep into bear habitats and increase the chances of unfortunate encounters. Mountain cyclists should carry a loud noisemaker and be particularly alert where shrubbery is thick or the berries are ripe.

Just don't let the thought of meeting a grizzly stop you from cycling the Rockies. One parks' report estimates that there is only one bear injury for every two million park visitors.

Cyclists face a far greater danger from the bear in the car behind them.

THE GRAND SLAM: LONG-DISTANCE LOOPS

The longest single tour in this book is rated about 3 1/2 to 4 1/2 days. Yet a number of single tours can be combined into exquisite loops or straight-line journeys for the long-distance cyclist.

BACKBONE OF THE ROCKIES: This is probably the single most outstanding long-distance tour and was part of the first international route selected by Bikecentennial, the non-profit U.S. bicycle touring organization.

From Jasper, take the Icefields Parkway south to Castle Mountain Junction (Tour 15). Then climb Vermilion Pass on Highway 93 (Tour 16) and cycle the Banff-Windermere Highway to Radium. At Radium, head south, still on Highway 93 (Tour 60) to Fort Steele and continue to Elko (Tour 59). At Elko turn east on Highway 3 (Tour 58) over Crowsnest Pass (Tour 37), then south on Highway 6 (Tour 36) to Waterton. From Waterton Lakes National Park, continue south on Highways 6, 17 and 89 (Tour 45) to St. Mary, Montana. Then traverse Logan Pass (Tour 47) to West Glacier, then west to Columbia Falls and Whitefish (Tour 49).

From Whitefish or Columbia Falls, cyclists may make the tour into a partial loop by turning north on Highway 93 to Eureka (Tour 50) and then back into Canada and up to Elko again (Tour 51).

Ambitious cyclists who have reached Whitefish or Columbia Falls could also continue south beside the backbone of the Rockies through Kalispell and Missoula, all the way to Yellowstone and Grand Teton national parks.

We don't personally recommend much of the cycling south of the Grand Tetons through Wyoming because it tends to be extremely windy and the terrain is relatively uninteresting from a bicycle seat. Colorado, however, is first-rate cycling country despite the high elevations and extremely lofty passes.

Bikecentennial has excellent maps and route guides for all these areas. Write them at P.O. Box 8308, Missoula, Mt. 59807 or phone 406-721-1776.

THE GRAND LOOP: Start at Castle Mountain Junction in Banff National Park, as for the Golden Triangle (Tour 16). Head south on the Banff-Windermere Highway 93 to Radium, then south again on 93 and 93A to Cranbrook (Tour 60). From Cranbrook head west on Highway 3 to Creston (Tour 56), then north and west on 3A, 31, and 31A to Kaslo and New Denver (Tour 55 and 54). Cycle north on Highway 6 to Nakusp (Tour 53) and up the Arrow Lakes to Revelstoke (Tour 52). Then turn east on the Trans-Canada up Rogers Pass to Golden (Tours 19 and 18) and through Yoho National Park over Kicking Horse Pass, back to Banff (Tour 16).

MOUNTAINS AND PRAIRIE LOOP: Start in Banff and cycle east on 1A towards Calgary (Tour 33). Before reaching Calgary, head north on Highway 22 from Cochrane, then west to Sundre and north on 22 again to Caroline. (In 1986, this involved a 33-kilometre stretch of gravel road.) Continue north on paved road to Rocky Mountain House. Turn west on Highway 11 to Nordegg and pick up Tour 38 to Saskatchewan River Crossing. Then cycle south over Bow Summit on the Icefields Parkway (Tour 15) to Banff.

Banff townsite, aerial view   TRAVEL ALBERTA

2

Day Tours in Banff, Yoho and Kootenay National Parks

Banff's 350 kilometres of paved roads link mountain scenery of stagger-ing beauty, exquisite lakes, two hot springs, two famous old hotels and a townsite with all services. There is something for every level of cycling. Although Banff is the gateway to the renowned Icefields Parkway tour and the Golden Triangle, it is also the best park for short day-trips. Here is the cycling hub of the Canadian Rockies.

There is a price for all this glory — crowds. Banff, situated just 130 kilometres west of Calgary on the Trans-Canada Highway, is the busiest and most crowded of the mountain parks. It is visited by four million annually (twice as many as Jasper National Park, which is larger in area). The townsite has a permanent population of about 7,000 swelling to 25,000 in summer.

The Trans-Canada, main highway through the park, is extremely busy and truck traffic is heavy. Even though shoulders are wide, we can-not recommend riding it between Calgary and Lake Louise.

Don't let these warnings put you off Banff. Once you pedal a kilometre or two on quiet tours recommended in this book, you can escape the crowds and experience the best of the park.

For those with leisurely pedalling in mind, half a dozen easy loops of an hour or two begin right in Banff townsite and lead to canyons, hot springs and mountain lakes.

Our top recommendations though are the tranquil Bow Valley Parkway (Tour 17), a delightfully level pedal with remarkable scenery; the strenuous Lake Minnewanka Loop (Tour 8), the loop up to Lake Louise (Tour 4) and the Lake Louise-to-Emerald Lake cycle (Tour 1), an outstanding and challenging day-trip over the Continental Divide and down past the famous Spiral Tunnels.

Adjoining Kootenay and Yoho national parks in British Columbia have less to offer day cyclists. No loop tours are possible because of the lack of paved side roads. The Banff-Windermere Highway through Kootenay National Park is spectacular and relatively quiet. Tours 12 and 13 are short out-and-back routes along it. In Yoho, Emerald Lake is the best destination. An enjoyable way to sample this park is to ride to Field and catch the train back to Banff.

Bicycles can be rented in Banff townsite. Trains and buses serve Banff and Yoho parks. Buses are the only public transport to Radium in Kootenay.

LAKE LOUISE TO EMERALD LAKE (RETURN)

TOUR 1

A GEM OF A TOUR

Distance	80 km (50 miles) return
Time	Full day
Rating	Strenuous
Terrain	Long, steep climb eastbound over Kicking Horse Pass; easier westbound
Elev. gain	345 metres (1132 feet) on return leg
Roads	Smooth, wide shoulders on Trans-Canada. Emerald Lake road narrower but in good condition
Traffic	Busy on Trans-Canada, especially in summer. Moderate, slow-moving traffic on Emerald Lake road
Connections	Tours 3, 4, 14, 15, 16, 17

This challenging daytrip takes the cyclist past some of the most dazzling peaks in Banff and Yoho national parks. You climb Kicking Horse Pass to arrive at Emerald Lake, placidly set under Emerald Glacier and Michael Peak.

You follow the busy Trans-

Canada most of the way. Shoulders are wide, however, and the scenery and historic railroad lore more than make up for traffic. The tour offers a look at the Spiral Tunnels, the Canadian Pacific Railway's answer to steep grades.

At Emerald Lake there are hiking trails, horseback riding and even swimming for the hardy. Rustic Emerald Lake Lodge was recently restored.

There are no grocery stores right on the route. Small grocery stores can be found by taking short side trips at the turnoff for Takakkaw Falls and at Field.

OPTION: Cyclists who want a more leisurely ride could stay overnight at West Lake Louise Lodge, Kicking Horse Campground or splurge at Emerald Lake Lodge.

Cyclists can also take the train between Field and Lake Louise, sparing themselves the stiff climb up the pass from the west. Phone Via Rail 1-800-665-8630 for schedule.

Highlights

Start at Lake Louise Village, turn west onto the Trans-Canada and begin a gradual climb. There are striking views of the snow-capped Lake Louise peaks. The ascent up to Kicking Horse Pass is gentle along braided river channels. Westerly winds are common here — good reason for getting an early start.

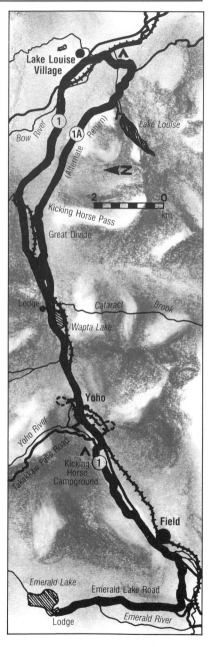

Kicking Horse Pass received its name from a nasty kick suffered by Sir James Hector near the Kicking Horse River on August 28, 1858. Sir James, a member of the Palliser Expedition, was the first white man to venture deeply into what are now Banff, Jasper, Yoho and Kootenay parks. As passes go, this is not a spectacular crossing of the Continental Divide — although what is to come makes up for it.

The road becomes level and the massive ramparts of Cathedral Mountain loom ahead. Cyclists might enjoy a rest stop at pretty Wapta Lake or West Lake Louise Lodge.

Now the exhilaration — a steep descent beside fast-moving Sherbrook Creek. On your left at km 69 is the Old Bridge on the Big Hill. This was part of the first CPR route through Kicking Horse Pass. Before the Spiral Tunnels were built, the Big Hill had the distinction of having the most severe grade of any railway in North America, dropping 400 metres from the Continental Divide.

A viewpoint explains the history of the tunnels. Up to 20 trains a day run in summer, so most cyclists will have a chance to see one wind its way through. The beautiful Yoho Valley extends beyond to the right.

It's a fast, steep descent down to the Yoho River, where the road suddenly levels off beside the braided channels. This can be an exhausting section if the westerlies are in force.

Just 1.6 km along the Emerald Lake Road is a natural limestone bridge carved by water. The bridge itself was once a waterfall, but cascading water cut a new channel underneath it.

The Yoho River has a high mineral content which attracts moose, elk and deer. A salt lick 0.8 km from the Natural Bridge is a good place to spot game.

The Emerald Lake road provides a smooth, easy cycle through lodgepole pine. Emerald Glacier and Michael Peak gleam ahead. Emerald Lake is well-named — if it looks familiar it may be because it adorned the 1954-71 issue of the Canadian $10 bill.

An easy 5.2-km hike leads around the lake. Moose can sometimes be seen feeding at dawn and dusk. Picnic tables a few steps down the trail mark a wonderful spot for a well-earned lunch.

Road Log Tour 1

0 km Start at Lake Louise Village, 56 km NW of Banff townsite. Elev. 1539 m, pop. 355, all services. Turn N on Trans-Canada (Hwy 1).

1.5 Jct. Icefields Parkway (Hwy 93). Keep straight on Trans-Canada.

2 Bow River Bridge.

9 Entering Yoho National Park. Kicking Horse Pass. Elev. 1647 m. Continental Divide. Boundary between

Alberta and British Columbia.

10 Picnic area.

13 Wapta Lake. West Lake Louise Lodge, accommodation and coffee shop (604-343-6311). No groceries.

16 Old Bridge on the Big Hill.

17 Spiral Tunnel Viewpoint. Interpretive display, view of tunnels and Yoho Valley.

24 Turnoff to Takakkaw Falls. Visitor information, Kicking Horse Campground (92 sites, showers). Cathedral Mountain Chalets, store, just up road (604-343-6442).

27 Field. Elev. 1242 m. Park administrative centre. Drinks, snacks at corner gas station. Fresh fruit, deli, takeout food at The Siding in town. No accommodation.

29 Picnic tables.

31 Turn right for Emerald Lake Road.

34 Natural Bridge Viewpoint. Picnic table.

40 Emerald Lake. Elev. 1302 m. Picnic tables, trails, horse stables, canoe rentals. Accommodation and dining at Emerald Lake Lodge, reservations 1-800-661-1367.

TRANS-CANADA HIGHWAY TO TAKAKKAW FALLS

TOUR **2**

A TOUGH ASCENT

Distance 28.4 km (18 miles) return

Time 2 hours up, 1 hour back

Rating Strenuous

Terrain Several very steep hills, remainder moderate

Elev. gain 153 metres (500 feet)

Roads Narrow. No shoulder. Good paved surface

Traffic Busy in summer. Moderate in off-season. No trucks or trailers

Connections Tours 1, 16

Takakkaw Falls are among the highest in North America—and the road up to the base of them is one of the toughest paved routes in the Canadian Rockies. While this is a beautiful tour up a narrow valley, cyclists seeking an easier day-trip

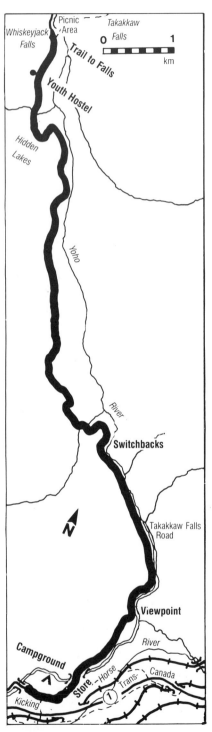

in the same area might consider the route from the Trans-Canada Highway to Emerald Lake (Tour 1).

Fortunately, most of the climbing is confined to a couple of steep sections. Many cyclists will want to dismount and walk up the hill.

The reward for all that exertion is passage up a rugged, steep-walled valley, superb views — and of course, the falls. In addition, the route leads to one of the best networks of hiking trails in Yoho National Park. At the end is a walk-in or wheel-in campground, especially for the likes of cyclists and hikers. The route, however, is probably better done as a day trip from Kicking Horse campground.

Highlights

Mountain goats can often be seen on the slopes of Mt. Field near the start of the route. Up on the same slopes is rubble from the old Kicking Horse Mine. The well-stocked store beyond the information centre provides the only supplies along this route.

The road ascends gradually from the Kicking Horse River to a viewpoint for the CPR's famous Spiral Tunnels. Mt. Stephen to the right and the Cathedral Crags to the left from the viewpoint are especially impressive above the railway. The ascent continues to a viewpoint called Meeting of the Waters, the tumultuous junction of the Kicking Horse and Yoho rivers. The latter is milky from nearby glaciers while the Kicking Horse is clearer since much of its silt settled further upstream.

The climb soon moderates and the road runs close to the Yoho River. The valley narrows with Wapta Mountain on the left and Mt. Ogden on the right.

The hardest part of the trip is the incredibly steep, 180-degree switchbacks up a rock step which blocks the valley. Most cyclists will push their bikes here. Views back down the valley become grand as you ascend.

The road continues high above the Yoho River, crossing numerous avalanche paths and tackling another steep pitch before reaching the falls.

Takakkaw means ''magnificent'' in Cree and the falls do not disappoint. While lacy streamers of spray can be seen from the parking lot, everybody has to get closer. An interpretive path leads for about 1 km towards the base of the falls which originate from meltwater of the Daly Glacier.

Road Log Tour 2

0 km Trans-Canada Hwy, 24 km W of Lake Louise Village, 3 km E of Field, elev. 1372 m. Turn N on sideroad to Takakkaw Falls. Yoho Park information centre. Picnic tables.

Takakkaw Falls, Yoho National Park
YOHO NATIONAL PARK

0.7 Cathedral Mountain general store and chalet, open June-Sept. (604-343-6442). Entrance Kicking Horse campground.

2 Kicking Horse River.

2.5 Steep climb.

3 Meeting of Waters point of interest. Picnic tables.

5.6 Extremely steep ascent on switchbacks.

7.1 Top of grade.

10 Steep climb.

12.5 Whiskey Jack youth hostel and trail to Yoho Pass.

14.2 Takakkaw Falls. Walk-in (wheel-in) campground 1 km. Picnic tables.

LAKE LOUISE TO VALLEY OF THE TEN PEAKS (RETURN) TOUR 3

VALLEY OF THE TEN PEAKS

Distance 28 km (17 miles) return

Time Half-day, with sightseeing

Rating Strenuous

Terrain Steep climb to Moraine Lake Road, then level until descent to valley

Elev. gain 361 metres (1184 feet)

Roads First 3 km rough in places, fair surface to Moraine, no shoulder

Traffic Busy first 3 km. Remainder is moderately busy summer weekends. Buses.

Connections Tours 1, 4, 14, 15, 16, 17

Today Moraine Lake is hardly unknown or unvisited, but it is still superb and unspoiled. Many prefer this small lake, cupped in the commanding Valley of the Ten Peaks, to the tourist-clogged splendour of nearby Lake Louise.

The climb to Moraine Lake is steep though not relentless, and is generally well-graded. While traffic is heavy on summer weekends, it is still quieter than the road to Lake Louise.

No camping or groceries are provided at the lake. There is a restaurant, lodge and chalets.

Moraine Lake is the centre of a superb network of hiking trails, making it an ideal base for those combining a hiking and biking holiday.

OPTION: An outstanding, though strenuous hike-and-bike outing can be had by first hiding bicycles well in the trees (lock them up) near the parking lot at Moraine Lake, then driving or hitch-hiking back to Paradise Valley trailhead. Hike the demanding 20.1 km trail over spectacular Sentinel Pass, ending at Moraine Lake. Then cycle back to your vehicle. The best time is early September when the larches are golden.

Highlights

The worst part of this tour is the first stretch. Out of Lake Louise Village the road is steep and often filled with bumper-to-bumper traffic. Traffic thins after the turn-off onto Moraine Lake Road.

From here the route climbs gradually through fir and spruce forest. Beautiful views appear over

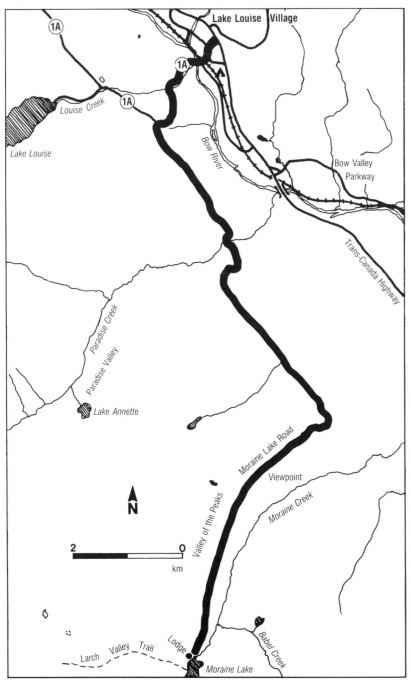

Lake Louise Village

1A

1A

1A

Louise Creek

Lake Louise

Bow River

Bow Valley Parkway

Trans-Canada Highway

Paradise Creek

Paradise Valley

Lake Annette

Moraine Lake Road

Viewpoint

Moraine Creek

Valley of the Peaks

N

2 0
km

Larch Valley Trail

Lodge

Babel Creek

Moraine Lake

the wide Bow Valley as you round the side of massive Mt. Temple, highest of the Lake Louise peaks.

The grade steepens after the trailhead for Paradise Valley, levelling off at km 7. Views open to the Wenkchemna Peaks, named for the Stoney Indian word for "ten". The final descent down to the parking lot is steep and exhilarating.

Moraine Lake, set against jagged peaks, is featured on the $20 bill. The lake owes its spectacular color to suspended rock particles ground up by glaciers.

The best-view can be enjoyed by a 15-minute walk up a rubble pile under the red-toned Tower of Babel. The trail begins at the south end of the parking lot, near the toilets, at the sign for Consolation Lakes. An easy 3.2-km walk skirts the west side of the lake, starting at the lodge. The best way to enjoy the beauty of the lake, however, is to rent a canoe, relax — and drift.

Road Log Tour 3

0 km Lake Louise Village, 56 km NW of Banff. Elev. 1,539 m, pop. 355, groceries, accommodation, campground. Take Lake Louise Road (Hwy 1A) over the tracks and Bow River. Steep climb.

3 Turn left on Moraine Lake Road. Picnic area. Gradual climb through trees.

7 Trail to Paradise Creek.

12 Superb views of Valley of Ten Peaks.

14 Moraine Lake. Elev. 1900 m. network of hiking trails. Canoe rentals. Restaurant, Moraine Lake Lodge and cabins, open June 9 to Sept. 21, 403-522-3733.

"I stood on a great stone of the moraine . . . and while studying the details of this unknown and unvisited spot, spent the happiest half hour of my life." Explorer-alpinist Walter Wilcox, 1893

LAKE LOUISE (LOOP)

TOUR 4

THE MOST FAMOUS LAKE

Distance 22 km (14 miles) loop

Time Half-day, with sightseeing

Rating Intermediate

Terrain Steep climb to lake, then mostly level or downhill

Elev. gain 193 metres (633 feet)

Roads Route to lake has switchbacks, pot-holes, no shoulder. Trans-Canada has good shoulder

Traffic Route to lake traffic-clogged but cars slow moving. Remainder of 1A is quieter. Trans-Canada busy

Connections Tours 1, 3, 14, 15, 16, 17

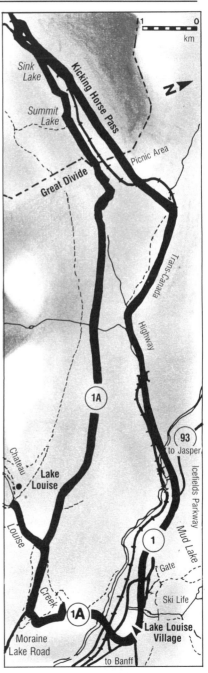

"As a gem of composition and coloring it is perhaps unrivalled anywhere," Sir James Outram wrote of Lake Louise. His assessment endures. A Florida newspaper recently called Lake Louise "the most beautiful lake in the Western Hemisphere." With Victoria Glacier at one end and stately Chateau Lake Louise at the other, the shimmering peacock-blue lake simply is the Canadian Rockies to many.

Cyclists, nonetheless, must be prepared for crowds, for near bumper-to-bumper traffic some days—and a grinding ascent from Lake Louise Village. Once you reach the lake, however, you can hike down the right side, quickly leaving the camera-clicking mobs behind. Or rent a boat and drift over the cold, placid waters.

And after the lake, traffic becomes lighter and you cross the Continental Divide twice and enjoy a smooth descent down from Kicking Horse Pass.

OPTION: Cyclists who climb to the Continental Divide past Lake Louise can take the thrilling option of a fast and glorious coast down the wide shoulder of the Trans-Canada through some of the best mountain scenery in the Rockies, past a viewpoint overlooking the famous Spiral Tunnels of the CPR. It's downhill for 15 km all the way to Field and you can do it almost at the speed of a car, if you wish.

At Field, take the eastbound train (check times in advance by calling Via Rail toll free at 1-800-665-8630) back to Lake Louise with your bicycle for only a few dollars. You get to pass through the Spiral Tunnels you viewed from the outside on the way down.

Highlights

The climb to the lake is pot-holed, busy and very steep. Many cyclists will be content to walk their bikes up. You can ride right up to the lake while motorists may spend some time finding a parking place and then trudging back to the chateau.

At the lake, the 3.8-km lakeshore trail is popular (but never too busy compared to the congestion around the hotel). For cyclists with an entire day, the 11-km (return) trail past the lake and up to Plain-of-Six-Glaciers is a wonderful introduction to the backcountry. Or you can hike the 3.5-km loop to Fairview Lookout or tour the fascinating Beehive area on the other side.

From Lake Louise, the quieter bypass to the Great Divide is a relief. You actually descend to the divide and can have a picnic right on the watershed between the Atlantic and Pacific. The quiet road then rejoins the Trans-Canada before a short, well-graded eastward climb to the top of Kicking Horse Pass and a smooth descent back to Lake Louise Village.

Road Log Tour 4

0 km Lake Louise Village, elev. 1539 m. All services. Campground. Nearest hostel at Corral Creek, 2 km S on Trans-Canada and 1 km S on Bow Valley Parkway, 403-283-5551 for reservations. Cross tracks and begin ascent for Lake Louise.

4 Moraine Lake Road. Keep straight.

4.5 Picnic ground. Ascent becomes less steep.

5 Paradise Bungalows.

5.5 Lake Louise turnoff. Gas station. Turn left.

6.5 Chateau Lake Louise and lake. Elev. 1732 m. Hiking trails, boat rentals. Cafeteria, restaurant, snack bar. After visit coast back to first junction.

7.5 Lake Louise turnoff. Gas station. Turn left on 1A for Great Divide.

13 Great Divide. Picnic area. Banff-Yoho

boundary.

15 Jct. Trans-Canada. Turn right (E) and begin well-graded climb.

17 Kicking Horse Pass. Elev. 1647 m. Continental Divide. Picnic area. Begin descent.

20 Jct. Icefields Parkway. Keep straight for Lake Louise Village.

22 Lake Louise Village.

BOW RIVER BY BIKE AND CANOE

PEDAL AND PADDLE ALTERNATIVE

Distance	28 km (17) miles or less by river, 27 km or less by bicycle
Time	1 day
Rating	Easy cycling. Paddlers need experience in manoeuvering canoes in fast current
Terrain	Bow Valley Parkway mostly level. Bow River is Grade I on this stretch
Elev. loss	100 metres (328 feet) by canoe
Roads	Well-paved, no shoulder
Traffic	Usually moderate and slow-moving
Connections	Tours 14, 15, 17

The canoe and the bicycle probably constitute the world's two best forms of transportation. You can combine them with advantage in the Rockies — and really see the countryside.

The beauty of the gentle, glacier-carved Bow Valley can be appreciated on a bicycle from the Bow Valley Parkway, certainly more than from a car seat. Yet you haven't really seen it until you've travelled on the Bow River itself. It's magic, especially on a clear day, the ramparts of Castle Mountain rising above the milky blue water.

A bicycle simplifies transportation arrangements for the canoeist and adds another dimension to travelling. Canoes can be rented in Banff. With a canoe and bike, you exercise both the upper and lower parts of the body.

Don't enter the water in or above Lake Louise townsite unless you are experienced in white water. In fact, the average paddler is better off starting way down the Trans-Canada where a number of launch sites can be found below Lake Louise. The easiest place for parking is a picnic site across the highway from the river. If you want to start higher for a fuller day, put in below the Trans-Canada bridge, south of the townsite. There's a

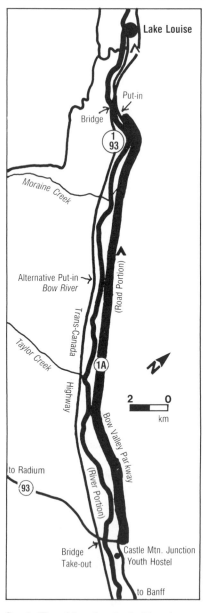

From then on, there are riffles but no rapids to trouble the paddler until after Castle Mountain Junction bridge. The river is fast-moving and does change direction frequently and the water is cold. So the canoeist must have ability enough to avoid sandbars and gravel patches and the occasional sweeper (a log jutting out into the river). Canoeists not experienced enough to steer in calm water without changing sides with their paddles should give the route a miss. It is not for beginners.

The canoeist/cyclist could continue beyond Castle Mountain Bridge, our recommended take-out point. But they should be prepared to run Redearth Creek rapids, 11 km below the bridge. It's usually Class II in June and July when water covers the rocks and sometimes Class III for intermediate paddlers later in the year when rocks are more exposed. The distance is 37 km from Lake Louise to the picnic area just upstream from the Trans-Canada Bridge, 8 km northwest of Banff.

OPTION: Cyclists/canoeists who want a leisurely and shorter day could put-in at the Trans-Canada bridge over the Bow River, just 8 km northwest of Banff. From there, the river winds and moves extremely slowly right into Banff townsite, an excellent route for seeing animals and contemplating the dogtooth peaks of the range opposite. Take out at the Banff

Grade II rapid under the bridge, but you can carry in your canoe and gear and launch below it.

boathouse. Do not go any further since the river speeds up quickly after the Banff Avenue bridge before plunging over Bow Falls. Return to the starting point by bicycle on the Trans-Canada, super-busy but with a wide shoulder.

Highlights

Leave your bicycles near Castle Mountain Junction, 28 km northwest of Banff, just off the Trans-Canada. They might be left, secured by a lock, at the hostel opposite the store, if you ask permission. Or you could just hide them in the trees near the river, chained to a substantial trunk with a note saying you'll be back soon, in case

somebody finds them and thinks they are abandoned.

Drive north on the Trans-Canada with your canoe and pick out a suitable launch site. Take lots of food and drink for the day. Canoeing generally takes longer than you expect and the river offers many sandy spots for a picnic.

After landing at Castle Mountain Junction bridge, hide your canoe in the woods, chained to a tree. Or leave someone with it while you cycle the 27 km or less back towards Lake Louise, preferably on the relatively quiet Bow Valley Parkway rather than on the Trans-Canada Highway. See Tour 17 for bicycle route.

BANFF TOWNSITE TO JOHNSTON CANYON (RETURN)

TOUR **6**

UP THE BOW

Distance	48 km (30 miles) return	**Roads**	Trans-Canada has wide shoulder. No shoulder on Bow Valley Parkway.
Time	Day trip for families and anyone doing extensive hiking, sightseeing or loafing. Half-day for faster cyclists	**Traffic**	Busy on the short stretch of Trans-Canada. Bow Valley Parkway quieter. Traffic slow moving and no trucks
Rating	Easy		
Terrain	Mostly level. One moderate hill where road splits	**Connections**	Tours 14, 15, 17, 33 and Banff townsite routes
Elev. gain	20 metres (69 feet)		

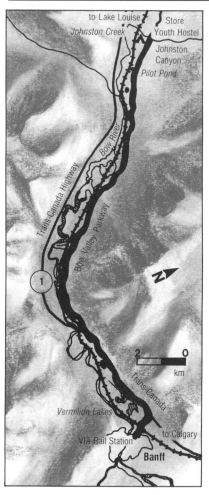

including a short visit to the canyon.

Interpretive stops along the way explain the evolution of the Bow Valley and give the inside story on mosquito-eating plants, landslides and meadows. You begin to pity the motorists hurrying by on the Trans-Canada on the other side of the river.

Highlights

Some cyclists find the first portion unpleasant as it involves seven kilometres on the brutally-busy Trans-Canada Highway outside Banff. But the shoulder gives you good separation from the traffic and the views are excellent to Vermilion Lakes, where moose can sometimes be seen, and back towards the writing-desk slope of Mt. Rundle behind Banff.

The parkway always comes as a relief. You'll often spot bighorn sheep near the road just after the turnoff. The mountains to the right are part of the sharp-toothed Sawback Range. Further along, you'll be able to see up to a dark hole in the side of Mt. Cory simply called Hole-in-the-Wall.

The valley floor is part of the dry montane zone, filled mostly with stands of lodgepole pine (which grew after extensive forest fires covered the area), mixed with aspen, white spruce and a few Douglas fir. The open meadows are excellent places to see deer and elk.

Johnston Canyon has a grocery store, restaurant, cabins and a camp-

Here is a restful, gentle cycle along the Bow River, ending at the most visited canyon in the Canadian Rockies. The trip makes a leisurely day-cycle with lots of time to hike up the gorgeous canyon past waterfalls, cascades and a natural tunnel. You can also picnic at one of several good sites along the Bow River. Faster cyclists can do it in a half-day,

ground. Be sure to hike at least part of the trail. It's 1.6 km return to the lower falls, 4.8 km to the Upper Falls and 11 km to and from the Inkpots. The path from the Lower to Upper Falls features seven waterfalls and an optional walk through a wet tunnel. You can stand at the base of the magnificent Upper Falls, twice the size of the lower ones.

Road Log Tour 6

0 km Banff townsite. Pop. 6,949, elev. 1383 m. All services. Campground and hostel (403-762-4122) above town on Tunnel Mountain Rd. From Via Rail station, turn N to Trans-Canada Hwy.

1 Left (W) on Trans-Canada for Lake Louise. Short hills.

7 Bow Valley Parkway. Turn right. Watch for mountain sheep.

8 Turnoff for Fireside picnic area, up steep paved road.

12 Muleshoe picnic area.

17 Sawback picnic area.

19 Road divides.

22 Two-way road resumes.

24 Johnston Canyon. Hiking trails, groceries, campground. Johnston Canyon Resort open May 15 - Sept. 20 Box 875, Banff, Alberta T0L 0C0, 403-762-2971.

BANFF TOWNSITE TO VERMILION LAKES (RETURN)

TOUR 7

MOOSE AND MUSKRATS

Distance	8 km (5 miles) return
Time	1/2 hour to 1 hour
Rating	Easy
Terrain	Level
Elev. gain	Negligible
Roads	No shoulder but fairly wide
Traffic	Busy summer weekends, but slow-moving; otherwise moderate
Connections	Tours 14, 15, 17, 33 and Banff townsite tours

The three scenic Vermilion Lakes are known for their rich wetlands habitat. Beaver, muskrat and a

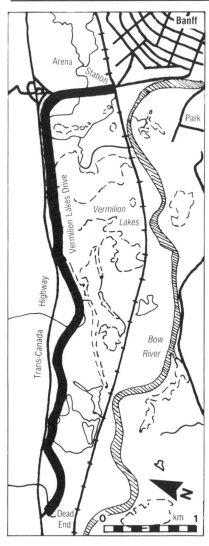

Highlights

Traffic can be busy from the Via Station in Banff to the turnoff. You may want to hike the Fenland Nature Trail along the way, a short self-guiding loop which explains the forest and pond environment.

After the turn-off, ride along the edge of the lakes. They provide a fairly typical feeding site for moose and a hospitable environment for muskrat and beaver. The lakes draw hundreds of bird species, including red-necked grebes and hooded mergansers. You may see bighorn sheep on the gravel slopes up from the Trans-Canada.

This is one of the most dramatic perspectives from which to view razor-edged Mt. Rundle. Sulphur Mountain, to its right, is believed to be the source of warm springs which surface at Vermilion Lakes and keep conditions so balmy on parts of the third lake that some ducks stay all winter.

In the 1950s, a few members of a Banff aquarium club once dumped tropical fish into Vermilion Lakes. While the aquarium fish flourished, they are now threatening the Banff longnose dace, an endangered species found only in these waters.

The tour ends at the turn-around under the Trans-Canada Highway.

variety of waterfowl are readily spotted. You may even see a moose, especially in early morning or at dusk.

The pace along the lakes is slow, although both car and foot traffic can be fairly heavy.

Road Log Tour 7

0 km Via Rail station, Banff townsite. Pop. 6,949, elev. 1383 m. Proceed

N to Norquay Rd; following signs for Trans-Canada. Turn right.

0.5 Fenland nature trail, 2-km interpretive loop.

1 Turn left on Vermilion Lakes Drive, just before Trans-Canada interchange.

4 Dead end. Return same way.

BANFF TOWNSITE TO LAKE MINNEWANKA (LOOP)

TOUR 8

A GHOST TOWN AND A LARGE LAKE

Distance	19 km (11 miles) loop
Time	2 to 4 hours
Rating	Intermediate
Terrain	Steady climb to lake, then level, steep descent
Elev. gain	92 metres (301 feet)
Roads	Generally good, some rough patches, no shoulder
Traffic	Fairly busy summer weekends but slow-moving
Connections	Tours 14, 15, 17, 33 and Banff townsite routes

Cycle under the cliffs of Cascade Mountain, wander through the remains of a ghost town and view the largest lake in Banff National Park. This is a first-rate, albeit strenuous, loop right from Banff townsite. Those with time might make a day of it, perhaps taking a cruise down Lake Minnewanka. Boats and fishing tackle can be rented.

OPTION 1: Cyclists could camp overnight at Two Jack main or lakeside campgrounds. These pretty campgrounds are situated near Two Jack Lake and are quieter than Tunnel Mountain Campground just above Banff townsite.

OPTION 2: This is a a fine bike-and-hike tour. The 8-km (return) Upper Bankhead Trail makes a steep but rewarding half-day hiking trip. A 4-km (return) walk to Stewart Canyon begins at Lake Minnewanka and leads to a scenic inlet. Serious hikers can enjoy the vistas (and curious bighorn sheep) at Aylmer Lookout. The 24-km hike is strenuous, so cyclists would be advised to camp at Two Jack and get an early start. The trailhead is at the boat access gate at Lake Minnewanka.

Highlights

The climb along the lower slopes of Cascade Mountain starts right after

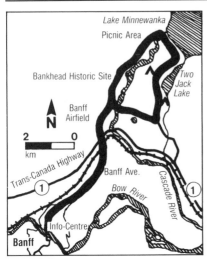

crossing the Trans-Canada. Once rich coal seams in this mountain sparked a thriving town; today all that's left of Bankhead are a few foundations. Wander down to the site which has a well-prepared interpretive walk and exhibits.

The gradient is fairly steady uphill to Lake Minnewanka. The 24-km-long lake did not start out this big — it was dammed once by Calgary Power in 1912 and a second time in 1941.

Minnewanka is an Indian name which translates to "Lake of the Water Spirit." Beneath its waters are spirits indeed — dams flooded the old resort town of Minnewanka Landing and the underwater site is now popular with scuba divers.

The lake is a fine place for picnicking, walking, renting a boat or taking a one-and-a-half hour cruise to Devil's Gap, where bighorn sheep are frequently

seen. Dinner cruises by reservation only, Minnewanka Tours, 1-403-762-3473.

Cycling is easy across the dam with views of the Palliser and Fairholme ranges. Capt. John Palliser made the first detailed survey of the region between 1857 and 1860.

The last portion is an enjoyable coast. If the day is hot, walk up the short trail just beyond the airfield parking lot and enjoy a cooling (some would say freezing) shower under Cascade Falls.

Road Log Tour 8

0 km Information centre in Banff townsite. Pop. 6949, elev. 1383 m. All services. Head N on Banff Ave. to Trans-Canada Hwy.

3 Intersection with Trans-Canada. Keep straight for Lake Minnewanka.

6 Cenotaph and below it remains of Bankhead. Exhibits, interpretive walk.

6.5 Access for Upper Bankhead trail on left, (8 km return). Climb.

10 Lake Minnewanka. Elev. 1475 m. Boat rentals, cruises, hiking, picnicking. Trailhead for Stewart Canyon and Aylmer lookout.

12 Two Jack main camp-

ground, 381 sites. Fairly
level.

13 Two Jack lakeside campground, 80 sites.

15 Turn left to rejoin main
road. Dirt road on right
before Trans-Canada
leads to airfield and base
of Cascade Falls.

16 Trans-Canada Hwy.
Keep straight for Banff
townsite.

19 Return information
centre.

Bankhead Yard
PROVINCIAL ARCHIVES OF ALBERTA

BANKHEAD

Crumbling deserted foundations and a few slag heaps are all that remain of Bankhead, once a thriving mining town.

A rich coal seam was discovered in the flanks of Cascade Mountain in 1883. In 1903, the Canadian Pacific Railway obtained a mining license in the national park and major production began. During Bankhead's heyday, more than 1,200 people lived here and 400 men worked to produce about 200,000 tons of coal annually. Facilities included tennis courts, a skating rink, a bakery, butcher shop and a Chinese laundry.

Decline began in 1912 with the first labour strike; falling markets and a general strike of 1922 spelled the end.

Coal mining is no longer allowed in Canada's national parks.

BANFF TOWNSITE TO SUNDANCE CANYON

TOUR **9**

SWIM, BIKE AND HIKE

Distance	10.4 km (6.5 miles)	**Elev. gain**	Negligible
Time	1/2 to one hour, not including optional hike or swim	**Roads**	Town streets, followed by paved roads reserved for use by cyclists and hikers
Rating	Easy		
Terrain	Mostly level		

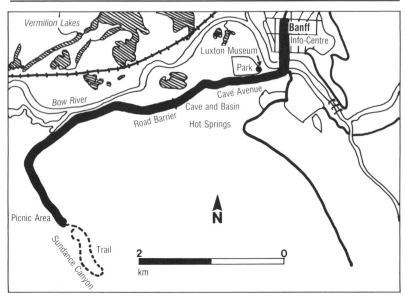

Traffic Moderate on streets. None past Cave and Basin

Connections Tours 14, 15, 17, 33 and Banff townsite tours

The short, easy tour to Sundance Canyon is one of the most popular cycles around Banff townsite. It leads past the renowned Cave and Basin hot springs, where Canada's national park system got its start.

The route follows a traffic-free paved road along the slow-moving Bow River with good views of the sharp-toothed Sawback Range and a chance to see waterfowl and possibly coyote, moose or elk along the banks. It ends at a fine picnic area where a 2.4-km trail loops through an impressive hanging canyon, past waterfalls and cascades.

Highlights

Luxton Museum, just across the Banff Avenue bridge, contains one of Alberta's finest collections of Plains Indian artifacts, plus wildlife exhibits. From there, it's only a short jaunt down Cave Avenue to the famous hot springs, restored for the national parks centennial in 1985. One hundred years before, three prospectors stumbled across a cave from which sulphurous vapor arose. Lowering themselves into the darkness, they found a deep pool of warm water — and enjoyed a good soak. Then they built a primitive bath house over the cave and tried to buy the land. But the federal government decided to reserve the land for itself. Thus began in 1885 what was to become the largest system of national parks in the world.

Today, you can browse through the Cave and Basin Centennial Centre, swim in the warm pool or take a couple of lavishly interpreted trails. One trail leads above the centre to the origins of the hot springs, the other heads below the centre through a fascinating variety of flora and fauna created by the hot springs, including an area where tropical fish thrive in a northern pond.

Beyond the hot springs, the road is closed to all motor vehicles except park personnel. It dips slightly to parallel the Bow River. Most prominent peak is the pinnacle of Mt. Edith directly opposite.

The road curves away from the river, climbs slightly and ends at a shady picnic area alongside Sundance Creek. From the end of the road, a highly-recommended trail leads past an overhanging cliff, ascends along the creek's beautiful cascades, finally loops higher to a viewpoint over the Bow Valley, then descends back to the picnic area. Walking time is one hour or less.

Road Log Tour 9

0 km Banff Information Centre. Cycle S on Banff Ave. over bridge, turn right on Cave Ave., passing Luxton Museum.

2 Cave and Basin hot springs. Interpretive trails. Pass building on right side and continue around road barrier.

5.2 Sundance Canyon picnic area. Hiking trail into canyon. Return same route.

SIDING 29: BANFF BEGINNINGS

Snow was falling, the air was crisp and the outline of Mt. Rundle loomed darkly above as the two journalists soothed away a day's work by soaking in Banff's Upper Hot Springs.

Suddenly the Easterner asked the Westerner: "Where do they heat the hot springs?"

The explanation — that the hot springs are natural, that the heat comes from the earth's central furnace — fell on disbelieving ears. Yet Banff National Park, indeed the country's vaunted national park system, owes its beginnings to the naturally-heated water spewing out of Sulphur Mountain.

Banff began as Siding 29, a small town with two general stores built along the Canadian Pacific Railway tracks in 1883. But change came rapidly after three railroad workers discovered the Cave and Basin in 1883 and immediately saw their chance to strike it rich with a bathing spa.

A legal battle over ownership ensued and the federal government was called in. Ottawa declared an area of 25.9 square kilometres around the springs a national reserve in 1885 and officially made it Canada's first national park in 1887.

Siding 29 was moved west about three kilometres to the new townsite of Banff. Now Banff has a permanent population of about 4,700 and a summer population that can exceed 25,000.

Yet park status alone would not have transformed Banff into a mountain playground. It took William Van Horne, the vigorous general superinten-dent of the CPR, to foresee the tourism potential of the park.

"If we can't export the scenery, we'll import the tourists," he declared. By 1887 he had made plans for a lavish hotel at the confluence of the Bow and Spray rivers. Banff Springs Hotel was the largest in the world when it opened in 1888; by 1900 the town boasted eight luxury hotels and a sanitarium.

Much of Banff Springs Hotel was destroyed by fire in 1926. But it was rebuilt and renovated over the years, still in the Scottish baronial style of Van Horne's vision.

Today the hotel enjoys 100-per-cent occupancy from May 1 to September 28 — and even a few ghosts, so the stories go.

BANFF TOWNSITE TO TUNNEL MOUNTAIN (LOOP) TOUR 10

HOODOOS AND VALLEY VIEWS

Distance 12 km (7.5 miles) loop
Time 2 hours with sightseeing
Rating Intermediate
Terrain Initial steep climb, mostly level or downhill afterwards
Elev. gain 80 metres (262 feet)
Roads Well-paved, some blind curves, no shoulder
Traffic Moderate for first 5 km, moderately heavy at times around campgrounds
Connections Tours 14, 15, 17, 33 and Banff townsite tours

Below, Banff townsite spreads out over the glacier-carved Bow Valley. Vermilion Lakes glimmer under the sharp-toothed Sawback Range. This is the vista from a bicycle seat only a few kilometres from the main drag.

Views never come easy on a bicycle, of course, and the loop over little Tunnel Mountain above Banff townsite is a tough one — for the

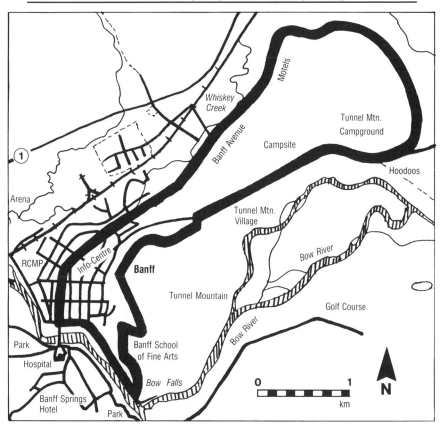

first three kilometres. After that, the road levels off and the last stretch is downhill.

The tour also provides access to a well-graded hiking trail that ascends Tunnel Mountain to even better viewpoints. It also passes Banff's hostel and the vast Tunnel Mountain "city" of campgrounds. Just beyond the campgrounds are the remarkable water-sculptured hoodoos atop the Bow embankment. The initial push may be worth the sweat.

Highlights

Don't go searching for the tunnel in Tunnel Mountain. It was named from an early Canadian Pacific Railway survey map that suggested tunnelling under this mountain. Later, a more cost-conscious surveyor chose an alternate route around the little mountain. As a cyclist, you go up and over its flanks.

As you begin to ascend the street above the Bow River, there's an almost magical view back to the baronial Banff Springs Hotel con-

Banff Springs Hotel addition under construction.
PROVINCIAL ARCHIVES OF ALBERTA

structed in 1888, then rebuilt in stages over the years. The Banff School of Fine Arts is on the left. Visitors can stop at the Walter J. Phillips Gallery in the Studio Building to view exhibits of paintings, ceramics, weaving and photography. Open year-round, 1 p.m. to 5 p.m. Free admission.

Tunnel Mountain Drive climbs again to the viewpoint where a trail leads off to the right to the summit of Tunnel Mountain. The road twists around the cliffs and descends slightly to Tunnel Mountain Village and the Banff hostel. Left is a direct route back to Banff townsite. Right are the campgrounds and the hoodoos, columns of silt, rock and gravel cemented together by dissolved limestone. The uncemented ground around them gradually eroded away, leaving these strange-looking pillars.

From the hoodoos, a new road curves uphill slightly, then descends smoothly to Banff Avenue near the Trans-Canada.

Road Log Tour 10

0 km Banff townsite. Start from Parks Information Centre on Banff Avenue. Turn left on Banff Ave. towards bridge.

0.2 At last street before bridge, turn left onto Buffalo, keep to right. View of Banff Springs Hotel. Moderately steep ascent.

2 Parking area. Trail to Bow River and campgrounds.

2.3 Banff School of Fine Arts. Climb continues.

3 Bow Valley overlook. Trail right to Tunnel Mtn. lookout.

4.9 T-junction. Store. Motels. Hostel straight ahead. 403-762-4122 for reservations. Left is direct route back to townsite. Turn right for continuation of tour.

7.4 Campgrounds.

8.4 Hoodoos. Scenic overlooks. New road curves left for brief ascent, then drops steeply to townsite.

10.5 Banff Ave. Left for town centre.

12 Banff information centre.

BANFF SPRINGS GOLF COURSE (LOOP)

VELVET GREENS

Distance	12 km (7.5 miles) loop
Time	1 to 2 hours
Rating	Easy
Terrain	Fairly level
Elev. gain	Negligible
Road	Narrow, rough in places
Traffic	Very light but watch for flying golf balls
Connections	Banff townsite tours

The Banff Springs Golf Course loop, dramatically set below Mt. Rundle on one side and the castle-like Banff Springs Hotel on other, makes a fine outing for cyclists of all ages.

Highlights

Start at the information centre, cross the Bow Bridge and ride up Spray Avenue. The impressive stone building at the end of the bridge is the park administration headquarters.

The Cascade Gardens behind the headquarters were developed as a Depression-era project. They make a colorful stop in summer. In the late 1800s, the site was occupied by the Brett Sanitarium, which pumped in water from the hot springs for its guests.

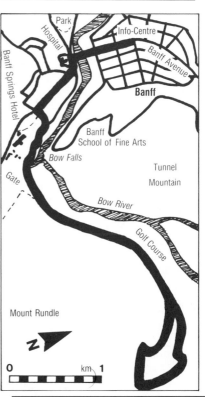

TOUR 11 BANFF SPRINGS GOLF COURSE LOOP

DISTANCE 12 km (7.5 miles)

At Bow Falls the river plunges over rock steps. The sight is particularly impressive in spring when water levels are high.

Continue on to the golf course, where the road can be bumpy in places. Glorious views across the fairways compensate for the rough ride. Construction of the course began in 1911. Stanley Thompson, one of the world's most renowned golf architects, redesigned it in 1927.

Wildlife occasionally wander here. Devil's Cauldron, on the eighth hole, is a green pond gouged by huge blocks of ice from retreating glaciers.

Cyclists may wish to complete their outing with a tour of Banff Springs Hotel. Tours are conducted several times weekly in summer. Call 762-2211 for times. High tea is served daily, from 2:30 to 4:30 p.m. in the Van Horne Room on the mezzanine level, July to September.

Road Log Tour 11

0 km Banff townsite information centre. Go S over bridge. Turn left on Spray Ave. towards Banff Springs Hotel (sign).

1.5 Turn left at sign for golf course. Go past Bow Falls and over Spray River. Follow main road through golf course.

10 Complete loop and return to townsite.

SULPHUR MOUNTAIN SOAK

The grind up the flanks of Sulphur Mountain will have cyclists in a sweat. The soothing springs, however, are warmer than the more easily-reached Cave and Basin and the views across to Mt. Rundle are marvellous.

Temperatures vary in the park's hottest springs, ranging around 38 degrees C. Bathing suits and towels can be rented. Hedonists — or those who have just completed cycling the Icefields Parkway — may want to book a massage. Call 403-762-2966 for an appointment.

The pool is open between 8:30 a.m. and 11 p.m. daily between mid-June and mid-September. Winter hours are 9 a.m. to 9 p.m. daily.

To take the 10-km return cycle, ride across the Bow River bridge, turn left and follow signs for the Sulphur Mountain gondola lift. You climb 190 metres above the town.

MARBLE CANYON CAMPGROUND TO NUMA CREEK (RETURN) TOUR 12

KOOTENAY HIKE AND BIKE

Distance 14 km (8.5 miles) return
Time 1 to 2 hours
Rating Intermediate

Terrain Gradual steady descent to Numa Creek, well-graded return

Road Fairly good con-
dition, wide
shoulders
Traffic Busy summer
weekends, other-
wise light to
moderate
Connections Tour 16

The Banff-Windermere Highway
between Castle Mountain Junction
and Radium Hot Springs is tailor-
made for cycling. The mountain
scenery is lovely, the road wide and
traffic lighter than on the Trans-
Canada.

Unfortunately for day cyclists,
there are no loops on the entire
stretch. If you only have time to
cycle part of this magnificent road,
this is the tour. It makes an ideal
afternoon or evening excursion for
those staying at Marble Canyon
Campground.

Stop to walk along the nature
trail at Marble Canyon, visit the
ochre Paint Pots and pack a picnic
to enjoy at Numa Creek. The return
involves a gradual but steady climb.

Highlights

You begin at Marble Canyon Campground, 7 km south of the Continental Divide which separates
Alberta and British Columbia and
Banff and Kootenay national parks.

Stop at Marble Canyon, a narrow
chasm where the limestone walls
have been dramatically scalloped by
Tokumm Creek. A 1.6-km nature
trail leads to Seventh Bridge, where

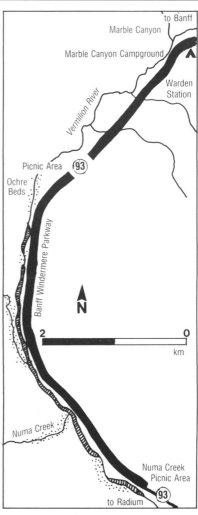

a 21-metre waterfall tumbles into a
foaming pool at the canyon head.

The jaunt to the Paint Pots is
short. An easy 1.6-km trail leads up
to the ochre pots, or cones, formed
by mineral deposits in the spring
water. The Indians regarded this as
a place of spiritual significance and
used the ochre color as a dye.

Back on the highway, riding is easy, with views of Vermilion Peak and Mt. Haffner to the east. Numa Creek offers a pleasant picnic spot.

Road Log Tour 12

0 km Marble Canyon Campground (29 sites). 19 km S of Castle Mtn. Jct. on Hwy 93S, the Banff-Windermere Hwy.

0.5 Marble Canyon. Nature trail, information. Picnic area.

1 Warden Station. Steady descent.

2.5 Paint Pots. Nature trail, picnic area.

7 Numa Creek picnic area.

McLEOD MEADOWS TO HECTOR GORGE (RETURN)

TOUR **13**

EASY CYCLE TO HECTOR GORGE

Distance 42 km (26 miles) return
Time Two hours to half-day
Rating Intermediate
Terrain Gradual climb to Hector Gorge
Elev. gain 30 metres (100 feet)
Roads Fairly good condition, wide shoulders
Traffic Busy summer weekends, otherwise moderate
Connections Tour 16

The entire 104-km Banff-Windermere Highway in Banff and Kootenay national parks is a dream to cycle. This section from McLeod Meadows Campground near Radium to Hector Gorge makes a leisurely jaunt for day cyclists, especially for those staying at the campground. Have a picnic lunch after viewing the gorge (which isn't spectacular) and enjoy an easy ride back to the campground.

Highlights

Begin at McLeod Meadows Campground, set in the woods near open meadows where moose, deer and elk are frequently seen. This campground does not fill up as quickly as some, and makes a pleasant, low-key stop.

Cycling is fairly level at first, following along the Kootenay River. Mt. Harkin dominates to the east at 2,983 metres, and Daer Mountain is immediately north.

You are following a travel route that goes back to pre-historic times. Archaeologists believe that Kootenai Indians used to gather at Radium Hot Springs and twice yearly trekked across the Rockies to hunt.

Sir George Simpson, governor of the Hudson's Bay Company, travelled through here in the 1840s, looking for a fur trading route across the mountains to the Columbia. The highway, opened in 1922, was the first motor road across the central Rockies.

Be prepared for steep climbing the last two kilometres to Hector Gorge. The sight of the aqua Vermilion River, set against snow-capped peaks and flowing south to join the Kootenay, is lovely. The gorge was named after Sir James Hector of the Palliser Expedition, who travelled over Vermilion Pass in 1858 looking for a good transportation route through the Rockies.

A good lunch spot is further ahead, down the steep hill at the Hector Gorge picnic area. Remember you'll have to climb back up afterwards.

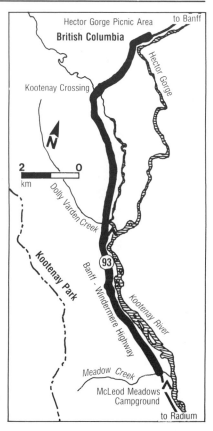

Road Log Tour 13

0 km McLeod Meadows Campground, 28 km NW of Radium on Hwy 93N, the Banff-Windermere Hwy. Elev. 1158 m. 100 sites, shelters. Fairly level cycling. Turn E towards Banff.

5 Cycle along Kootenay River.

15 Kootenay Crossing. Viewpoint and warden station.

17 Climb stiffens.

19 Hector Gorge, elev. 1188 m. Viewpoint of Vermilion River flowing to join the Kootenay River. Steep downhill.

21 Hector Gorge picnic area. Return.

TRAVEL ALBERTA

3

The Icefields Parkway

The Icefields Parkway connecting Banff and Jasper in the shadow of the Great Divide is surely one of the great cycling tours of the world. To spend four or five days bicycling amidst turquoise lakes, castellated mountains, waterfalls, snow-capped peaks and tumbling rivers is one of Canada's paramount outdoor experiences.

The route can not be properly experienced by driving. Even people who have motored the road many times experience it anew on a bicycle. Whenever we cycle it, we want the smooth roadway to go on forever.

Many call the Icefields Parkway the best cycling route on the continent. Bikecentennial, a non-profit U.S. organization, selected it as the focus of their first international bike route. We've met cyclists along the way from the Maritimes, southern U.S. and Europe.

The Icefields Parkway is so important as a cycling route that we have described it both northbound and southbound.

The route passes from the montane forest with Douglas fir, white spruce, lodgepole pine and occasional aspens to the higher subalpine forest of Engelmann spruce and fir. At the two passes, it approaches the upper limit of trees. You can take an out-of-this-world stroll through alpine tundra on Parker Ridge above the roadway. Indeed, there are dozens of superb hikes from 30 minutes to a whole day for cyclists with time and energy to spare.

Few other places along a highway provide such a close and varied glimpse of wildlife: mule deer, elk, bighorn sheep, mountain goats, coyotes, ospreys, herons, beaver, muskrats, occasionally even black bears. (We've never heard of a bear chasing cyclists along here, although it has happened on the Alaska Highway.)

Seventeen campgrounds are situated between Banff and Jasper. Ten hostels are conveniently spaced for cyclists. There are, in addition, five privately-operated hotels, inns or sets of cabins, not counting the tourist villages in Jasper, Lake Louise and Banff townsites.

However, the only sure place to get groceries between Lake Louise and Jasper is at the Saskatchewan River Crossing where most of the space is given over to a huge cafeteria and gift shop. We've talked to cyclists all over North America who remark on how skimpy the food supplies can be at this vital and isolated point.

Transportation

If anything discourages cyclists from travelling the 290-kilometre route between Banff and Jasper, it is the difficulty of getting transportation back to the starting point.

You can take the train to Banff or Jasper with your unboxed bicycle and just start cycling. The problem comes at the end.

Cyclists have worked out many creative ways of dealing with the problem. A few just spend a day or two resting and sightseeing in Jasper or Banff — and then cycle back to their starting point. Others ride their bikes a few kilometres out of town and try to hitchhike, hoping that someone with a pickup truck or vehicle big enough to hold their bikes will stop for them. In the U.S., at least, we have found that hitchhiking can often be easier with a bicycle than without one. Motorists feel they know who you are. Sometimes they stop because they think you've had a mechanical breakdown and they want to help. But most vehicles on the parkway are tourists taking their time and hitching can be more difficult. Of course, hitchhiking is by no means completely safe and we can't wholeheartedly recommend it.

The ideal solution is to get someone with a vehicle to meet you at your destination. Or travel with a club, with a commercial or hostel tour (see appendix) and these problems are all looked after for you.

An excellent new alternative is to rent a fully-equipped touring bicycle in either Banff or Jasper townsite and drop it off at the other end. Spoke 'n' Edge in Banff and Mountain Air Sports in Jasper co-operate to offer this much-needed service. The two stores rent new, good-quality touring

bicycles, mostly 18-speeds, complete with front and back panniers and water bottles. There is a reasonable daily fee and drop-off charge. Reserve ahead. Call the Spoke 'n' Edge at 403-762-2854 or Mountain Air Sports at 403-852-3760.

For cyclists with their own bicycles, probably the most direct solution is to travel back between Jasper and Banff by one of the frequent Brewster tour buses which make the trip in about 4 1/2 hours from the bus depots in the two towns. The hassle is that bikes must be boxed, although there's no extra charge for them. Phone 1-800-332-1419 toll free for latest information and schedule. In Banff, Spoke 'n' Edge sold bike boxes for $3 each in 1985.

If you plan to box your bike in either Jasper or Banff phone ahead to a bike store (see appendix) and ask if a bicycle box could be saved for you.

An easier way is to box your bicycle at home. Then drive (you could also use public transportation) to either Banff or Jasper and catch the first Brewster bus to the other end of the parkway. Set up your bike and begin the trip. Your own vehicle awaits at the destination.

Another possibility at the end of your trip is to take your bike with you on one of the daily trains between Banff and Calgary or between Jasper and Edmonton. Passenger train service no longer exists between Edmonton and Calgary, although unboxed bikes can be handled as an express shipment, while you make other arrangements.

Greyhound will take boxed bicycles to and from Banff or Jasper, or between Edmonton and Calgary at no extra charge, provided you don't exceed their luggage limits. For cyclists, this is usually no problem. One way around the boxing hassle is to take the luxurious Red Arrow bus service which goes between the CN Tower in Edmonton and the Via Rail Station in downtown Calgary. They do not require you to box your bikes, unlike Greyhound. This could change so it's advisable to check. Phone 403-424-3339 in Edmonton and 269-2885 in Calgary. There is an additional charge for bicycles.

Don't let these transportation hassles discourage you. The trip would be worth twice the effort.

Best Time to Go

We used to recommend fall at the best season. Traffic is amazingly quiet after Labor Day and September is usually drier than June. But one fall we were out on the roads and snow came early, very early. Everything was suddenly cold, damp and slippery. Now we strongly recommend June.

In June, you can still get snow while crossing the two passes but it is less likely to cover the valleys. The evenings are better for camping because it stays light for a long time. Traffic doesn't build up much until school vacation begins. Do try to avoid the weekend of the international Banff-to-Jasper relay race, involving 100 running clubs from all over North America. It's usually around the middle of June. Check with parks information. See appendix. While the relay is a great sporting event, it doesn't mix with cycling. How would you like to have hundreds of runners and their support vehicles cluttering up your cycling shoulder?

While late spring and early fall are the optimum times for travelling the route, most cyclists do the trip in July or August because of their vacation schedules. The weather is warmer, of course, a considerable advantage. It seldom gets hot enough to make cycling uncomfortable.

The major disadvantage in the peak season is the heavy traffic — an amazing daily armada of RVs, trailers and private cars. On the plus side, big trucks are banned on the parkway. The cyclist has a huge, wide shoulder, isolated from the driving lane, although motorists do pull off frequently to admire the scenery or to view wildlife. Beware of drivers so engrossed in the scenery, they don't watch the road properly.

It's a good idea to wear bright clothes and a white helmet. Consider using orange flags for the back of your bike. Ride in single file on the outside of the shoulder. And plan your days so you arrive at a hostel or campground with daylight to spare. The road is fairly quiet after dark but we don't recommend it — and you miss all the scenery.

Accommodation

Cyclists who stay in hostels don't have to carry heavy tents and stove, something to be appreciated when climbing Sunwapta Pass and Bow Summit. The hostels are located within a few hours' cycling of each other and are especially welcome in rainy weather.

Hostel reservations along the route are handled partly by the Edmonton headquarters, partly by Calgary. The Banff townsite hostel has its own reservation number, as well. See the road logs for phone numbers.

Many prefer to camp. The campgrounds are low-key compared to the vast camper cities in Banff and Jasper. Check with park officials to find out how early campgrounds tend to fill up. Cyclists can usually squeeze in somewhere, however. Be bold. You can always ask other cyclists or anyone who looks sympathetic if you can share their campsite. Cyclists are not likely to be turned away from a full campsite. At the same time, cyclists should realize they can't camp anywhere they want, using a full campground as an excuse. Camping is not allowed along the roadway, except at campgrounds.

For a super-light, luxurious trip, make reservations far in advance for the peak season and stay at some of the cabins, lodges and hotels along the parkway. See road logs for phone numbers. Take food for your lunch but eat breakfast and dinner in their restaurants. Sleep in a soft bed. Take scores of showers. Sit by the fireplace in the lounge, recounting your adventures. One of these years, we're going to try it.

Day trips

While most cyclists travel the Icefields Parkway as one continuous tour, it is possible — and much easier — to divide the tour into a number of day trips or even half-day trips. The cyclist need not carry anything more than a lunch and perhaps a raincoat and sweater.

The disadvantage is that unless cyclists have someone in a vehicle to pick them up, they'll have to return the way they came each day. Fifty kilometres out means 50 kilometres back and there's not the same sense of freedom, or exploration.

Better for day trips are the tours around Jasper, Banff and Lake Louise. See day-trip sections. A few of these can be done as circular trips.

BANFF
TO JASPER

THE SUMMIT
OF ADVENTURE

Distance 290 km (180 miles)

Time 3 1/2 to 4 1/2 days average. With sightseeing and some side-trail hiking, it could be extended to a week. Trips often consist of a half-day at the start and finish. That's the model for this description. Cyclists may shorten the trip by 57 km by starting at Lake Louise instead of Banff

Rating Strenuous

Terrain Many short hills to climb, a number of long, fairly level stretches beside rivers, two steep passes followed by long downhills

Elev. gain See individual sections

Roads Well-engineered highway with huge paved shoulder. However, the shoulder is frequently interrupted on hills and before turn-offs to allow an extra driving lane, leaving the cyclist with little room. A fairly safe route, with slow-moving traffic and wide road.

Traffic Light to moderate, busy between July 1 and Labor Day with a nearly constant stream of cars, trailers and RVs (but no trucks). Hwy 93A and 1A (Bow Valley Parkway) are quieter although there's no shoulder

Connections Tours 1, 3, 4, 5, 15, 16, 20, 21, 33, 38 and townsite tours in Banff and Jasper

Highlights

Section 1
Banff to Lake Louise
Distance 57 km (35 miles)
Terrain Mostly Level

The first stretch on the busy, noisy Trans-Canada beyond Banff is mercifully short. Some cyclists pedal all the way to Lake Louise on this main road because it is faster and more level than the Bow Valley Parkway. It's recommended only for those who don't mind exhaust fumes, near bumper-to-bumper traffic in summer and dangerous stretches where the shoulder disappears to almost nothing to provide for a passing lane.

The Trans-Canada has no campgrounds or hostels on this stretch while Bow Valley Parkway is well provided. Although the Bow Valley Parkway has no shoulder, it seems tailored for cycling as traffic is slow-moving and the road winds invitingly past viewpoints and exhibits, traversing a dry, montane forest of mainly lodgepole pine and aspen that is home to a considerable population of deer, elk, mountain sheep and smaller game.

The Trans-Canada leads above Vermilion Lakes and you can look back to the "writing desk" slope of Mt. Rundle beyond Banff townsite. The Bow Valley Parkway is mostly level, highlighted by Johnston Canyon, a short, popular trail that leads past waterfalls, a natural tunnel and close-up views

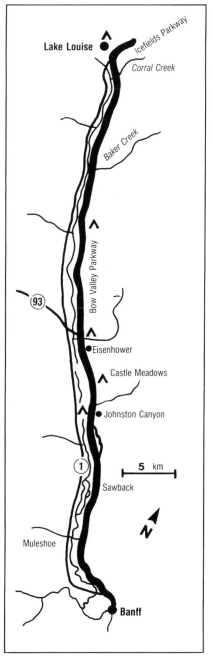

of the effect of water erosion. The parkway is the original route between Banff and Lake Louise completed in 1920 and finally superseded as the major route by the completion of the Trans-Canada Highway in the late 1950s.

Exhibits along the parkway outline the history of the valley, where once a saloon-filled mining town boomed and died. They tell how the U-shaped valley was carved by glaciers and point out features such as Hole in the Wall in the face of Mt. Cory, the meadows that attract big game and the names of the dogtooth peaks above.

After Castle Mountain Junction, the road continues more or less straight on new pavement through even corridors of lodgepole pine and past numerous picnic areas and campgrounds. The most prominent peak is Castle Mountain, formerly Mt. Eisenhower, a good example of a castellated peak. Horizontal layers of Cambrian limestone have eroded to leave turret-like spires.

The parkway ends at the Trans-Canada, two kilometres south of Lake Louise Village where there are good views west to the great bulk of Mt. Temple. Cyclists with lots of time should take the steep, 4-km road from Lake Louise townsite to the teeming tourist mecca at the spectacular lake and gothic chateau. The sidetrip to Valley of the Ten Peaks is also recommended (Tour 3). Many prefer this beautiful valley and lake because it isn't such a tourist trap as Lake Louise.

Road Log Tour 14

Section 1—Banff to Lake Louise

0 km Banff. Pop. 6949, elev. 1387 m. All services. Via Rail station. Campground and hostel above town on Tunnel Mountain Rd. (403-762-4122 for hostel reservations). From Via Rail head N to Trans-Canada.

1 Left (W) on Trans-Canada for Lake Louise. Short hills.

7 Bow Valley Parkway. Turn right. Watch for mountain sheep.

8 Turnoff for Fireside Picnic area, up steep paved road.

12 Muleshoe picnic area.

17 Sawback picnic area.

19 Road divides.

22 Two-way road resumes.

24 Johnston Canyon. Hiking trails, groceries, campground. Johnston's Canyon Resort open May 15 - Sept. 20 Box 875, Banff, Alta. T0L 0C0 403-762-2971.

26 Castle Meadows group campground.

30 Castle Mountain Campground.

31 Castle Mountain Jct. Store, hostel (283-5551 for reservations). Closed Wed. nights. Castle Mountain Village chalets, 762-3311. Keep straight on Bow Valley Parkway.

42 Protection Mtn. Campground.
45 Baker Creek picnic area.
Baker Creek Bungalows,
522-3761.
54 Corral Creek picnic
area. Hostel, call
283-5551 for reserva-
tions. Closest hostel to
Lake Louise. Closed
Mon. nights.
55 Jct. Trans-Canada. Turn
right on busy highway
for Lake Louise.
57 Lake Louise turnoff.
Elev. 1539 metres.
Groceries, accommoda-
tion, food. Campground.
Via Rail station. Scenic
lake is 6 km W, with
steep climb. Keep
straight on Trans-
Canada for Icefields
Parkway.

Highlights

Section 2

Lake Louise to Rampart Creek
> **Distance** 90 km (56 km
> miles)
> **Terrain** Gradual climb of
> 550 metres,
> steep towards
> end, 300-metre
> drop

Stock up on supplies in Lake Louise
Village and continue north on the
Trans-Canada for two kilometres
until the turn-off. Here begins the
famous Icefields Parkway alongside
slabs of orange rock, 600 million
years old, oldest in the park. You
leave truck traffic behind and begin
the 42-km ascent to Bow Pass,
highest point on the parkway. The
climb is about 550 metres (1,800
feet) and is mostly gradual, although
steeper at the end.

The views compensate for the
effort, however. Green Hector Lake
is seen below with the Balfour
Glacier behind it. The dry, montane
forest of the lower Bow Valley gives
way to denser, wetter, subalpine
forest of tangled spruce and fur. To
your left, numerous glaciers tumble
down steep cliffs from the heights
of the Continental Divide.

Bow Lake is a jewel, its turquoise waters reflecting glaciers and
the massive limestone cliffs of
Crowfoot Mountain behind it.
Beside the lake is historic red-roofed
Num-Ti-Jah Lodge which used to be
accessible only by an arduous,
40-km horse trail from Lake
Louise.

From the lake, the climb to the
pass is more gruelling, although the
over-all ascent is easier in this direction than from Jasper. The meadows
on either side of the road are partly
a product of thermal inversion. Cold
air sweeps down from the glaciers
above and pools in this valley, making it colder than the forested slopes
above.

The pass itself is not especially
spectacular. For views, you need to
take the 10-minute walk to Peyto
Glacier viewpoint where the vista
is among the best on the parkway.
Below is the stunning, opaque blue-
green of glacier-fed Peyto Lake.
Beyond the lake, you can look down

the long Mistaya Valley, which you'll soon be travelling. From here, hiking trails lead up into alpine tundra and down to the lake.

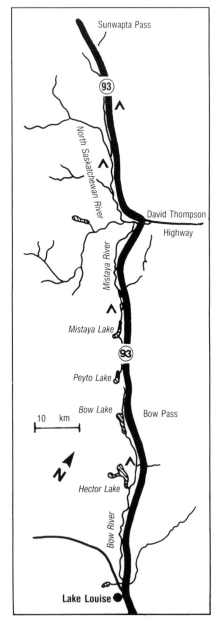

Put on warm clothing for the fast, exhilarating descent of 7 km past Snowbird Glacier viewpoint to the beautiful Waterfowl Lakes Campground. The descent continues more gradually along the clear Mistaya River. Fine views abound especially left to the impressive, multi-layered tower of Mt. Chephren, sometimes called the Matterhorn of the Rockies. On the opposite side of the valley is the broad-shouldered, massive Mt. Murchison.

A few kilometres before the Saskatchewan River crossing is a short, interesting trail that leads in 15 minutes to where the Mistaya River plunges into a deep, narrow canyon in the limestone.

The route descends to the North Saskatchewan River and the easy part is over, for now. Across the bridge, you climb past a lookout over the historic Howse Valley, crossed by explorer David Thompson. The Howse River route over an easy pass into British Columbia was once seriously considered for the transcontinental highway.

Just beyond the junction of the Icefields Parkway and the David Thompson Highway (see Tour 38) is a motel, cafeteria and gift shop, beautifully situated under the cliffs of Mt. Wilson. Cyclists should be warned that while there are groceries, the variety is extremely limited. Most of it is snack food and it sometimes takes considerable imagination to devise meals from the stock. The lack of supplies at this remote and important stop is a source of conversation among experienced cyclists (who talk mostly of food, anyway) from here to Wyoming.

From this development, the tour continues to climb gradually alongside the North Saskatchewan River under the high limestone cliffs of Mt. Wilson (3240 metres) where waterfalls scour the rock in spring. Then it continues along the broad gravel flats of the North Saskatchewan River to little Rampart Creek Campground and hostel.

Road Log Tour 14

Section 2

Lake Louise to Rampart Creek

(57) 0 km Lake Louise Jct. Elev. 1539 m. Continue N on Trans-Canada.

(59) 2 Jct. Icefields Parkway. Turn right (N) for Jasper. Begin gradual climb.

(62) 5 Herbert Lake picnic area.

(83) 26 Mosquito Creek Campground. Hostel 403-283-5551 for reservations. Closed Tues. nights.

(88) 31 Crowfoot Glacier viewpoint. Hiking trails.

(93) 36 Bow Lake picnic site and viewpoint.

(96) 39 Bow Lake viewpoint. Turnoff for hiking trail and Num-Ti-Jah Lodge (Box 39, Lake Louise, Alta., T0L 1E0, call Calgary mobile operator and ask for lodge at 135-9002.)

(99) 42 Bow Summit. Elev. 2088 metres (6,850 ft). Exhibits, hiking trails, outstanding viewpoint. Begin descent.

(107) 50 Snowbird Glacier viewpoint.

(116) 59 Waterfowl Lake Campground. Hiking trails.

(133) 76 Warden Station and Saskatchewan River Bridge.

(134) 77 Howse River viewpoint.

(135) 79 Saskatchewan River Crossing. Limited groceries. Cafeteria. Parkway Lodge (403-721-3920).

(147) 90 Rampart Creek Campground and hostel. For hostel reservations phone 403-283-5551 in Calgary.

Highlights

Section 3
Rampart Creek to Beauty Creek
  Distance 56 km (37 miles)
  Terrain Steep 365 metres climb, 300-metre drop

This is a short day in terms of distance travelled. But it's the day you ascend steeply to Sunwapta Pass and Athabasca Glacier. It's a day of extraordinary scenery, a chance to do some hiking — and visit a toe. Many cyclists, of course, will want to push further.

The road leads gradually higher, following the North Saskatchewan River through Graveyard Flats, a braided river channel formed by accumulations of sediments brought down from the mountains by the torrents of early summer.

The climb steepens after the Alexandra River and you pass Cirrus Mountain Campground and a viewpoint for the huge limestone wall decorated with cascades.

Prepare yourself for the worst. From here the highway rises very steeply for about 300 metres to Sunwapta Pass, an ascent known to generations of travellers as the ''Big Hill.'' You cross over a spectacular gorge, make a sharp turn right and begin the relentless ascent.

The going is glorious, however, at least when you stop to rest. Views down the valley of the North Saskatchewan are awesome. Near the top, you can take a 30-minute hike from the uppermost viewpoint to Panther and Bridal Veil Falls. The trail descends from the lower end of the parking area near the sign showing mountain profiles.

OPTION: If the weather is good, don't pass up a stroll on Parker Ridge near the top of the pass, starting from a parking area before Hilda Creek Hostel. You quickly leave the stunted fir trees behind and traverse an alpine zone of stunted, twisted shrubs and hardy alpine flowers. The bare ridge overlooks the huge Saskatchewan Glacier and all the peaks of the Icefield area.

Once atop the Big Hill, the road leads on an easier grade to the top of Sunwapta Pass — about 2042 metres (6,700 feet) — dividing the waters of the North Saskatchewan and Athabasca river systems. You descend through open meadows, cross into Jasper National Park and pass two campgrounds just before the famous Athabasca Glacier.

The Columbia Icefield, which feeds these glaciers, covers 389 square kilometres and is the largest icecap south of the Arctic. Most of its ice and snow is out of sight high on the Continental Divide. The Athabasca Glacier which grinds down from the main ice mass is perhaps the most accessible glacier in North America. You can walk up to it on a short trail opposite the information centre and touch its icy toe.

The icefield is a strange spot, scenic with the glorious peaks of Mt. Athabasca (left of the glacier) and Mt. Kitchener (right) yet also stark with huge, gloomy masses of moraine tumbled everywhere. It has the unfinished look of a massive construction site.

An insignificant-looking bump to the right above the Athabasca Glacier is Snow Dome, the hydrographic apex of the continent. Water from it drains three ways: to the Athabasca River flowing north and northeast to the Mackenzie River and then the Arctic Ocean; to the North Saskatcehwan River flowing to Hudson Bay; and to the Columbia River flowing to the Pacific.

Above the toe is a visitor's centre with exhibits, a hotel and cafeteria (but no groceries) and a commercial tour operation that takes vehicles out onto the glacier.

There is one more slope to climb before the long downhill run to Jasper. Sunwapta Canyon Viewpoint provides good vistas back to massive Mt. Athabasca. Best of all for cyclists is the look of the steep, downhill grade ahead. Think of all the potential energy you've built up. Button up for the fast, chilly run down to the valley of the Sunwapta and relatively level gravel flats leading to Stanley Falls and Beauty Creek Hostel.

Road Log Tour 14

Section 3
Rampart Creek to Beauty Creek

(147) 0 Rampart Creek.

(162) 15 Cirrus Mtn Camp-ground.

(169) 22 Viewpoint. Steep ascent.

(173) 25 Viewpoint. Steep ascent.

(174) 26 Viewpoint. Steep ascent, trail to Panther and Bridal Veil falls.

(176) 29 Parker Ridge Trail, 5-km round trip above tree-line.

(177) 30 Hilda Creek Hostel. For reservations, phone 403-283-5551. Closed Thurs. nights.

(181) 34 Sunwapta Pass. Banff-Jasper boundary. Elev 2,042 metres.

(182) 35 Wilcox Camp-ground, hiking trails.

(184) 37 Icefield Camp-ground.

(186) 39 Icefield Centre. Short road to toe of glacier. Glacier Rides concession. Information Centre. Exhibits. Back-country permits. Columbia Icefield Chalet and cafeteria open June 1 to Labor Day, 403-762-2241.

(190) 43 Tangle Falls picnic area.

(203) 56 Beauty Creek Hostel. For reser-

vations phone
Edmonton HQ
403-439-3089.
Closed Thurs.
nights in summer;
key system
otherwise.

Highlights

Section 4

Beauty Creek to Jasper
> **Distance** 87 km (54
> miles)
> **Terrain** Rolling with
> gradual descent
> of 400 metres

The road slopes gradually downhill, following the gravel flats of the Sunwapta River, past Jonas Creek Campground and a short, paved turnoff to Sunwapta Falls, a fine sidetrip that doesn't take long. This section is a prime place to spot elk and other game, especially in the morning. Mountain goats are often found by a natural mineral lick at Goat Viewpoint.

Once you reach the Athabasca River, the terrain changes, offering less steady descent and more ups and downs above the river. Athabasca Falls is always worth a stop, the water boiling and foaming 25 metres into a narrow gorge.

OPTION: Many cyclists will prefer to take the alternate route Highway 93A starting at Athabasca Falls for the last stretch into Jasper. The old road is about the same length as the newer main highway but carries less traffic, although there's no shoulder.

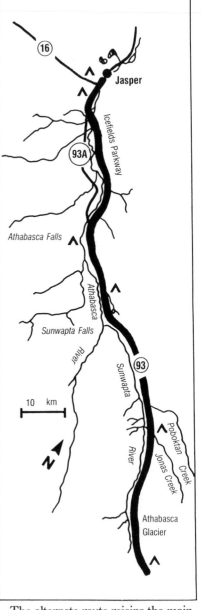

The alternate route rejoins the main highway nine kilometres south of Jasper.

The alternate road follows the Athabasa River closely past a picnic ground and pleasant Wabasso Campground before climbing, for the last time, to the junction with the Edith Cavell Road. (The trip up this steep, 15-km road isn't recommended for cyclists, although there's a hostel near the end and a glorious hike opposite the groaning Angel Glacier.) From there, it's a fast descent back to Highway 93.

From Athabasca Falls, Highway 93 (the main route) leads up and down high above the Athabasca River, passing a couple of viewpoints before linking with the 93A south of Jasper. The main highway then leads past the vast Wapiti and Whistlers campgrounds and into Jasper townsite, passing the turnoff for Whistlers Hostel.

You've made it! Treat yourself to a pig-out in Jasper. Tokyo Tom's behind Marmot Lodge (852-3780) is popular and specializes in sukiyaki and so forth. The Tonquin Prime Rib (852-4987) is probably the place for red meats. The No. 1 action spot is the Athabasca bar, right in the middle of town. There's a lounge and disco and you can get burgers in what the locals refer to as the Dead Animal Room (because of all the stuffed heads).

Road Log Tour 14

Section 4
Beauty Creek to Jasper

(203) 0   Beauty Creek Hostel.

(212) 9   Jonas Creek Campground.

(217) 14 Sunwapta Warden Station.

(229) 26 Bubbling Springs picnic area.

(234) 31 Sunwapta Falls turnoff. 10 minutes to upper falls. Sunwapta Falls Bungalows and cafeteria 403-852-4852.

(236) 33 Trail to Buck and Osprey Lakes.

(237) 34 Honeymoon Lake Campground.

(241) 38 Ranger Creek group camping.

(247) 44 Goat picnic area.

(251) 48 Goat viewpoint.

(254) 51 Mt. Kerkeslin Campground.

(257) 54 Athabasca Falls Hostel. 403-439-3089 for reservations. Closed Tues. nights.

(259) 55 Athabasca Falls turnoff. Elev. 1173 m. Viewpoint and picnic area 0.5 km. Jct. 93 A, alternate route N.

OPTION: (259) 55- Continue past falls on 93A, towards Jasper.

(260) 56 Turnoff for Geraldine Lakes trail.

(268) 64 Whirlpool Fire Road. Historic route of fur traders into British Columbia across Athabasca Pass to Columbia River.

(270) 66 Wabasso Campground.

(278) 74 Edith Cavell Rd.

(285) 81 Jct. Hwy 93, rejoining main route. Turn left to Jasper.

(259) 55 Athabasca Falls turnoff. Continue straight on Hwy 93 for Jasper.

(261) 58 Horseshoe Lake.

(273) 69 Picnic area.

(281) 78 Jct. 93A.

(284) 81 Wapiti Campground.

(286) 83 Turnoff left for Whistlers Camp-

ground in 0.5 km and steep climb to Whistlers Mountain Hostel in 2.5 km and The Whistlers tramway. Phone 403-439-3089 for hostel reservations.

(288) 85 Jct. Yellowhead Hwy. 16. Keep straight for Jasper.

(290) 87 Jasper townsite. Pop. 3970, elev. 1060 m, all services. Via Rail Station. National Parks information centre on Connaught Dr., almost opposite station.

JASPER TO BANFF

TOUR **15**

THE SUMMIT OF ADVENTURE

Distance 290 km (180 miles)

Time 3 1/2 to 4 1/2 days average. With sightseeing and some side-trail hiking, it could be extended to a week. Trips often consist of a half-day at the start and finish. That's the model for this description. Cyclists may shorten the trip by 57 km by finishing at Lake Louise instead of Banff

Rating Strenuous

Terrain Many short hills to climb, a number of long, fairly level stretches beside rivers, two steep passes followed by long downhills

Elev. gain See individual sections

Roads Well-engineered highway with huge paved shoulder. However, the shoulder is frequently interrupted on hills and before turn-offs to allow an extra driving lane, leaving the cyclist with little room. A fairly safe route, with slow-moving traffic and wide road.

Traffic Light to moderate, busy between July 1 and Labor Day with a nearly constant stream of cars, trailers and RVs (but no trucks). Hwy 93A and 1A (Bow Valley Parkway) are quieter although there's no shoulder

Connections Tours 1, 3, 4, 5,

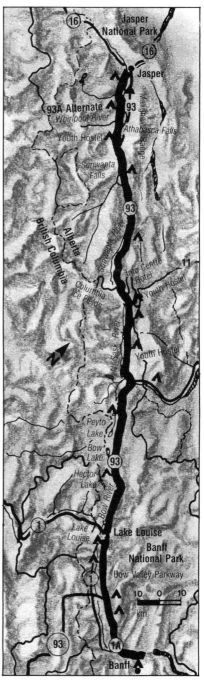

15, 16, 20, 21,
33, 38 and
townsite tours in
Banff and Jasper

Highlights
Section 1
Jasper to Beauty Creek
> **Distance** 87 km (54
> miles)
> **Terrain** Rolling with
> gradual climb of
> 400 metres

The Icefields Parkway is fairly gentle for the first stretch south of Jasper townsite along the fast-moving Athabasca River, passing the two giant campgrounds called Whistlers and Wapiti.

OPTION: At the 9-km mark you'll have to decide whether to continue on main Highway 93 or head off right on 93A, a quieter and narrower road that rejoins the parkway at Athabasca Falls.

Highway 93A is only three kilometres further than the main highway and is usually is quieter and more intimate. There's no shoulder but traffic is lighter and you get a better sense of the country. It also leads past Wabasso Campground, one of the most pleasant in the Jasper area. The disadvantage is that the alternate road begins with a stiff climb from the Athabasca River up the lower flanks of Mt. Edith Cavell.

The alternate route passes the turnoff to Mt. Edith Cavell. (The trip up this steep, 15-km road isn't recommended for cyclists, although there's a hostel near the end and a glorious hike opposite the Angel Glacier.) The road descends from the Cavell turnoff and then follows the west side of the Athabasca to the falls.

The main road rolls along more gently and climbs to viewpoints above the river.

Athabasca Falls is always worth a stop, a mighty surge of water forced between a narrow gap and over a steep step.

The road has so far gained only 100 metres over-all in 32 km from Jasper. The ascent continues relatively gently with some ups and downs following the Athabasca River. This section is a good place to spot elk and other game, especially in the morning. Mountain goats are often found by a natural mineral lick at Goat Viewpoint.

After a longer ascent and descent, there's a short turn-off to Sunwapta Falls, a good sidetrip that doesn't take long. From here, the cycling is pleasant, the river on one side and forests of lodgepole pine under the Endless Chain Ridge on the other. The massive peaks of the Columbia Icefield appear ahead as you reach Jonas Creek Campground and Beauty Creek Hostel.

Road Log Tour 15
Section 1
Jasper to Beauty Creek
> **0 km** Jasper. Pop. 3970, elev.
> 1060 m, all services.

Via Rail Stn. National Parks information centre on Connaught Dr., almost opposite railway station. Turn W on Connaught and cycle through town, under railway tracks.

2 Jct. Yellowhead Hwy. 16. Keep straight.

4 Turnoff left for Whistlers Campground in 0.5 km and steep climb to Whistlers Mtn Hostel in 2.5 km and The Whistlers tramway. 403-439-3089 for hostel reservations.

5.5 Wapiti Campground.

9 Jct. 93A alternate route S to Athabasca Falls and Banff. Main route goes straight.

OPTION:

9 Turn right on 93A, ascending steep slope on side of Mt. Edith Cavell. Alternate route is quieter than 93 although it's 3 km further and there's no shoulder.

16 Edith Cavell Rd. Begin descent.

24 Wabasso Campground.

26 Whirlpool Fire Road. Historic route of fur traders into British Columbia across Athabasca Pass to Columbia River.

34 Turnoff for Geraldine Lakes trail.

35 Athabasca Falls. View-

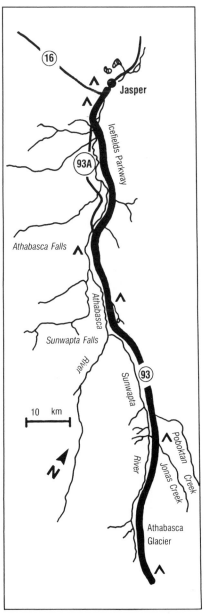

points and picnic tables. Continue to jct. with main highway and turn right.

END OPTION

18 Picnic area.

29 Horseshoe Lake.

32 Athabasca Falls. Viewpoint and picnic area 0.5 km. Jct. 93 A.

33 Athabasca Falls Hostel. 403-439-3089 for reservations. Closed Tues. nights.

36 Mt. Kerkeslin Campground.

39 Goat viewpoint.

43 Goat picnic area.

49 Ranger Creek group camping.

53 Honeymoon Lake Campground.

54 Trail to Buck and Osprey Lakes.

56 Sunwapta Falls turnoff. 10 minutes to upper falls. Sunwapta Falls Bungalows and cafeteria 403-852-4852.

61 Bubbling Springs picnic area.

73 Sunwapta Warden Station.

78 Jonas Creek Campground.

87 Beauty Creek Hostel. For reservations phone Edmonton HQ 403-439-3089. Closed Thurs. nights in summer; key system otherwise.

Highlights

Section 2

Beauty Creek to Rampart Creek
Distance 56 km (37 miles)

Terrain Steep 300 metre climb and 365 metre drop

This is a short day on distance and long on work. But it's the day you ascend to Athabasca Glacier and Sunwapta Pass, a day of extraordinary scenery, a chance to do some alpine-hiking — and visit a toe. Many cyclists, of course, will want to push further.

After the hostel, the route continues along the gravel-choked braids of the Sunwapta River before the real climbing begins with a grade of about eight per cent and a few stretches of almost ten per cent, steepest on the generally well-graded parkway.

Of course, the views grow fabulous as you ascend and leave the Sunwapta Valley plain behind. Athabasca Glacier finally appears ahead with smaller Dome Glacier high to the right. Sunwapta Canyon viewpoint provides good vistas ahead to massive Mt. Athabasca. The road descends steeply to the rubble below Athabasca Glacier which used to extend right down to the highway. Then the road climbs again slightly to a well-equipped park interpretive centre, a hotel with cafeteria (but no groceries) and a commercial outfit providing rides out onto the Athabasca Glacier.

The Columbia Icefield, which feeds these glaciers, covers 389 square kilometres, largest icecap south of the Arctic. Most of its ice and snow is out of sight high on the Continental Divide. The Athabasca

Glacier which grinds down from the main ice mass is perhaps the most accessible glacier in North America and you can walk up to it on a short trail opposite the information centre and touch the icy toe.

The icefield area is a strange spot, both scenic with the glorious peaks of Mt. Athabasca (left of the glacier) and Mt. Kitchener (right) and also stark with huge, gloomy masses of moraine tumbled everywhere, giving it the unfinished look of a massive construction site.

An insignificant-looking bump to the right above the Athabasca Glacier is Snow Dome, hydrographic apex of the continent. Water from it drains three ways: to the Athabasca River flowing north and northeast to the Mackenzie River and then the Arctic Ocean; to the North Saskatchewan River flowing to Hudson Bay; and to the Columbia River flowing to the Pacific.

From the glacier, the tour passes two campgrounds and tackles the last slopes of Sunwapta Pass, nothing compared to what came before. Near the top, you move into Banff National Park, oldest in Canada. You've made it! The elevation is about 2042 metres, close to the upper limit of the subalpine forest.

OPTION: If the weather is good, don't pass up a stroll on Parker Ridge near the top of the pass, starting from a parking area after Hilda Creek Hostel. You quickly leave the stunted fir trees behind and traverse an alpine zone of of stunted, twisted shrubs and hardy alpine flowers. The bare ridge overlooks the huge Saskatchewan Glacier and all the peaks of the icefield area.

Button up for the long, thrilling descent of the Big Hill into the valley of the North Saskatchewan. Consider stopping at the first viewpoint for a 30-minute hike to Panther and Bridal Veil Falls. The trail descends from the lower end of the parking area near the sign showing mountain profiles.

Views down the valley are awesome as the highway smoothly loses about 300 metres in 11 km. Below and beyond rise the massive limestone walls of Cirrus Mountain, decorated with waterfalls.

After a huge curve at the bottom of the hill, the grade becomes gentle, passing Cirrus Mountain Campground and following the North Saskatchwan River through Graveyard Flats. The braided river channels are formed by intense accumulation of sediments brought down from the mountains, especially in spring and early summer. The route reaches Rampart Creek Campground and hostel.

Road Log Tour 15
Section 2
Beauty Creek to Rampart Creek

- **(87) 0 km** Beauty Creek Hostel.
- **(100) 13** Tangle Falls picnic area.
- **(104) 17** Icefield Centre. Short road to toe

of glacier. Glacier Rides concession. Information Centre. Exhibits. Backcountry permits. Columbia Icefield Chalet and cafeteria open June 1 to Labor Day, 403-762-2241.

(106) 19 Icefield Campground.

(108) 21 Wilcox Campground, hiking trails.

(109) 22 Sunwapta Pass. Banff-Jasper boundary. Elev. 2,042 m.

(113) 26 Hilda Creek Hostel. For reservations, phone 403-283-5551. Closed Thurs. nights.

(114) 27 Parker Ridge Trail, 5 km round trip above tree-line.

(117) 30 Viewpoint. Steep descent.

(128) 41 Cirrus Mountain Campground.

(143) 56 Rampart Creek Campground. Hostel, reservations. 403-283-5551.

Highlights

Section 3

Rampart Creek to Lake Louise
 Distance 90 km (56 miles)
 Terrain Steep 300-metre climb, 500-metre drop

From Rampart Creek, the route descends gradually past the high limestone cliffs of Mt. Wilson where waterfalls scour the rock in spring and early summer. Keep straight for Banff at the junction with the David Thompson Highway where a motel, store and large cafeteria are located under the cliffs of Mt. Wilson.

There's only a small selection of groceries in the back of the gift shop. Most of it is snack food and it sometimes takes considerable imagination to devise meals, if you are depending on what you buy here. The lack of supplies at this remote and important stop is a source of conversation among experienced cyclists (who talk mostly about food, anyway) from here to Wyoming.

Just past the junction is a viewpoint over the historic Howse Valley, crossed by explorer David Thompson. The Howse River route over an easy pass into British Columbia was once seriously considered for the trans-continental highway.

The route descends to the North Saskatchewan River crossing — and the easy part is over, for now.

The climb from the river is stiff; then the grade relents. For the next 30 km or so, the rise will be fairly gradual following the clear, green Mistaya River. A few kilometres above the bridge, a 15-minute trail leads to where the Mistaya River plunges into a deep, narrow canyon in the limestone.

The climb continues with the huge grey and yellow mass of Mt. Murchison left and Mt. Sarbach right. Beyond it is the impressive, multi-layered tower of Mt. Chephren, sometimes called the Matterhorn of the Rockies.

The tour leads alongside beautiful Waterfowl Lake with the well-situated campground at its south end and then passes Snowbird Glacier viewpoint. The real work begins, last of the entire trip. The final seven kilometres or so to Bow Summit has a grade of about eight per cent, steep enough to make some cyclists push their heavily-loaded bikes.

The pass itself is not an especially spectacular place. For views, you need to take the 10-minute walk to Peyto Glacier viewpoint where the vista is among the best on the parkway. Below is the stunning, opaque blue-green of glacier-fed Peyto Lake. Beyond the lake, you can look down the long Mistaya Valley, which you just ascended. From the viewpoint, hiking trails lead up into alpine tundra and down to the lake.

The summit divides the North and South Saskatchewan river systems. And best of all, from here, it's gloriously downhill, a thrilling coast much of the way to Lake Louise. Put on some extra clothes.

The meadows on either side of the road down to Bow Lake are partly a product of thermal inversion. Cold air from the glaciers pools in this valley, making it colder than the slopes above which can sustain

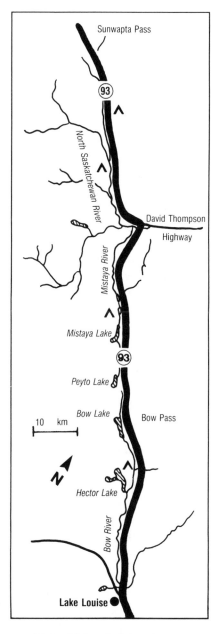

a fairly thick subalpine forest.

Don't let the pleasure of coasting prevent you from stopping at Bow Lake. It is a jewel, turquoise waters reflecting the glaciers and massive limestone cliffs of Crowfoot Mountain behind it. Beside the lake is red-roofed Num-Ti-Jah Lodge formerly accessible only by an arduous, 40-km horse trail from Lake Louise. A level trail leads around the north side of the lake and then rises slightly to fine viewpoints.

Further down the parkway is green Hector Lake with the Balfour Glacier behind it. The route leads gradually down — with a few annoying uphills — to the Trans-Canada and two kilometres more to the teeming tourist masses of Lake Louise Village. We always react to this outpost of "civilization" with mixed feelings. It's so busy from here on that there's less sense of exploration.

Road Log Tour 15

Section 3

Rampart Creek to Lake Louise

0
(143) km Rampart Creek Campground and hostel.

(154) 11 Jct. David Thompson Hwy. Limited groceries, cafeteria. Parkway Lodge, open all year, 403-721-3920.

(156) 13 Howse River viewpoint.

(157) 14 Warden Station and North Saskatchewan River bridge. Begin ascent.

(159) 16 Mistaya River Canyon trail.

(174) 31 Waterfowl Lake Campground, hiking trails.

(183) 40 Snowbird Glacier viewpoint.

(191) 48 Bow Summit. Elev. 2088 m (6,850 ft.) Exhibits, trails and Peyto Lake viewpoint. Begin descent.

(194) 51 Bow Glacier viewpoint. Turnoff to Num-Ti-Jah Lodge, snack bar, restaurant, hiking trails and accommodation, call Calgary mobile operator and ask for lodge at 135-9002.

(197) 54 Bow Lake picnic site.

(207) 64 Mosquito Creek Campground. Hostel 403-283-5551 for reservations. Closed Tues. nights.

(228) 85 Herbert Lake picnic area.

(231) 88 Jct. Trans-Canada Hwy. Keep straight for Lake Louise. Road level.

(233) 90 Lake Louise access. Elev. 1539 m. Via Rail Stn. accommodation, campground.

Scenic lake is 6 km W, with steep climb.

Highlights

Section 4:

Lake Louise to Banff

Distance 57 km (35 miles)

Terrain Level to rolling, little over-all elevation change

Cyclists with enough time should take the steep, four-kilometre road from Lake Louise townsite to the teeming tourist mecca at the spectacular lake and gothic chateau. See Tour 4. Perhaps a better tour is to Valley of the Ten Peaks which, many believe, is just as scenic as Lake Louise. And it's certainly less tourist-clogged.

Otherwise, continue on the Trans-Canada until the turnoff for Highway 1A, the Bow Valley Parkway, just 2 km south of town. The Trans-Canada Highway route to Banff is not recommended — too many exhaust fumes, near bumper-to-bumper traffic in summer and dangerous stretches where the shoulder disappears to almost nothing to provide for a passing lane. The Trans-Canada has no campgrounds or hostels on this stretch while the Bow Valley Parkway is well provided.

Although the Bow Valley Parkway has no shoulder, it seems tailored for cycling as traffic is slow-moving and the road winds invitingly past viewpoints and exhibits

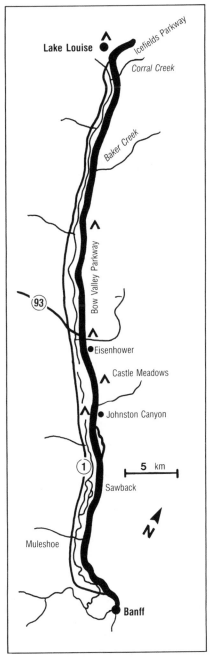

through a dry, montane forest of mainly lodgepole pine and aspen.

87

TRAVEL ALBERTA

From the Trans-Canada, the parkway continues straight on new pavement through even corridors of lodgepole pine, past numerous picnic areas and campgrounds. The most prominent peak ahead is Castle Mountain, formerly Mt. Eisenhower, a good example of a castellated peak formed from horizontal layers of Cambrian limestone that have eroded to leave turrets.

The route leads past Castle Mountain Junction where there is a store, cabins and hostel, past Johnston Canyon, and numerous picnic areas before finally rejoining the Trans-Canada. The last stretch on the busy road is mercifully short.

The Trans-Canada leads quickly into Banff past viewpoints overlooking Vermilion Lakes and ahead to the distinctive "writing desk" slope of Mt. Rundle. Take the first turn-off for Banff.

You've made it! Treat yourself to a pig-out in town. Ticino (205 Wolf, 762-3848) features Swiss-Italian cuisine, notable veal dishes and beef and cheese fondues. The Magpie and Stump at Bear and Caribou (762-2014) has good Mexican food.

But the best way to unwind, in our opinion, is to soak in one of Banff's hot springs: the newly-restored and conveniently-located Cave and Basin, or the hotter Upper Hot Springs, five kilometres up the side of Sulphur Mountain. After a long soak, cleaning away all those miles, we usually fall asleep during dinner anyway.

These open woods are home to a considerable population of deer, elk and smaller game.

The Bow Valley Parkway is mostly level, highlighted by Johnston Canyon, a short, popular trail that leads past waterfalls, a natural tunnel and close-up views of the effects of water erosion.

The parkway is the original route between Banff and Lake Louise completed in 1920. It was finally superseded as the major route by the completion of the Trans-Canada Highway in the late 1950s.

Exhibits along the parkway outline the history of the valley, where once a saloon-filled mining town boomed and died. They tell how the U-shaped valley was carved by glaciers and point out features such as Hole in the Wall in the face of Mt. Cory, the meadows that attract big game and the sharp dogtooth peaks above. It's a fascinating and restful cycle.

Section 4
Lake Louise to Banff

(233) 0 km Lake Louise. S on Trans-Canada for Banff.

(235) 2 Turn left on 1A Bow Valley Parkway.

(236) 3 Corral Creek picnic area. Hostel, call 403-283-5551 for reservations. Closest hostel to Lake Louise. Closed Mon. nights.

(245) 12 Baker Creek picnic area. Baker Creek Bungalows, 403-522-3761.

(248) 15 Protection Mountain Campground.

(259) 26 Castle Mountain Jct. Store, hostel (403-283-5551 for reservations). Closed Wed. nights. Castle Mtn. Village chalets, 403-762-3868. Keep straight on Bow Valley Parkway.

(260) 27 Castle Mountain Campground.

(264) 31 Castle Meadows group campground.

(266) 33 Johnston Canyon. Hiking trails, groceries, campground. Johnston Canyon Resort open May 15 - Sept. 20, 403-762-2971.

(278) 45 Muleshoe picnic area.

(282) 49 Turnoff for Fireside picnic area, up steep paved road.

(283) 50 Jct. Trans-Canada Hwy. Head SE for Banff.

(289) 56 Jct. Banff townsite access road. Turn right for Banff. Bus and railway station on left.

(290) 57 Banff townsite. Pop. 6,949, elev. 1387 m. All services, VIA Rail stn. Campground and hostel above town on Tunnel Mountain Road. Hostel reservations, 403-762-4122.

TRAVEL ALBERTA

89

Banff Springs Hotel

4
The Golden Triangle

CASTLE MOUNTAIN TO RADIUM TO GOLDEN (LOOP)

THE GOLDEN TRIANGLE

Distance 313 km (195 miles) loop

Time 3 or 4 days or longer depending on sightseeing

Rating Strenuous

Terrain Three mountain passes, many long but well-graded climbs, level stretches along rivers, varied. Narrow steep gorge from Golden to Yoho park boundary

Elev. gains 225 metres (738 feet) Castle Mtn. Jct. to Vermilion Pass 327 metres (1072 feet) McLeod Meadows to Sinclair Pass 857 metres (2,811 feet) Golden to Kicking Horse Pass

Roads Wide shoulders and mostly good surfaces in national parks, which extend between Castle Mountain and Radium and Yoho park boundary to finish. Narrow, no shoulder outside parks, mostly good surfaces.

Traffic Busy summer weekends in national parks. Light to moderate traffic Radium to Golden. Busy out of Golden on Trans-Canada

Connections Tours 1, 2, 3, 4, 14, 15, 17, 18, 60

Here is cyclists' gold. Not long ago, long-distance touring in the Canadian Rockies meant the Icefields Parkway. Today, the peak-rimmed, three-legged tour dubbed the Golden Triangle is quietly gaining popularity among the wheelie crowd.

There's good reason. The tour, a personal favorite, is far less travelled than the parkway, but as rich in wildlife and remote scenery. Almost every kilometre offers a sense of discovery.

The pristine landscape of peaks, forests, waterfalls and clear rivers doesn't disappoint. You conquer three mountain passes, travel

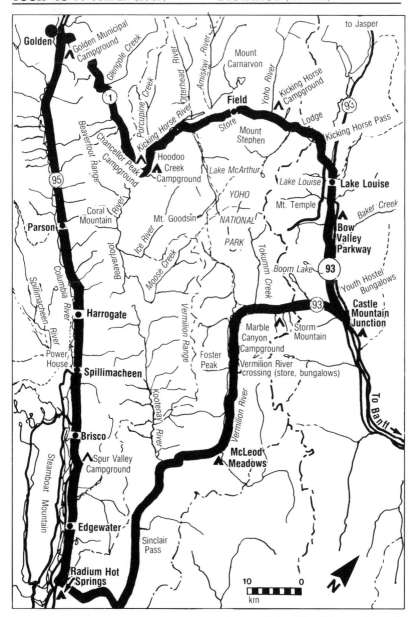

through three spectacular Rocky Mountain national parks — Banff, Kootenay and Yoho — follow the sleepy Columbia River through tumbledown hamlets and twice bisect the Continental Divide.

JOHN DODD

Continental Divide, Vermilion Pass, Banff and Kootenay National Parks

Attractions include a scalloped limestone canyon, Sinclair Canyon and the Iron Gates, Hector and Kicking Horse gorges, an historic railroad town and natural hot springs.

The trip is less strenuous than the Icefields Parkway. Passes are lower. The tour is also easier to organize than the parkway because it is a loop, not a ribbon.

Yet the Golden Triangle has two flaws. The first is the twisting, busy section along a steep gorge on the Trans-Canada above Golden. The shoulder sometimes disappears on this stretch, and there are logging trucks to contend with.

That portion is short, however. Cyclists should remember that they are legally entitled to one lane of traffic when the shoulder disappears. Tackle the gorge portion early in the day if possible and dismount when in doubt. It's not as bad as it sounds.

The other flaw is lack of accommodation. There is one set of cabins on the Banff-Windermere Highway between between Vermilion Pass and Radium. Otherwise, the cycle to Radium makes a long first day, especially since a hard climb is required up Sinclair Pass. Accommodation on the other legs of the tour is also limited, although cyclists who plan ahead (see road log) could spend each night in a soft bed.

The day-to-day breakdown here is designed for cyclists who carry a tent and sleeping bag. It provides fairly equal cycling for four days. Many cyclists take only three days. If you plan to hike and sightsee, the tour could easily be extended to a week.

McLeod Meadows is the suggested first night's stop. Cyclists who want to go further should be cautioned that only one campground in Radium accepts tents — and that campground (Redstreak) is a grind up a long hill. (However, a fairly level trail leads from the Radium Aquacourt to Redstreak and cyclists can save themselves the climb by walking their bicycles along it.)

On the next section between Radium and Golden, we prefer to rough camp, that is to find our own secluded place off the road. This is not difficult as there are plenty of meadows and streams. (Water must be purified.) That allows us to climb through the Kicking Horse gorge while relatively fresh and then camp in one of Yoho's lovely campgrounds on the third night. The new campground at Spur Valley, or the municipal campground at Golden, are other options on this portion.

Some cyclists will want to stay at Kicking Horse Campground in Yoho because it is the only one with showers.

Groups larger than ten may now reserve the Ottertail Group Camp in Yoho.

There is a hostel at Castle Mountain Junction (closed Wednesday nights). No hostels are provided in Kootenay and the only one in Yoho is at Takakkaw Falls, a long, hard climb from the highway.

Those who want to travel light can do so in some style. Castle Mountain Village, at the starting point, is clean, quiet and comfortable — a fine place to treat yourself to a bed, shower and perhaps an outdoor barbecue at the end of the trip. The proprietors are friendly and run a well-stocked store with groceries in small quantities. Rustic Emerald Lodge in Yoho has just been restored to its former splendor. (See Tour 1.) There are plenty of motels in Radium. Taliesin Guest House on Highway 95 near Parson is a secluded log lodge overlooking the Columbia Valley and the Selkirks. See road log for phone numbers.

Strong cyclists might consider a Grand Slam, Canadian Rockies-style, for five to 10 days of the best cycling North America has to offer.

Begin in Jasper townsite, cycle the Icefields Parkway, Tour 15, and cap that renowned trip with the Golden Triangle. Or begin in Banff, cycle the triangle, then the parkway and end in Jasper. To make planning easier, bicycles complete with panniers and water bottles can be rented in Jasper and dropped off in Banff at a reasonable fee. See appendix.

The Golden Triangle begins at Castle Mountain Junction, 30 km northwest of Banff townsite. If starting from the townsite, take the quieter Bow Valley Parkway, rather than the Trans-Canada, to the starting point. (Tour 17.) Vehicles may be left, with permission, at the parking lot for the hostel.

The loop can, of course, be tackled from either direction. We recommend the clockwise approach because it avoids the horrendous northbound approach up Sinclair Pass. It also takes advantage of frequent westerlies from Golden on.

However you plan your trip, take adequate food supplies and water purification tablets. Weather can change rapidly. Be on guard for hypothermia and take extra clothing as well as standard safety gear.

The Golden Triangle is cycled en masse each spring in Alberta's largest bicycling tour. The trip is organized by Calgary's Elbow Valley Cycle Club and cyclists rave about the sense of camaraderie along the way — not to mention the luxuries of a sagwagon and great food.

The tour is scheduled for the Victoria Day long weekend, usually the third weekend in May. Newcomers are welcome, but must reserve in advance. The popular tour is limited to 250 riders. See appendix for the club's address.

The Castle Mountain-Radium portion of the tour is included in longer group tours organized by the Alberta Hostelling Association and Bikecentennial. See appendix.

Highlights

Sir James Hector, first white man to travel over Vermilion Pass, gave the descriptive handle of Castle Mountain to the mountain which dominates the starting point. It was renamed after Gen. Dwight D. Eisenhower in 1946. Happily, the 1858 name has been restored, although Ike still has his name on the southernmost tower of the mountain.

Begin the wide-shouldered Banff-Windermere Highway with a blood-warming climb up Vermilion Pass. Storm Mountain Lodge, opposite Storm Mountain, which is usually topped by clouds, is one of the older lodges in the park.

The effects of the devastating forest fire of 1968 are soon apparent. Some 6,000 acres were scourged by fire in four days. At the Continental Divide, you can take the short Fireweed Trail which shows the effects of the fire and nature's response. In summer, magenta fireweed lights the hillside, and lodgepole pines push through the deadfall.

At Vermilion Pass, waters run west to the Pacific via the Columbia River; waters to the east empty into the Bow River and ultimately Hudson Bay via the Saskatchewan and Nelson rivers.

Long and Narrow Kootenay

Indians hunted in the Kootenay Valley for hundreds of years before the white man. Pictographs suggest that a favorite native congregating place may have been Radium Hot Springs.

The great geographer David Thompson was the first white man to travel through the Kootenays. Sir George Simpson, governor of the Hudson's Bay Company, passed by here in the 1840s, seeking a fur route through the mountains to the Columbia River.

In 1858, Sir James Hector, geologist and naturalist with the Palliser Expedition, explored the area and became the first white man to cross Vermilion Pass.

Kootenay, the anglicized version of an Indian word meaning "strangers" or "people from beyond the hills," became Canada's tenth national park in 1920.

The park is 96 kilometres long but only about 30 kilometres wide. Earlier this century, the federal government decided it wanted another national park in the region, but could only convince British Columbia to cede the land if a highway were built through it.

On June 30, 1923, the gates officially swung open to the new Banff-Windermere Highway. More than 1,200 people awaited their chance to cross the Rockies in their cars.

No record seems to exist of the first cyclist to cross the Rockies, a grave omission indeed.

At Marble Canyon, a 30-minute walk leads along a deep gorge to Seventh Bridge, dramatic spot to view a 21-metre waterfall.

Lock your bicycles to a tree and walk past ochre-colored meadows to the ochre Paint Pots. This was a place of spiritual significance to Indians, who believed the Red Clay Spirit lived there. They used the vermilion color for rock paintings and decoration of bodies and clothing.

The ochre clay was mixed with water, kneaded and shaped into flat cakes. The cakes were then baked, ground into a powder and mixed with fish oil or animal grease to produce an indigenous "oil paint" that defied weathering.

Cycling is mostly downhill for the next portion. The valley is bounded by glaciated peaks, whose flanks are cloaked in subalpine forest. Purple aster, yellow columbine, fireweed and heart-leafed arnica fringe the road.

Vegetation in Kootenay National Park ranges from moist subalpine forest in the eastern half to drier Douglas fir terrain beyond McLeod Meadows. Clouds tend to release rain and snow over the Columbias, leaving the western part of the park dry. The two climatic zones provide a varied environment that allows for a greater range of wildlife.

There are several pleasant picnic spots along the Vermilion River. Note that the store at Vermilion Crossing sells only limited groceries and is open only between June 1 and Sept. 30.

Watch for mountain goats on the lower elevations at Mt. Wardle. It's a stiff but short climb up to the Hector Gorge viewpoint. Enjoy a long, easy coast and level cycling to McLeod Meadows campground.

This woodsy campground is low-key and slower to fill than many in the national parks. Moose, elk and mule deer graze the meadows at dawn or dusk.

It pays to be fresh for the climb up Sinclair Pass. Rewards are great — a long glide down a narrow canyon, past stands of western red cedar and the Iron Gates which are limestone and dolomite cliffs colored by hot mineral waters over the centuries.

Check your brakes before descending the grade. Also be wary of bighorn sheep, which skitter along the road causing traffic jams.

The natural hot springs at the Aquacourt make a wonderful place to soothe away the weary miles. Lock your bicycle to the railing above the pool and bliss out. Subterranean heat keeps the water between 35 to 47 C degrees, depending on the season. A cool pool, cafeteria and outdoor patio are also provided.

From the Aquacourt, cyclists can walk their bicycles along a fairly level trail through the woods to Redstreak, a fine national park campground. If you don't take the trail, access to the campground involves a steep climb from the main highway below. All other campgrounds in the Radium area prohibit tenting.

Radium is the last major supply point until Golden. There are fruit stands on Highway 95. Dorothy's Bakery, on the south side of the highway, offers sausage rolls, muffins and whole-wheat buns. The fast-food-lined access road to Radium, however, may seem a shock after the national park. Most will be relieved to head out of town.

Out of Radium another delightful world unfolds. The scenic road to Golden can be eerily quiet as it threads along the Columbia River Valley. To the west, the Columbia meanders at the bottom of the Rocky Mountain Trench. Beyond it, the snow-covered peaks of the Purcell Mountains and the Bugaboos gleam in the distance.

Little farms and sleepy hamlets have a 1950s look, as though the world has passed them by. The road has such a slow, mellow feel it needs to be cycled to be appreciated.

The shoulder on this section occasionally disappears. Road conditions are not as ideal as in the national parks, and hot blustery winds can impede progress. If that happens, rest somewhere and wait for the wind to drop, as it usually does by evening.

Golden has numerous shopping centres, a museum and a municipal campground situated beside the Kicking Horse River. Watch for wheel-gobbling railway tracks on the road leading out of town.

The first 21 kilometres out of Golden are the trip's hardest. Fill water bottles before leaving town on a steep climb out of the trench. The

Radium Aquacourt
KOOTENAY NATIONAL PARK

Trans-Canada ahead is narrow and climbs steeply, at an eight-per-cent gradient in places, along ledges high above the Kicking Horse River.

Traffic in summer can be very heavy and includes logging trucks. Approach this section well-rested, take your time, and if in doubt, pull over or stop completely to let traffic by. While cyclists are entitled by law to a full lane of traffic when the shoulder disappears, they need to remember that motor vehicles are bigger than they are. We don't suggest arguing with truck drivers, especially the guys in logging trucks.

Mercifully, the climb is not that long. Views are marvellous and the experience evokes some understanding of the difficulties encountered by the early railroad builders.

It is a relief to enter Yoho National Park, smallest in the Rockies and for many, the most intimate. Its name is the Cree word for ''awe''.

Chancellor Peak Campground is the smallest in the park, and a fine place to spend the night, especially on river-front campsites. Don't pitch your tent too near the railway tracks in the woods or you'll be awakened every time a train passes, which is often on this main trans-continental route.

Cycling is fairly easy to the historic railroad town of Field. The Siding, a small store in the town, has a deli, take-out food and salads and is open daily. There is also a well-stocked, small general store near the turn-off to Takakkaw Falls.

The falls are among the highest in the world and are situated in Yoho Valley. The climb up, however, is only for strong. See Tour 2.

After Field, begin the infamous climb up Kicking Horse Pass — a climb worse in anticipation than reality. Stop along the way to view the Spiral Tunnels, where the CPR licked the steep grade by spiralling two tunnels upwards inside mountains on either side of the highway. The scheme required nine kilometres of tunnels and reduced the grade by more than half, to a manageable 2.2 per cent. Trains that needed four locomotives to make the grade at five miles per hour used only two locomotives to go five times as fast. Up to 20 trains a day go through the tunnels.

Cyclists, however, have only their own organic engines and no spiral has been built on the highway to give relief from the tough grade. But by the time you pass the excellent viewpoint for the spiral tunnels, the worst is over. You pass pretty Wapta Lake and West Louise Lodge to reach the forested, unspectacular pass.

It's smooth sailing from here.

OPTION: Cyclists who want to see Lake Louise should veer off on Highway 1A shortly before the top of the pass. See Tour 4. The alternate highway climbs to the famous, tourist-clogged lake and then descends steeply on switchbacks to Lake Louise townsite.

The main highway descends smoothly to Lake Louise Village. The going is level back to Castle Mountain Junction and we recommend the quiet Bow Valley Parkway rather than the busy, noisy Trans-Canada. The parkway leads off the Trans-Canada a couple of kilometres south of Lake Louise townsite and passes a hostel and campground and several exhibits. It then traverses a dry montane forest of lodgepole pine along the Bow River. A relaxing end to a golden trip.

Kicking Horse Pass, Yoho National Park
GAIL HELGASON

Sir James Hector (seated) and Edward Whymper, Field B.C.
PROVINCIAL ARCHIVES OF ALBERTA

Kicking Horse Pass

The colorful name given to the forested pass straddling the Continental Divide ten km west of Lake Louise is based on an actual incident.

In 1858, Sir James Hector, a young Scottish doctor, led a party of six into the uncharted terrain that is now Kootenay and Yoho national parks. The group was part of the Palliser Expedition, appointed by the Royal Geographical Society of Britain to explore British North America between the Great Lakes and the Rockies.

"The going was rugged," Hector recounted in his journals. He was probably given to understatement.

When the group started to cross a turbulent stream near Wapta Falls, one horse had to be rescued from the river and another bolted into the bush. The 24-year-old Hector approached the frenzied animal and for his troubles received a severe kick in the chest, causing extreme pain but not seriously hurting him.

The stream became known as the Kicking Horse River. The name carried over to the 1647-metre pass selected as the CPR's route to the Pacific.

Road Log Tour 16

Section One
Castle Mountain Junction to McLeod Meadows

0 km Castle Mtn Jct., 30 km NW of Banff townsite on Trans-Canada Hwy. Elev. 1425 m., store. Castle Mountain Hostel, accommodates 40, open to non-members. Closed Wed. nights. Reservations through Calgary office 403-283-5551. Groceries at Castle Mtn. Village chalets, 403-762-3868. Cars may be parked in lot by hostel, but ask permission. Turn SW to Trans-Canada.

1 Take overpass above Trans-Canada to Hwy 93. Start climb to Vermilion Pass.

7 Top of long grade. Storm Mountain Lodge. Rustic log cabins, dining, open June 1-Sept. 17, 403-762-4155.

8 Boom Creek picnic area.

9 Vista Lake viewpoint. 90-minute return walk to lake, views of burn.

11 Vermilion Pass, elev. 1650. Continental Divide, boundary between Banff and Kootenay national parks and Alberta and British Columbia. Views of Storm Mtn. left, Mt. Whymper right, short interpretive nature trail.

18 Marble Canyon. Campground, 29 sites. Picnicking, information, interpretive trail at canyon.

21 Paint Pots. 1.6-km return interpretive trail, picnicking.

25 Numa picnic area. Scenic falls on Vermilion River.

37 Vermilion River Crossing. Open June 1-Sept. 30, limited groceries, licensed dining, Vermilion Crossing Bungalows, Box 958, Banff, Alta. T0L 0C0.

42 Monument to Simpson.

43 Animal lick. Mule deer, elk and moose often observed early morning or evening.

46 Wardle Creek picnic area.

50 Hector Gorge picnic area beside Vermilion River. Steep uphill.

52 Hector Gorge viewpoint. Views of Vermilion River flowing to join Kootenay River. Mt. Wardle W.

56 Kootenay River crossing and warden station.

66 Level cycling along river.

71 McLeod Meadows Campground, elev. 1158 m. 100 sites, shelters. Recommended camping spot for first night.

Section 2
McLeod Meadows to Harrogate

(71) 0 km McLeod Meadows Campground.

(72) 1 McLeod Meadows picnic area.

(75) 4 Kootenay River picnic area. Start climb.

(83) 12 Viewpoint overlooking Kootenay Valley, Mitchell and Stanford ranges.

(86) 15 Olive Lake, Sinclair Pass summit, elev. 1485 m. Beginning of long, steep descent. Picnicking. Olive-hued lake nearby.

(89) 18 Sinclair Creek picnic area.

(100) 29 Iron Gates tunnel.

(101) 30 Aquacourt. Radium Hot Springs. Hot and cool pools, cafeteria, outdoor patio. Wooded trail to Redstreak national park campground.

(102) 31 Leaving Kootenay National Park. Information Centre.

(104) 33 Radium. Pop 1,000, elev. 808 m. All services. Jct. with Hwy 95. Turn right (N) following signs for Golden.

(For Redstreak National Park campground, leave park and turn S on Hwy 95 a short distance. Watch for signs.)

(114) 43 Edgewater. Edgewater Inn cabins and campground, 58 sites, showers, store, May 15-Sept. 15., 604-347-9403.

(123) 52 Spur Valley Campground. 32 sites, store, four cabins, four motel units, 604-347-9822. Recommended spot for second night for those taking four nights and not wishing to rough camp.

(132) 61 Brisco. Groceries.

(143) 72 Spillimacheen. Groceries.

(151) 80 Harrogate. Groceries and take-out food. Rough camping recommended hereabouts for small groups.

Section Three
Harrogate to Chancellor Peak

(161) 0km Castledale. No services.

(166) 5 Turn 2 km up steep gravel road for Taliesin Guest

House. Log construction, shared bath/shower, some meals, 604-348-2247.

(172) 11 Parson. Supplies uncertain.

(175) 14 Rest area, outhouses.

(208) 47 Golden. Pop. 3,500, elev. 790 m. All services. Museum. Camping: Golden Municipal Park on Kicking Horse River (90 sites, showers, includes group camping, 604-344-5412). Golden KOA Campground, 1.6 km E on Hwy 1, (106 sites, store, 604-344-6464). Last supply point until Field. Follow signs out of town for Trans-Canada. Turn right.

(209) 48 Visitor Information Centre. Picnicking.

(210) 49 KOA Campground, see above. Begin long, twisting climb.

(213) 52 Entering canyon.

(214) 53 Most narrow, treacherous part of gorge. Sharp curves and virtually no shoulder in places.

(215) 54 Levels off, then up again.

(218) 57 Bridge. Begin climb. Shoulder often disappears.

(225) 64 Level, beside Kicking Horse River. Picnic table by river.

(226) 65 Bridge over Kicking Horse River. Small shoulder but less threatening.

(229) 68 Top of grade! Sheer drop into gorge.

(233) 72 Park boundary, national parks permits and information centre.

(239) 78 Access for Chancellor Peak Campground on Kootenay River, recommended campground for those camping three nights. 64 sites, some on river.

Section Four

Chancellor Peak to Castle Mountain Junction

(239) 0 km Chancellor Peak Campground.

(240) 1 Hoodoo Creek Campground, 106 sites.

(242) 3 Picnicking, views of Mt. King.

(248) 9 Picnicking

(257) 18 Picnicking

(260) 21 Field. Elev. 1,242 m. Drinks, snacks at corner gas station. Fresh fruit, deli, smoked meat, salads and takeout food at The Siding in town, open daily in summer, 9 a.m. to 7 p.m.

(263) 24 Turnoff to Takakkaw Falls. See Tour 2. Visitor information. Kicking Horse Campground, 92 sites, showers, just up road. Cathedral Mountain Chalets, by Kicking Horse River has small though well-stocked store, 604-343-6442. Whiskey Jack Hostel is 13 km further along extremely steep and narrow Takakkaw Falls Road. Showers. Reservations through Calgary office, 403-283-5551. Begin steep climb.

(270) 31 Spiral Tunnel Viewpoint. Interpretive display, view of tunnels and Yoho Valley. Climb continues.

(271) 32 Old Bridge on Big Hill.

(274) 35 Wapta Lake and West Louise Lodge. Coffee shop. 604-343-6311.

(275) 36 Jct. Hwy 1A, direct route to Chateau Lake Louise and Lake. Keep straight for Lake Louise Village.

(277) 38 Picnic area.

(278) 39 Kicking Horse Pass. Elev. 1647 m. Continental Divide. Leaving Yoho National Park, entering Banff National Park.

(285) 46 Bow River bridge.

(287) 47 Jct. Icefield Parkway (Hwy 93). Keep straight on Trans-Canada.

(288) 48 Lake Louise Village. All services.

(290) 50 Turn left onto 1A (Bow Valley Parkway).

(291) 51 Corral Creek picnic area, hostel. Accommodates 50, call Calgary 403-283-5551 for reservations.

(300) 60 Baker Creek picnic area.

(303) 63 Protection Mountain Campground, 44 sites.

(314) 74 Return Castle Mountain Jct.

5

Extended Tours in the Rockies and the Selkirks

Tours in this chapter lead from dry montane forests, filled with Douglas fir, grasslands and lodgepole pine, to the dank interior rain forest of giant skunk cabbage, spiny Devil's Club, mosquitoes and frothy torrents.

They offer everything from the most famous—and surely the most tourist-clogged lake in North America (Lake Louise)—to the mysterious, cloud-shrouded monarch of the Canadian Rockies (Mt. Robson) to an historic pass that continues to oppose the passage of man (Rogers Pass). Here the cyclist finds adventure and challenge.

Most of these tours can be linked with others for extended trips. Banff-Lake Louise (Tour 17), for example, can be combined with the last leg of the Golden Triangle (Tour 16) to traverse the famed Kicking Horse Pass and descend through Yoho National Park and the difficult Yoho gorge to Golden, B.C.

From Golden, Tour 18 leads steeply over rainy Rogers Pass, connecting to Tour 19, a thrilling descent to Revelstoke, B.C. where cyclists may turn south into the Kootenays on Tour 52.

To the north at the end of the Icefields Parkway (Tours 14 and 15), cyclists can cross easy Yellowhead Pass and descend to Mt. Robson Provincial Park (Tour 20). Cyclists with plenty of time and energy might even continue from Robson to Tete Jaune Cache and then south on the Yellowhead Highway along the North Thompson River to Canada's drylands around Kamloops. From there, cyclists could return on the hurly-burly of the Trans-

Canada back over Rogers Pass and the Kicking Horse. Or better yet, turn southeast into the gorgeous Okanagan country and then into the lonely, serene Arrow Lakes and all the tours outlined in Chapter Eleven.

BANFF TO LAKE LOUISE

TOUR **17**

THE BOW VALLEY PARKWAY

Distance 158 km (98 miles) return

Time 2 days

Rating Intermediate

Terrain Gently rolling or level

Elev. gain 156 metres (512 ft)

Roads Newly-paved and realigned Bow Valley Parkway has no shoulder. Two short stretches on Trans-Canada which has wide paved shoulder

Traffic Trans-Canada busy. Bow Valley Parkway has moderate, slow-moving traffic

Connections Tours 1, 3, 4, 5, 14, 15, 16, 33 and Banff townsite routes

The Bow Valley Parkway seems made for cycling — and this tour travels its entire length. It leads through dry montane forest past a popular canyon, waterfalls, camp-grounds, a castle of a mountain, through meadows where deer and elk often graze and by numerous exhibits and trails.

There's a wide choice of campgrounds, hostels, restaurants, cabins, stores and hiking trails. And it ends at the tourist mecca below the famous Lake Louise from where cyclists may take the gorgeous loop up to the glacier-bounded, aquamarine lake. Other cycle routes from Lake Louise lead to equally-scenic Moraine Lake or over the Continental Divide into Yoho National Park.

For cyclists who only have a couple of days, not enough time to cycle the entire Banff-Jasper route, this tour through some of the most gorgeous mountain scenery on the continent is highly recommended.

The trip can be shortened to a one-day outing by starting from Castle Mountain Junction. Ask permission at the hostel to leave your car. Most cyclists will prefer to return from Lake Louise on the relatively quiet parkway. Others will want to make it something of a loop by returning on the other side of the river on the Trans-Canada. One's

TOUR 17 BANFF TO LAKE LOUISE

DISTANCE 158 km (98 miles)

a route for nature; the other for speed.

Highlights

For the first 24 km from Banff, see the description for Tour 6, Banff to Johnston Canyon.

After the canyon, views of the gothic towers of Castle Mountain begin to appear ahead. Formerly Mt. Eisenhower, it is a good example of a castellated peak formed from horizontal layers of Cambrian limestone that have eroded to leave turrets.

You soon pass the site of the once-thriving Silver City. It boomed in 1882 after a Stoney Indian showed prospector J.J. Healy a chunk of ore high in silver and copper. Healy staked a claim and word got around. By 1883, there were 175 wooden buildings along here, including five stores, three hotels, two saloons and three barbershops. But no silver. By 1885, Silver City was a ghost town.

The parkway passes a quiet campground and reaches Castle Mountain Junction where a spur connects with the Trans-Canada and the Banff-Windermere Highway. The road climbs to good vistas over the Bow River and passes the trailhead for Castle Mountain Lookout, a 7.2 km (return) hike. It goes by another quiet campground, a good picnic area, cabins and a

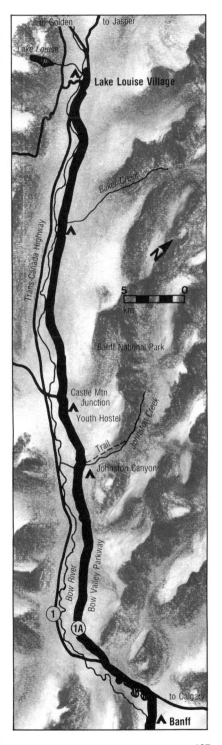

107

hostel before crossing the Bow and emerging onto the Trans-Canada for a short stretch to Lake Louise Village.

The large Lake Louise campground is the most convenient overnight stop. There's no camping near the lake or down at Valley of the Ten Peaks. For the route to Lake Louise, see Tour 4.

Road Log Tour 17

0 km Banff townsite. Pop. 6949, elev. 1383 metres. All services. Campground and hostel (403-762-4122 for hostel reservations) above town on Tunnel Mountain Rd. From Via Rail station, head N to Trans-Canada Hwy.

1 Left (W) on Trans-Canada for Lake Louise. Short hills.

7 Bow Valley Parkway. Turn right. Watch for mountain sheep.

8 Turnoff for Fireside picnic area, up steep paved road.

12 Muleshoe picnic area.

17 Sawback picnic area.

19 Road divides.

22 Two-way road resumes.

24 Johnston Canyon. Hiking trails, groceries, campground. Johnston Canyon Resort open May 15 - Sept. 20 (Box 875, Banff, Alberta T0L 0C0, 403-762-2971).

26 Castle Meadows group campground.

30 Castle Mountain Campground.

31 Castle Mountain Jct. Store, hostel (403-283-5551 for reservations), Castle Mountain Village chalets, 762-3311. Keep straight on Bow Valley Parkway.

42 Protection Mtn Campground.

45 Baker Creek picnic area. Baker Creek Bungalows, 522-3761.

54 Corral Creek picnic area. Hostel, 403-283-5551 for reservations. Closest hostel to Lake Louise.

55 Jct Trans-Canada. Turn right for Lake Louise.

57 Lake Louise turnoff, elev. 1539 metres. All services. Campground. Scenic lake is 6 km W, with steep climb.

TRAVEL ALBERTA

GOLDEN TO ROGERS PASS

TOUR **18**

THE GREAT CANADIAN CHALLENGE

Distance	77 km (48 miles) one way
Time	1 day westbound. Half-day eastbound.
Rating	Super-strenuous
Terrain	Continuous climb for most of trip, sometimes steep
Elev. gain	530 metres (1738 feet)
Roads	Well-paved, large shoulder
Traffic	Often heavy
Connections	Tours 16, 19

Climb steeply to historic, avalanche-scarred Rogers Pass under sharp peaks and great sheets of perpetual ice. Here is the only practical highway route through the formidable Selkirks, discovered in 1881 by Major A.B. Rogers, surveyor for the Canadian Pacific Railway.

"Such a view!" wrote A.L. Rogers, nephew of the explorer. "Never to be forgotten. Our eyesight caromed from one bold peak to another for miles in all directions. The wind blew fiercely across the ridge and scuddy clouds were whirled in their eddies behind

TOUR 18 GOLDEN TO ROGERS PASS   **DISTANCE** 77 km (48 miles)

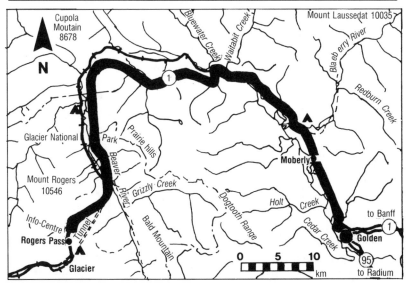

109

the great towering peaks of bare rock. Everything was covered with a shroud of white, giving the whole landscape the appearance of snow-clad desolation.''

The price for such a sight then and today is hard work. The ascent from the Columbia River to a point above the Beaver River Valley requires the CPR to put six extra locomotives on its heavy-tonnage westbound trains. And the trains only have to ascend to the Connaught Tunnel. Cyclists go 400 metres higher — and work harder than the lumbering trains, relatively speaking. And there's rain on the average two out of every three days in summer.

The Selkirk mountains are some of the most rugged in North America and continue to oppose the challenge of man, even man with 15 gears.

Highlights

Enjoy the first 25 km out of Golden because this is the only easy stretch. While traffic can often be heavy, the shoulder is wide and well-paved most of the way, except when it disappears on steep sections to make way for an extra driving lane.

Golden used to be a rip-roaring place optimistically called Golden City. It began in 1883 as a motley collection of tents, to which were gradually added cabins, stores and a huge number of saloons and with dance halls. The railway reached town in 1884. After the railway construction was finished, many of the boom towns along the tracks dwindled away. Golden, in a strategic location at the junction of the Columbia and Kicking Horse rivers, settled down to growth and respectability.

The highway passes close to the mosquito-filled bottomlands of the Columbia River past Golden. This valley is part of the Rocky Mountain Trench, a major geological fault line that follows the west edge of the Rockies for 1,500 km up through British Columbia. Getting out of a trench is never easy.

The highway finally crosses the Columbia, here only a modest river on a wide floodplain. It begins the dreaded ascent, leaving behind the cottonwoods and moving quickly up into Douglas fir, spruce and lodgepole pine. The highway climbs the rounded end of the Dogtooth Range, part of the Purcells, while the railway remains closer to the Columbia, before turning directly up the Beaver River.

It wasn't until 1956 that construction began on the Trans-Canada Highway through Rogers Pass, although the railway had been there since 1885, plagued by snowslides as well as the steep grade. The highway opened in 1962.

There's a brief stretch that's almost level before the highway swings south up the Beaver and begins a very strenuous ascent once again. The prominent peak directly ahead is Mt. Macdonald while Mt. Shaughnessy looms on the right side in front of Mt. Rogers.

The road finally crosses Beaver River just above the entrance to the

CPR's eight-kilometre Connaught Tunnel which passes under Mt. Macdonald. The views grow spectacular, compensating for the hard work. Note the many avalanche paths down the side of the pass ahead, pale green strips (in summer) through the darker forest. These mountains average almost 10 metres of snow every winter, making the Rogers Pass highway one of the most bombarded of main routes anywhere.

Painted circles along the shoulder indicate placements for the 105mm Canadian Forces howitzer that's used in winter to trigger avalanches. This is done to avoid the surprise avalanche that could bury traffic. It doesn't always work. Every winter is snow wars in Rogers Pass and every winter sees the highway closed for varying periods. Man never wins.

The highway soon passes through five rather dark snowsheds built of concrete under some of the more active avalanche paths. The tunnels have small shoulders and enough light from either end to provide some visibility. Cyclists, nonetheless, should be careful since drivers may be momentarily blind when entering the sheds from bright sunlight.

The grade finally relents as the highway approaches the lavish Rogers Pass Centre, 1.3 km east of the actual summit. It has a large fireplace, theatre, exhibits showing the history and geology of the area, outdoor displays and an information desk. Next to it is a lodge with a 24-hour cafeteria and a gas station with a limited supply of groceries.

A short trail right from the centre leads 1.3 km on an abandoned railway bed to the summit monument, passing the ruins of abandoned snowsheds.

Road Log Tour 18

0 km Golden, B.C. (Pop. 3,500, elev. 790 m. Camping at Golden Municipal Park in town on river (604-344-5412); KOA Kampground, 1.6 km E of town, below Hwy 1. Tourist info booth on Hwy 1. CP Rail service from Banff and Revelstoke. For Rogers Pass, turn W on Hwy 1. Road nearly level.

9 Moberley. Gas station.

12 Turnoff 1 km for Blaeberry Campground (604-344-2683), showers, laundromat, store, cook shelter (fee).

14 Blaeberry River.

16 Doyle Creek rest area. Views over Columbia River.

25 Columbia River bridge. Begin ascent.

35 Picnic area. Still climbing.

39 Road is more level.

41 Quartz Creek.

46 Turnoff 4 km for for Big Lake Resort and campground. Store, boat rentals, fishing (604-344-2000).

47 Steep climb resumes.

54 Time zone change: clocks go back 1 hour. Picnic tables. Enter Glacier National Park. Descent.

57 Bottom of hill. Mountain Creek (national park) campground, 306 sites, kitchen shelters.

59 Picnic area. Well-graded ascent.

60 Park gate.

64 Beaver River.

66 Ascent steepens. Excellent views.

67 Viewpoint. Steep climb.

70 Enter Rogers Pass.

71 First of 5 snowshed tunnels. Use lights, if possible.

74 End of snowsheds.

75 Picnic area.

77 Rogers Pass information and interpretive centre. Elev. 1320 m. Lodge (604-837-2126). 24-hour cafeteria, limited groceries at gas station June to mid-October. Hiking trails. Illecillewaet campground 4 km W.

THE GREAT BARRIER

"The walking is dreadful, we climb over and creep under fallen trees of great size and the men soon show that they feel the full weight of their burdens. . . The dripping rain from the bush and branches saturates us from above. Tall ferns sometimes reaching to the shoulder and devil's clubs through which we had to crash our way make us feel as if dragged through a horsepond and our perspiration is that of a Turkish bath. The devil's clubs may be numbered by millions and they are perpetually wounding us with their spikes against which we strike. We wade through alder swamps and tread down skunk cabbage and prickly aralias and so we continue until half-past four when the tired-out men are able to go no further."
— Sir Sanford Flemming on bushwacking in the Illecillewaet Valley

Step off the paved highway for an instant and you'll see that the valley hasn't changed since Flemming's day. Take a few steps from the trail and instantly appreciate what the early pathfinders Walter Moberley, Major A.B. Rogers and Flemming went through. For the Selkirks were — and remain — a barrier to Canadian unity more formidable than the Rockies. Here the mountains are usually made of harder rock than the peaks to the east. The great walls are slower to decay and remain perpendicular while in the Rockies sliding scree tends to reduce the grades.

The result is that while there are plenty of low, well-graded passes through the Rockies, only Rogers Pass provides a practical traverse through the rugged central Selkirks.

And there man must still battle every winter to keep the route open.

The search for a pass through the Selkirks began seriously after 1871 when British Columbia joined Canada. Part of the deal was that Canada would build a transcontinental railway to link B.C. with the rest of the country.

The railway was built across the Prairies, up the Bow River valley and over Kicking Horse Pass, a route long known to explorers. But at the Columbia River, the railway builders feared they might have to take their line up the "Big Bend" of the Columbia River, a considerable detour around the mountains rather than through them.

No route had yet been discovered through the Selkirks. In 1864, Moberley had pushed up the Illecillewaet from what is now Revelstoke. His assistant, Albert Perry, got even further the next year but had to turn back before reaching the head of the valley. Finally, in 1881, railway surveyor Rogers, by all accounts a rough, profane and ambitious man, reached the headwaters of the Illecillewaet and glimpsed the pass that would bear his name.

The railway was completed through the pass in 1885 — but the Selkirks still challenged. Winter after winter, great avalanches blocked the rails for long periods. On March 4, 1910, an avalanche caught a snow-clearing crew under Cheops Mountain and 62 men died.

Rogers Pass, Glacier National Park
TOURISM BRITISH COLUMBIA

The CPR soon began construction of the Connaught Tunnel under Mt. Macdonald, the longest railway tunnel in Canada that would enable the trains to avoid some of the steep grades and most especially the avalanches. Even that wasn't enough for speedy transportation of freight through the Selkirks. By the 1980s, the railway was again at work on a longer tunnel which would reduce grades in the pass. The Mt. Macdonald Tunnel is to stretch 14.7 km, longest in North America.

No road was built through the pass until the Trans-Canada Highway was completed in 1962. There again, the battle against avalanches meant a state of war. Numerous snowsheds had to be constructed under some of the worst slide paths. Earth dams, dikes, mounds and catch basins were constructed above the highway to block or divert slides. And each winter the road is closed occasionally while a 105mm army howitzer is brought in to bombard known avalanche trigger zones above the highway. No surrender.

ROGERS PASS TO REVELSTOKE

PASSAGE THROUGH THE SELKIRKS

Distance 67 km (42 miles)

Time Half-day westbound, 1 day eastbound

Rating Moderate westbound. Super-strenuous eastbound.

Terrain Gradual to steep grade

Elev. change 873 metres (2864 ft)

Roads Well-paved, large shoulder

Traffic Often heavy

Connections Tours 18, 52

Descend through a rain forest of cedar and hemlock, past a hot springs, along an historic valley, the road winding above a cascading river through some of the most rugged terrain in Canada. That's the glide from Rogers Pass down the Illecillewaet River Valley to the junction with the Columbia River at Revelstoke. For the westbound cyclist, it's downhill almost all the way — and cyclists need to resist the temptation to do this leg in one thrilling, non-stop flash. That's the motorists' way and they miss so much. For the eastbound cyclist, it's one of the longest ascents in Canada, although the road grades are seldom extremely steep.

Highlights

From the information and interpretive centre and lodge, it's only a slight ascent to the summit monument where there are views across the road to the sharp and deeply-glaciated Mt. Sir Donald Range and behind to the snowy Hermit Range. The view south down the road is to the Asulkan Glacier, among the more than 100 glaciers in the well-named park. The vista north takes in the Swiss Glacier between Mt. Rogers and Hermit Mountain. The closer peak to the right is Mt. Tupper.

Once the railway went right over the summit of the pass with a station where the hotel is today. The Connaught Tunnel, completed in 1916, enables the trains to avoid the steep, avalanche-prone climb over the top.

The vegetation here represents the interior subalpine forest of mountain hemlock, subalpine fir and Engelmann spruce. Behind the momument, a trail leads for 25 minutes along the old railroad bed for 1.3 km, ending back at the interpretive centre.

Bundle up well for the glorious descent from the summit. Just below is Illecillewaet campground, best in the park, and the hub of one of the most concentrated networks of hiking trails anywhere in the western mountains. These beautifully-engineered trails leading to impressive ridges and aerial viewpoints are a legacy of early trail builders who operated out of Glacier House, a big CPR resort open from 1887 until 1925. For hiking information, a brochure called ''Footloose in the Columbias: A Hiker's Guide to Glacier and Mount Revelstoke National Parks'' is available at the interpretive centre.

The descent becomes more gradual as the road leads above the Illecillewaet River. Past Loop Brook campground are three snowsheds built over some of the more active avalanche paths along the highway, just some of the 96 that menace traffic in winter through the park. You can see other avalanche paths on the far side of the river and more snowsheds protecting the railway. On these light green streaks on the hillside, grizzlies may sometimes be seen feeding in spring. The yellow avalanche lily, which blooms in spring soon after the snow melts, is a favorite food for the grizzly.

Albert Canyon Hot Springs is worth a stop, especially in cool weather when cyclists will especially welcome the 40 degrees C (105 F) hot mineral soak.

While Mount Revelstoke National Park has no campgrounds, it provides a number of picnic areas and roadside attractions such as the Giant Cedars Trail. In damp forests, Western red cedars and Western

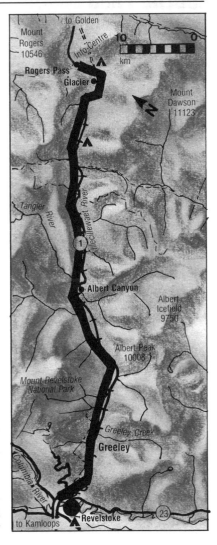

hemlock can grow to 2.4 metres across and 7.7 metres around.

Step away from the highway clearing anywhere and you'll appreciate that this landscape is far removed from the dry, semi-open montane forest of the lower Rockies.

Here, it's a tangle of devil's club, thimbleberry, false box and ferns, even pungent skunk cabbage that grows chest high in some places. Imagine the effort of explorers such as Walter Moberly or Major A.B. Rogers as they pushed their way up this valley through nearly impenetrable undergrowth.

On the outskirts of Revelstoke, the highway passes the start of the 26-km gravel road which switches back steeply up to the 1938-metre summit of Mt. Revelstoke, a route not recommended for cyclists, although some do it each year.

Revelstoke is just off the highway to the left and this beautifully-situated and friendly community is recommended for a stopover. The downtown has a deli, natural-food store and the Revelstoke Cycle Shop at 120 Mackenzie Avenue. (604-837-2646).

OPTION: From Revelstoke, a long side trip leads north up the Columbia River on the well-paved Big Bend Highway past Revelstoke Dam, eight kilometres north. It goes all the way to the Mica Dam, 144 km from town, largest earth-filled dam in the western world.

The Big Bend road carries little traffic and provides excellent views up many of the valleys to the glaciers above. While the highway generally follows the river, there are many long ascents and descents. Supplies are available at the small community of Mica Creek at the end and there's camping at Downie Creek at about the halfway point.

Road Log Tour 19

0 km Rogers Pass information and interpretive centre on Trans-Canada Hwy, 77 km W of Golden. Elev. 1320. Lodge (604-837-2126), 24-hour cafeteria, limited groceries at gas station June to mid-October. Interpretive trails.

2 Rogers Pass summit monument. Elev. 1330 metres. Begin descent.

4 Paved turnoff for Illecillewaet campground (National Park) in 1.5 km, 58 sites, kitchen shelters. Steep downhill. Grand views.

5 Leaving Rogers Pass. Road levels.

6 Turnoff for Loop Brook campground

7 Illecillewaet River. Gradual descent.

15 Picnic area.

20 Picnic area beside river. Leaving Glacier National Park.

21 First of three snowsheds.

31 Seven-per-cent grade descent.

34 Road levels. Turnoff for Canyon Hot Springs. Camping, natural hot pool and swimming pool. Cafe, store. Open May to Sept. (604-827-2526)

39 Woolsey Creek.

40 Entering Mt. Revelstoke National Park. Giant Cedars picnic area. Nature trail. Up-and-down cycling.

51 Park gate

53 Illecillewaet rest area. Gradual descent.

64 KOA Kampground (837-2085), store, laundromat. Niedersachsen campground (837-5387), store, laundromat.

65 Revelstoke turnoff. Descent.

66 Turnoff for 26-km gravel road which switches back steeply up to the 1,938-metre summit of Mt. Revelstoke.

67 Revelstoke (pop. 9,682, elev. 457 m). All services. Via Rail connections to Vancouver and Banff. Smokey Bear campground (604-837-2546) 5 km W on Hwy 1, laundromat, store. Canada West campground (837-4420) 4 km W, pool, store, laundromat. Williamson Lake (municipal) campground (837-2968), beach swimming.

JASPER TOWNSITE TO Mt. ROBSON (RETURN)

MONARCH OF THE CANADIAN ROCKIES

Distance 166 km (102 miles) return

Time 1 to 2 days

Rating Intermediate

Terrain One relatively easy pass, numerous level stretches, long descent into Mt. Robson Park

Elev. loss 235 metres (770 feet) to Robson

Roads Wide shoulder, good condition

Traffic Moderate to busy

Connections Tours 14, 15, 39

Mighty Mt. Robson is the highest peak in the Canadian Rockies, a monarch at 3,954 metres, an inspiring sight from the Yellowhead Highway — on one of those rare days when cloud doesn't cover the summit. The cycle from Jasper townsite to Mt. Robson Provincial Park is relatively easy. There are great peaks, lakes, vast forests and profusions of wildflowers along the way.

Although bicycle clubs often use this tour as a one-day training sprint, it is recommended as an over-nighter for all but the strongest. Note that there are only two campgrounds at Mt. Robson and they can fill up quickly on weekends. Cyclists can usually squeeze in somewhere,

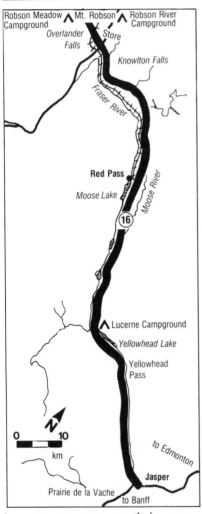

townsite. The Whistlers are on the left; to the north are numerous small lakes and the Victoria Cross ranges. Undemanding grades make for leisurely cycling.

Yellowhead Pass at 1130 metres was once known as Leather Pass and is among the lowest crossings of the Continental Divide. The pass marks the boundary between Alberta and British Columbia. From here, waters to the east go into the Miette, Athabasca and Mackenzie rivers and on to the Arctic Ocean; to the west, water flows into the Fraser and on to the Pacific.

This gap was used as a route to the Cariboo gold rush in the 1860s and the Canadian Pacific considered it as a route west. But they rejected it in favour of the Kicking Horse Pass, although the Grand Trunk and Canadian Northern (later Canadian National Railway) built their trans-continental line over the pass in 1915.

At Yellowhead Lake, Mt. McFitzwilliam is prominent to the south and Yellowhead Mountain and Lucerne Peak rise across the water to the northwest. Longer Moose Lake is, not surprisingly, a good place to spot moose in early morning or at dusk. In mid-summer, the roadside is fringed with daisies, asters and Indian paintbrush. The prolific paintbrush is usually found among other plants because it is a parasite. Its roots penetrate other plants and rob their food.

however, or camp on their own (unofficially) in the surrounding forest.

Take water purification tablets and ample food supplies, as selection is limited at the small store at the park.

Highlights

Cycling is easy out of Jasper

118

The glide down to the camp-grounds in Mt. Robson Provincial Park is exhilarating. You can't see famous Mt. Robson until almost opposite it — and then only if the weather is good. In 1913, Austrian guide Conrad Kain was the first to attain the summit. Cyclists who catch sight of the summit are fortunate — Robson's lofty altitude crowns it with wispy clouds for all but a dozen days a year. Yet even without views of Robson, this remains a first-class tour.

Road Log Tour 20

0 km Information Centre on Connaught Dr. in Jasper townsite, pop. 3970, elev. 1060 m, all services. Go right (W) down main street and continue under tracks.

2 Turn right (W) onto Yellowhead Hwy 16 at jct. with Hwy 93. Begin gradual climb.

26 Alberta-British Columbia border. Yellowhead Pass, 1130 m. Enter Mt. Robson Provincial Park, picnicking.

30 East end of Yellowhead Lake, picnicking.

34 Lucerne campground, 32 sites, picnicking. Water bottle fill-up.

36 W end of lake, picnicking.

53 Moose Lake.

65 Red Pass, park headquarters.

83 Mt. Robson. Elev. at information centre 825 m, picnicking, sparsely-stocked store, hiking. Turn left (S) for Robson Meadows campground, 127 sites, visitor centre. Follow road to right of main highway to Robson River campground, 19 sites. Return to Jasper by same route.

GAIL HELGASON

Medicine Lake, Jasper National Park   GAIL HELGASON

6

Day Tours in Jasper National Park

Jasper National Park is where the cyclist goes to relax. Compared with the parks to the south, the traffic isn't as heavy, nor the tourist facilities so elaborate. This is a stunning land of wilderness, ice caps and elk on the main street.

Here is the largest and most northerly of the Canadian Rocky Mountain national parks. It covers more than 10,800 square kilometres (4,170 square miles). Two chains of mountains — the Front Ranges and the Main Ranges — cut through it, gouging a spectacular land of glaciers, broad valleys, lakes and rivers.

Jasper townsite, which has a population of about 4,000, is generally less accessible than Banff, Yoho or Kootenay parks. It lies at the end of the Icefields Parkway but it is 362 kilometres from Edmonton, the closest city. However, transcontinental VIA Rail service links Jasper with east and west and there is daily bus transportation to Vancouver and Edmonton. Brewster Transport has frequent bus service down the parkway to Banff and will carry boxed bicycles.

Jasper lacks the variety of day cycling trips to be found in Banff. The scenery around the townsite, where most of the day-trips are based, lacks some of the drama of Banff, although it is tranquil and relaxing.

On the other hand, traffic is lighter — and the pressure is off. Here the cyclist can lose himself in contemplation of crystal clear lakes, water-falls and canyons. Most of the day-trips are on roads with light to moderate traffic, except on summer weekends when everything is busier.

The most strenuous and perhaps the most rewarding day-trip is the ascent to Maligne Lake, everyone's ideal of what a mountain lake should look like. See Tour 21. An excellent and less strenuous tour is the loop south of Jasper townsite to Athabasca Falls — Tour 26. There's also a family or short tour around some of the tiny lakes south of the townsite that is partly on roads blocked to motor vehicles — Tour 22. Plus a bike-and-canoe option on the Athabasca River and an out-and-back trip up onto the benchlands behind the townsite, ending at a pleasant lake.

And no visitor should miss a visit to Maligne Canyon. Here pounding water has swirled, pummelled and shaped the limestone into a narrow, pot-holed gorge as delicate and powerful as a work of art.

JASPER TOWNSITE TO MALIGNE LAKE (RETURN) TOUR 21

CLIMB TO MARY SCHAFFER'S LAKE

Distance	96 km (60 miles) return
Time	4 hours up, 2 hours back
Rating	Strenuous
Terrain	Steep climb
Elev. gain	620 metres (2,034 feet)
Roads	Mostly new paving. No shoulder.
Traffic	Busy summer weekends, light to moderate otherwise
Connections	Tours 22, 23, 39

The picture that represents Alberta (or at least Jasper National Park) in the minds of many, shows tiny Spirit Island and the impressive peaks and glaciers above the deep blue of Maligne Lake. Everybody wants to see it but cyclists should take warning: Getting to the lake is a long, hard, uphill grind.

Views do compensate for the low-gear toil as do the many scenic picnic spots. At Maligne Lake, you can rent a canoe, go on a two-hour cruise to Spirit Island, recuperate on the sunny balcony of the day lodge, or if energy remains, take an easy nature walk.

Another reward comes late in the day with an exhilarating descent. Note that there is no camping anywhere along this route. The only accommodation is at Maligne Youth Hostel near the start.

OPTION: Those with less time could have a pleasant outing by only going as far as Medicine Lake at km 32 (an elevation gain of 400 metres) where there are fine views and picnic spots.

Highlights

Cycling is flat and easy on Highway 16 to the Athabasca River crossing, a good place to spot game in the early morning. Roche Bonhomme of the toothy Colin Range towers ahead. South is the forested, round top of Signal Mountain and behind it red-brown Mt. Tekarra, part of the Maligne Range.

The climb begins after you cross the Athabasca. Maligne Canyon, a narrow limestone gorge hewn by the Maligne River, is not to be missed. A 20-minute self-guided walk leads to the canyon's steepest parts and ends at a tea house.

Traffic thins after the canyon turnoff. The grade is generally steep along the Maligne River although some easy bits provide momentary relief. This part of the river usually carries little water. Most of the drainage from Medicine Lake above runs underground. The jagged peaks ahead are part of the oldest rock formations in the park, dating back 600 million years.

Depending on the time of year, Medicine Lake may or may not be scenic. But it will almost certainly be interesting. (See box.) There are fine views across the water to the slate-grey Queen Elizabeth Range.

The road is relatively level along the lakeshore, then begins to climb again. The Maligne River is more spectacular here with cascades and violent rapids. At km 42 there are some particularly well-situated

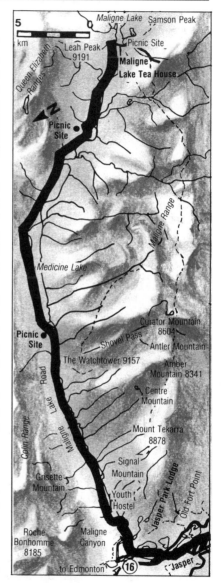

picnic tables by the river.

To the left rise the pink-topped Opal Hills, named by early explorer Mary Schäffer. In 1908 she became the first white woman to view Maligne Lake. To the right are the Bald Hills, traversed by the Skyline Trail, one of Jasper's prime backpacking trips. These hills are some of the southernmost grazing grounds of the caribou.

At Maligne Lake, a 3.2-km trail loops from the promenade by the boathouse down the lake and back through forests of lodgepole pine to an area of kames and kettles, mounds and depressions formed by glaciers. Lake cruises are fairly expensive but undeniably scenic. Call 403-852-3370 for rates and reservations.

Road Log Tour 21

0 km Information Centre on Connaught Dr., in Jasper townsite. Pop. 3,970, elev. 1060 m, all services. Turn E.

4 Jct. Hwy 16. Turn left (E)

6 Bridge over Athabasca River. Cross and turn left at end of bridge for Maligne.

12 Maligne Canyon. Elev. 1160 m. Sightseeing, nature walks, teahouse. Maligne Youth Hostel on right across from canyon. Closed Wed. Reservations through Edmonton office: 403-439-3086.

19 Picnic table by Maligne River.

25 Medicine Lake, elev. 1460 m. Views, picnic tables.

32 Jacques Lake trail. Picnic tables.

42 Maligne River. Picnic tables.

48 Maligne Lake, elev. 1680 m. Cafeteria, rentals of canoes, rowboats and fishing tackle, hiking, lake cruises, 403-852-3379 for rates and reservations. No camping. Return to Jasper by same route.

A Disappearing Lake

The calm waters of Medicine Lake hide one of Jasper's most fascinating geological phenomena, a puzzle which intrigued researchers for decades before finally being solved in 1956: Why does Medicine Lake disappear in fall and winter?

The depth of the lake varies by as much as 20 metres through the year. The Indians knew where to put the blame — they called the vanishing lake "Bad Medicine." Later, one park warden dumped magazines into the lake to see where they would end up. Results were not conclusive.

A French scientist, Jean Corbel, finally unravelled the mystery. He discovered that Medicine Lake drains into what may be the world's largest underground stream, an inaccessible cave network whose passages lead down to Maligne Canyon 15 km below.

JASPER TOWNSITE - Lac BEAUVERT — LAKE ANNETTE - LAKE EDITH **22**

PLACID LAKES AND A PRINCELY LODGE

Distance	19 km (12 miles) return
Time	1 to 2 1/2 hours with sightseeing
Rating	Easy
Terrain	Mostly level
Elev. gain	Negligible
Roads	Narrow, partly on roads blocked to through-motor traffic
Traffic	Mostly slow-moving tourist traffic
Connections	Tours 14, 15, 20, 21, 39 and Jasper townsite routes

This is the recommended short day tour from Jasper townsite. It is an almost level if unspectacular ride by glassy green lakes, mixed forest and luxurious Jasper Park Lodge. You can spend an hour or two or a day, perhaps renting a boat, swimming in Jasper's warmest waters or hiking. Or pack some champagne. It's that kind of tour.

Highlights

Head out of Jasper townsite and cross the Athabasca River. A trail on the right leads up the knoll dubbed Old Fort Point. Take a few minutes to walk up the steps, where a cairn commemorates early geographer David Thompson. Views of Mt. Edith Cavell and the winding river are impressive on clear days. To the north are the quartz sandstone cliffs of Pyramid Mountain above the Jasper benchland.

No fort ever stood on this knoll. Henry House, a small shack erected by the Northwest Fur Co. in 1811, may have been situated nearby.

There's a small rocky beach to the left on Lac Beauvert (much frequented by scuba divers) before the road is blocked to motorized traffic and winds through the plush golf course around the lake.

Jasper Park Lodge has had its share of prestigious guests, including Princess Margaret. The original lodge of felled logs was built in 1922 by the CNR and burned down in 1952. Only nine of the original cabins are still in use and are much sought after by guests. Paddle boats, rowboats, sailboats and bicycles can be rented at Sandy's at the front of the lodge at lakeside.

The lodge offers an expensive but memorable outdoor patio lunch in summer. Snacks are available in the Copper Kettle. Or splurge in the Beauvert or Tonquin room (reservations, 403-852-3301).

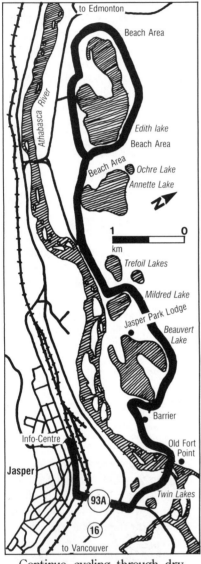

Continue cycling through dry, semi-open montane forest. There are popular beaches at both Lake Annette and Lake Edith, the warmest waters around, although they still feel chilly to flatlanders.

Their clarity makes them popular with scuba divers.

The beautiful log cabins visible through the trees at Lake Edith are privately owned. Beachfronts, including those in front of cottages, are public.

Cyclists have the option of returning the same way, or continuing on to Maligne Canyon and looping back to Jasper townsite on Highway 16. (See Tour 23.)

Road Log Tour 22

0 km Jasper townsite information centre on Connaught Dr. Pop. 3,970, elev. 1060 m. All services. Head W on Connaught Dr., pass railway station and go left on first turn, Hazel Ave.

0.5 Cross tracks.

1 Cross over Hwy 16.

1.2 Turn left on Lac Beauvert Rd. Sign says Lac Beauvert-Old Fort Point Rd.

2 Bridge over Athabasca River. Old Fort Point Trail.

3 Pass barrier. Paved road is blocked to motorized traffic. Proceed along Lac Beauvert.

4 Jasper Park Lodge. Dining, bike rentals, boat rentals, stables, 403-852-3301.

4.5 Mildred Lake.

6.5 Lake Annette. Beach, swimming, boat rentals. (NOTE: Paved path for wheelchairs and pedestrians is banned to bicycles.)

7.5 Lake Edith. Beaches, swimming, boat rentals south end-obtain keys in town. Continue right around east side of lake, where road is blocked to cars.

9.5 Beach, swimming. Follow bike route on west side to circle lake. Return same way.

19 Return information centre.

THOMPSON, THE GREAT MAPMAKER

"Here let us stand and say,
Here was a man — full sized — whose fame
Shall never pass away."
— Bliss Carman, 1922

Born in London, England in 1770, David Thompson became the first to map comprehensively Canada's western territories. The Welsh student began as an apprentice to the Hudson's Bay Company and studied surveying while recovering from a broken leg. By 1797 he had left that company and mapped most of the posts of its rival, the North West Co. He took on extra duties as a trader and by 1806 embarked on opening trade with Indians west of the Rockies. Here he mapped the uncharted Columbia River basin and explored the passes west from the Athabasca and Saskatchewan rivers.

Thompson retired from exploration in 1812 and continued as a surveyor and mapmaker. The failure of his businesses led him to publish the journals of his early explorations. He died in poverty at age 87. Today, he is regarded as one of the world's greatest geographers.

GAIL HELGASON

JASPER TOWNSITE TO MALIGNE CANYON (LOOP)

CANYON, LODGE AND LAKES

Distance	24 km (15 miles) loop
Time	2 to 3 hours, with sightseeing
Rating	Intermediate
Terrain	Mostly level. Long climb to Maligne Canyon
Elev. gain	100 metres (328 feet)
Roads	Hwy 16 wide shoulders, others are narrower
Traffic	Maligne Road traffic often fairly busy
Connections	Tours 14, 15, 20, 39 and Jasper townsite tours

The scalloped limestone gorge that is Maligne Canyon makes an exhilarating destination for the day cyclist. The climb is steady to the canyon; the remainder of the tour loops gently along green lakes and past Jasper Park Lodge back to the townsite.

Highlights

The first portion of the tour to the bridge over the Athabasca River is an easy pedal. Forested Signal Mountain is to the south with rougher Mt. Tekarra, named after Sir George Simpson's Indian guide,

behind. The toothy Colin Range is to the left after you cross the bridge, where a gradual ascent begins.

The canyon is well worth a stop. A 0.8-km interpretive walk leads from the end of the parking lot to Second Bridge, the canyon's deepest part, where the drop is 50 metres.

After viewing the canyon, you may want to stop at the teahouse before a glide down to Lake Edith and Lake Annette. These are Jasper's warmest lakes and have several sand beaches. Numerous picnic spots can be found along the way.

The route skirts Mildred Lake and Jasper Park Lodge, where boats (and bicycles) can be rented.

Road Log Tour 23

0 km Information centre in Jasper townsite, on Connaught Dr. Pop. 3970, elev. 1060 m, all services. Go E on Connaught.

4 Jct. Hwy 16. Turn left.

6 Bridge over Athabasca River. Cross and keep left at end of bridge for Maligne Canyon.

12 Maligne Canyon. Elev. 1160 m. Nature walks, teahouse. Maligne

Hostel on right across from canyon (Closed Wed. Reservations through Edmonton office, 403-439-3086). After canyon visit, head down hill again.

16 Turn on first road left after canyon to join Lake Edith Road.

16.5 Turn right (S) on Lake Edith Road for fastest return. A peaceful alternative is to turn left to go round the lake on the other side.

17 S end of Lake Edith. Beach, swimming. Obtain keys for boat rentals from town.

18 Lake Annette. Beach. swimming, picnicking. Paved trail around lake for foot and wheelchair traffic only.

19 Mildred Lake.

19.5 Jasper Park Lodge. Bike and boat rentals, stables. Reservations 403-852-3301.

21.5 Old Fort Point. Cross bridge over Athabasca River.

22 Turn right (N) on Hwy 93A.

22.5 Cross Hwy 16.

23.5 Cross over tracks. Turn right on Connaught Dr. to return to information centre.

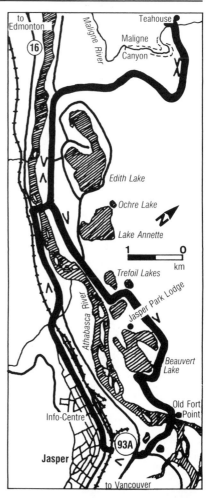

Maligne Canyon, Jasper National Park
TRAVEL ALBERTA

129

JASPER TOWNSITE TO PYRAMID LAKE (RETURN)

CLIMB A BENCH

Distance	14 km (8 miles) return
Time	1/2 hour to 1 hour
Rating	Intermediate
Terrain	Fairly steady ascent, sometimes steep to lake, fast descent coming down
Elev. gain	140 metres (394 feet)
Roads	Winding, no shoulder, some rough pavement
Traffic	Usually moderate
Connections	Tours 14, 15, 20, 39 and Jasper townsite tours

The road up to Pyramid Lake requires a fairly steep climb. Persevere. There's much to see and do at the destination. There's no camping at the lake, although cyclists could stay at Pyramid Bungalows. Strong cyclists, however, can ride up in less than an hour and enjoy a nearly effortless coast back down.

Highlights

This forest-fringed route wastes no time gaining altitude. It levels off in places and crosses Cottonwood Creek, best place to see a moose hereabouts. The 5-km Patricia Loop trail begins on the west side of the road from Pyramid Riding Stables. Although it doesn't afford many views of Patricia Lake, the hike is fairly easy and a good place to see moose and beaver. Birdwatchers frequent Cottonwood Slough, where hummingbirds, warblers and yellowthroats are spotted in summer.

Patricia Lake was the site of an odd war-time experiment — Operation Halakkuk. The idea was to use ice for a ship's hull, with the ultimate aim of using ice to construct North Atlantic airfields. The war ended before the fascinating idea could be applied.

Ahead is the distinctive quartz sandstone peak of Pyramid Mountain, with its microwave tower. Continue to Pyramid Lake, which is swimmable, although colder than either Edith or Annette.

You can picnic at the south end. We recommend Pyramid Island at the end of the road. Cross a rustic bridge to the tiny island, where there are picnic tables and a gazebo. A special place.

Road Log Tour 24

0 km Jasper Information Centre on Connaught Dr. Pop. 3970, elev. 1060 m, all services. Go E on

TOUR 24 JASPER TOWNSITE TO PYRAMID LAKE (RETURN)

DISTANCE 14 km (8 miles)

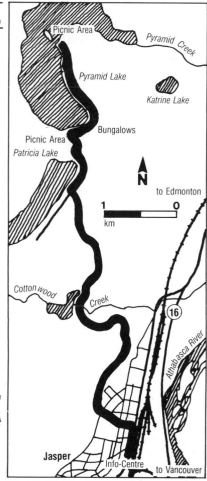

Connaught and turn left at first turn, Cedar Ave.

0.5 Keep straight to join Pyramid Lake Road where it intersects Bonhomme.

5.5 Patricia Lake, elev. 1200 m, picnicking, hiking, riding, boat rentals.

6 South end, Pyramid Lake. Turn left 0.5 km for picnic and beach area, short hiking trails.

6.2 Pyramid Lake Bungalows. Restaurant, boat, canoe, windsurfing and fishing tackle rental, 403-852-3536.

7 Pyramid Lake Island picnic site. Return same route.

ATHABASCA RIVER BY BIKE AND CANOE

TOUR **25**

AN ATHABASCA ALTERNATIVE

Distance About 25 km (16 miles) by river, 30 km (19 miles) by road, depending on where you land

Time Full day. Get an early start

Rating Paddlers must be proficient in manoeuvring the canoe and

131

	avoiding gravel bars. The second part is an easy and pleasant cycle, though many paddlers may be tired by this point
Terrain	River gradient gentle. Road mostly level
Elev. loss	Negligible
Roads	Hwy 16 well-paved with excellent shoulder
Traffic	Hwy 16 usually moderate
Connections	Tours 14, 15, 20, 39 and Jasper townsite tours

Below Jasper townsite, the Athabasca River is fast-moving yet without rapids. It winds below great limestone peaks, under cliffs, past sand dunes and into a large, shallow lake. This was once the route of explorers and fur traders like David Thompson.

A bicycle and canoe make an ideal combination. Leave the bike hidden in the woods, chained to a sturdy tree near your landing place. Have a rather effortless outing on the river, letting the current do most of the work (the current dies at the start of Jasper Lake). Then ride your bike down the broad shoulder of the Yellowhead Highway back to Jasper where you started — and you've sampled the world's two best forms of transportation.

Highlights

You need a vehicle for this route, as well as bike and canoe. Travel Highway 16 to Jasper Lake, about 25 km northeast of Jasper townsite. If the wind is strong or if you're hesitant about facing the shallow waters of Jasper Lake, leave your bike near the Athabasca River bridge. Otherwise pick a spot along the lakeside. Hide your bike in the bush, locked to a sturdy tree with a note saying you'll be back for it later. Otherwise, someone might find the bike and think it was abandoned or stolen. Once you've found your landing spot — and that shouldn't be difficult — stand by the lake a minute and fix in your mind where you want to go. Remember the shoreline will look different from the water.

After hiding your bikes, drive back to Jasper. From Highway 16, turn left at the first road beyond the entrance to the townsite. Turn left again to Old Fort Point bridge. There's a convenient launch site on the other side of the bridge and cars may be left here for the day.

The river flows gently past numerous islands. Take the channels that seem to have the most water. The river passes the Maligne Road bridge and leads out past interesting rock formations. At km 15, canoeists can stop and climb the bank through a few trees to an open field where John Moberley's old cabin, built in 1896, is situated. He was the son of Henry Moberley, factor at Jasper House until 1881.

TOUR 25 ATHABASCA RIVER BY BIKE AND CANOE

DISTANCE 25 km (16 miles)

John, like his brother Ewan, homesteaded in the valley until the national park was established. Then they sold their holdings to the government and moved to Grande Cache.

The river passes the confluence with the fast-moving Snaring River and crosses under Highway 16. This is the alternate pull-out point. The grey-rock mountain on the right is Morro, a favorite practice peak for climbers. The Athabasca widens into Jasper Lake and the paddler is in for some interesting going. The lake is so clogged with sand that only a couple of inches of water may be left under the keel. You might even have to get out and pull the canoe along for awhile. From this point, paddlers could keep to the right for the most direct route to the pull-out point. Those with more time might enjoy keeping left to explore the sand dunes on the north bank.

At the highway, you can either hide your canoe in the bush, chained to a tree or leave someone to guard it while you take the two- or three-hour cycle back to Jasper.

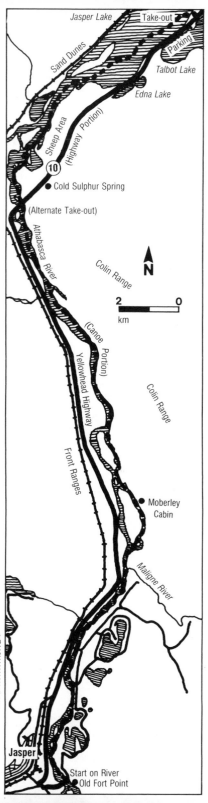

JASPER TOWNSITE TO ATHABASCA FALLS (LOOP)

ALONG THE ATHABASCA VALLEY

Distance 67 km (41 miles)
Time Day tour
Rating Intermediate
Terrain Hilly along Hwy 93, two long climbs on return
Elev. gain 162 metres (531 feet)
Roads Hwy 93 wide, protected and well-paved shoulder which disappears to allow extra lane of traffic at turn-offs. Hwy 93A no shoulder, rough in places
Traffic Hwy 93 busy in summer, quiet in spring and fall. Hwy 93A traffic moderate in summer, quiet in spring and fall
Connections Tours 14, 15, 20, 39 and Jasper townsite tours

Turbulent Athabasca Falls is one of Jasper's prime tour attractions. That's a secondary reason for riding this scenic loop, however.

A better reason is that the Athabasca Falls loop offers the best longer daytrip from Jasper townsite.

Most lengthier daytrips in the Jasper area dictate a steady uphill climb followed by a fast coast back down. This route goes up and down like a roller coaster in places, but has relatively little over-all elevation gain.

Pack a great picnic — there are no services along the route. The tour can be done as an overnighter by camping at Wabasso or staying at the Athabasca Falls Hostel.

Highlights

Cycling starts off easily. You follow along the Athabasca River with The Whistlers to the west and the Maligne Range to the east. Cyclists who are also canoeists might enjoy stopping at Becker's Bungalows for a look at the impressive rapids at a riverbend there.

Wapiti Campground has some camping spots along the Athabasca River and makes a more low-key place to stay than mammoth Whistlers.

At Horseshoe Lake, a short trail leads to a pretty pond under the reddish, quartz sandstone outcroppings of Mt. Hardisty. Mt. Kerkeslin, at 2983 metres, dominates to the south.

Athabasca Falls boils and foams 25 metres down into a narrow gorge. Signs explain the geology of

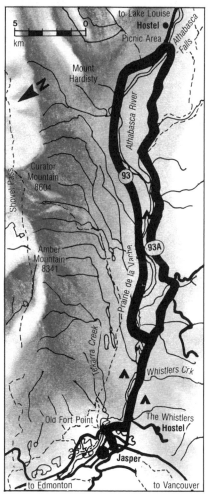

1811. He was looking for a safer fur trade route across the Rockies as an alternative to Howse Pass to the south. He managed to reach the Continental Divide with dog teams through deep snow, blazing a trail that was used for 50 years before being abandoned in favor of Yellowhead Pass to the north.

Along the Athabasca, you pass a pleasantly-situated picnic site at Leach Lake, a warden station and Wabasso Campground before starting a steep ascent along the flanks of Mt. Edith Cavell.

At the top is the turn-off to Angel Glacier. It's a steep, difficult climb of 14 km to the glacier, not recommended for average cyclists. Those who consider this option may stay at Edith Cavell Hostel on the road near the top. (Reservations through Northern Alberta office, 403-439-3089.)

After the Edith Cavell Junction, the descent is exhilarating across the Astoria River and down an open slope with views across the Athabasca Valley.

Road Log Tour 26

0 km Jasper townsite at information centre on Connaught Dr. Pop. 3,970, elev. 1060 m. Head W on Connaught.

0.3 Turn left at first street (Hazel) and cross tracks.

1 Cross over Hwy 16.

the area and a short walk leads to an abandoned gorge where the falls originally plunged. Sir James Hector travelled here in 1859, looking for a way across the mountains.

Undulating Highway 93A is usually quiet. The Whirlpool fireroad is the access to the valley which early geographer David Thompson mistakenly followed in

1.2 Lac Beauvert Rd. Keep straight.

3.5 Turnoff for Whistlers Campground 0.5 further and Whistlers Hostel 2.5 km further. (Accommodates 50, reservations through Edmonton office, 403-439-3089). Keep straight.

5.5 Wapiti Campground (340 sites, showers)

9 Jct. 93A. Alternate route S to Athabasca Falls.

18 Picnic area.

29 Horseshoe Lake.

32 Jctn 93A. Turn right.

32.5 Athabasca Falls. Elev. 1173 m. Picnicking. Athabasca Falls Hostel 1 km N, accommodates 40. Reservations 403-439-3089). Continue past falls on Hwy 93A back towards Jasper.

33 Turnoff for Geraldine Lakes trail. Dirt road is 6 km (steep) to trailhead. First lake is 1.8 km, second lake 5 km.

41 Whirlpool Fire Rd. Historic route of fur traders into British Columbia across Athabasca Pass to Columbia River.

43 Wabasso Campground, 238 sites.

51 Edith Cavell Rd.

58 Jct. Hwy 93, turn left to return to Jasper on same route.

67 Return Jasper townsite.

7

Day Tours in Kananaskis Country

Kananaskis Country is Alberta's well-kept secret. The province does not widely advertise its attractions to the outside world. This mountain recreation area is to be preserved for Albertans while out-of-province visitors flock to better-known mountain areas like Banff and Jasper.

Well, the Kananaskis is a secret we can't keep. The opportunities for both day trips and long-distance cycling are simply too good.

Kananaskis Country is situated on the eastern slopes of the Rockies, 90 km west of Calgary and 60 km southeast of Banff. It encompasses 4,000 square kilometres of peaks, clear rivers and lakes, bisected by Highway 40 which leads to Upper Kananaskis Lakes and Highwood Pass, the highest paved road in Canada. The shoulders on Highway 40 are wide, the grade gentle and the surface excellent.

Three provincial parks are encompassed within the boundaries of Kananaskis Country — Peter Lougheed, Bow Valley and Bragg Creek. Development of Kananaskis Country began during the province's oil boom in the 1970s, and facilities are more lavish than in any other wilderness area we've visited.

The few cedar buildings are unobtrusive, campsites are well-planned and remarkably private, and there are lots of picnic stops. K-Country has one of the world's best golf courses and Mt. Kidd RV Park (open to tenters), probably the best-equipped public campground in Canada. It even has saunas, whirlpools and tennis courts.

Kananaskis is the only Rocky Mountain park planned from the start with cyclists in mind. Four paved (yet short) bicycle-only paths are provided — more than in Banff, Jasper, Waterton, Kootenay, Yoho, Glacier or Revelstoke national parks combined.

These bike paths include three short, leisurely rides, suitable for families, at Upper Kananaskis Lakes. Mountain bicycles may be rented nearby at Boulton Trading Post.

At Ribbon Creek, the Evan-Thomas Trail, also a paved bicycle path, is well-suited for those staying at Mt. Kidd campground. Bikes can be rented at the campground.

Highway 40 leads through the pristine Kananaskis Valley where the peaks seem more intimate than in Jasper or Banff. An outstanding day-trip, for those seeking challenge, is from Peter Lougheed Provincial Park to Highwood Pass.

While K-Country does not have as many day-trips as Banff, the possibilities for mountain biking are excellent. See Chapter One for recommended areas.

Cyclists should be aware that campgrounds at Upper Kananaskis Lakes often fill up by Thursday afternoon in summer. There is a limited reservation service at the lakes. Call 403-591-7222. For Mt. Kidd reservations, call 403-591-7700.

TRAVEL ALBERT

UPPER KANANASKIS LAKE BY MOUNTAIN BIKE

AN INTRODUCTION TO MOUNTAIN BIKES

Distance	7.6 km return (5 miles)
Time	1 1/2 hours
Rating	Easy mountain bike trail
Terrain	Fairly level
Elev. gain	None
Road	Wide, smooth trail for first stretch, ending in difficult boulder field which can be walked or avoided (Backcountry campsite at end)
Traffic	No motor vehicles
Connection	Tour 32

The short trail around the north shore of Upper Kananaskis Lake is the only off-road, mountain-bike tour in the book. Although mountain biking is not the province of this publication, here is a brief introduction to this exciting and fast-growing new sport that makes almost anyone feel like a kid again.

Peter Lougheed Provincial Park is a good place to start because, at time of writing, mountain bikes had not been restricted as in some national parks. In addition, good-quality mountain bikes are available for rental, by the hour or by the day, at the Boulton Trading Post in the park near the beginning of the trail.

While this tour will seem ridiculously easy and short to experienced off-road cyclists, its smooth, wide trail, good scenery and relatively level terrain will introduce beginners to the sport. Cyclists who rent bikes at Boulton near the end of the park road can leave their cars at the store and follow the paved Lakeside bicycle path (Tour 32) and then turn right on the main road to the North Interlakes parking lot. This may be the most strenuous section of the trip. Some might prefer to drive with their bikes right to the parking lot.

The trail crosses the narrow strip between Upper and Lower Kananaskis lakes and then turns west, keeping close to the shore with only gentle ups and downs. The beach offers good spots for a picnic amid the twisted driftwood.

The trail soon enters a boulder field under the cliffs of Mt. Indefatigable and the trail becomes rough and somewhat steep. Many cyclists will just turn back at this point. Those who push on will soon reach a viewpoint over the lake. Just beyond is the turnoff for the free North Point backcountry campground, which has 20 sites used

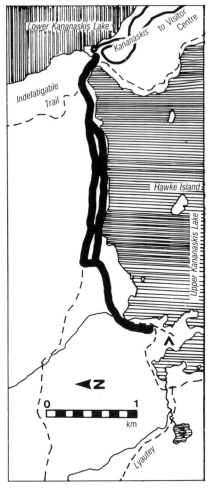

mainly by canoeists. Cyclists are welcome as well.

The remainder of the trip around the lake, while beautiful, is narrower and steeper with many rocks and roots. It is not officially approved for mountain bikes by park authorities.

Road Log Tour 27

0 km North Interlakes parking lot at end of road in Peter Lougheed Provincial Park (formerly Kananaskis). Follow signs for Three Isle Lake-Upper Lake trail across end of Upper Kananaskis Lake.

1.1 Turn left towards lake, descending slightly to stay on Upper Lake Trail.

3.2 Enter boulder field.

3.8 Turnoff for North Point backcountry campground. Return same route.

KANANASKIS VISITOR CENTRE TO HIGHWOOD PASS (RETURN)

TOUR **28**

HIGHEST RIDE OF ALL

Distance 42 km (26 miles) return

Time Half-day or

more, with sightseeing

Rating Strenuous

Terrain	Gradual ascent. Downhill on return
Elev. gain	566 metres (1856 feet)
Road	Good condition, wide shoulders
Traffic	Moderately busy on summer weekends
Connections	Tours 30, 34, 35

Highwood Pass offers strong cyclists the opportunity to conquer Canada's highest paved road. You pedal high into rugged subalpine terrain seen more often by backpackers than bicyclists. The grade on the wide road is mostly gentie and the mountain scenery awesome. In early September when the larch trees are gold and skies blue, there can be no more beautiful ride.

This road is closed to motor vehicle traffic between December 1 and June 15, not necessarily because of snow but to minimize man's impact on bighorn sheep herds in the area. The closure should not deter cyclists who can walk around the barrier, if the road is still snow-free. Just don't bother the sheep.

Make a day of it by exploring several of the nature trails along the way. Take adequate supplies as no facilities are provided.

OPTION 1: Campers may want to spend the night at Elbow Lake, a walk-in campground with 20 sites. It's located 1.4 km from Elbow Pass Junction at the 16-km mark. The initial section is steep but soon levels off.

OPTION 2: Cyclists with access to a vehicle may enjoy being driven up to the top of the pass and coasting back down.

Highlights

Begin at the Kananaskis Visitor Centre. The road descends steeply through the pines, then ascends after Pocaterra Lodge. The Opal Range rises ahead.

Turn right at the junction with Highway 40. The road climbs gradually at first, affording splendid views over Peter Lougheed Provincial Park. To the right, the north end of the Spray Range meets the south end of the Kananaskis Range.

The real climbing starts at km 7. The valley narrows and begins to look more Swiss, with avalanche paths visible on steep slopes and subalpine meadows reaching down to the road. You cycle under the great serrated walls of Mt. Elpoca and veer away from the main Kananaskis Valley.

Elbow Pass Junction is a pleasant rest spot just under timberline. You have reached the alpine threshold where snow may fall by mid-September or earlier. Note the larches on the right. Larches are the only coniferous trees which shed their needles. The short Rock Glacier Trail provides a look at a moving rock formation.

At Highwood Pass you'll find delicate subalpine Highwood

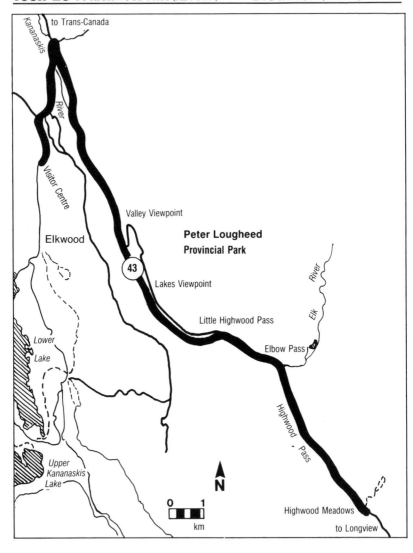

Meadows. Mt. Tyrwhitt is on the right, Mt. Rae on the left and Mt. Arethusa to the south. Congratulations! Few on-pavement bicycles in Canada climb higher than this, except in airplanes.

A short 1-km trail, explaining the alpine environment, leads through Highwood Meadows. The Cirque Trail, one of the most interesting in K-Country, is a two-hour, 5-km hike through an ancient forest.

Road Log Tour 28

0 km Kananaskis Visitor Centre, 4 km from turnoff with Hwy 40 in Peter Lougheed Provincial Park. Turn right (E) onto road. Steep descent.

2 Pocaterra Lodge.

4 Jct. Hwy 40. Turn right (S).

7 Climbing starts.

9 Valleyview Trail. Picnic area (up steep grade).

10 Elpoca Creek.

16 Elbow Pass Jct. Picnic tables, hiking, 1.3-km hike to Elbow Lake Campground.

19 Rock Glacier Nature Trail.

21 Highwood Pass, elev. 2253 m. Hiking, Highwood Meadows. Return same way.

RIBBON CREEK TO WEDGE POND (RETURN)

TOUR **29**

THE EVAN THOMAS TRAIL

Distance	19.6 km (12 miles) return
Time	1 1/2 to 2 hours
Rating	Easy
Terrain	Mostly level or rolling
Elev. gain	Negligible
Roads	Asphalt bicycle path
Traffic	No motorized vehicles, one highway crossing
Connections	Tour 34

Mountains, trees and ease. A leisurely bicycle path, suitable for all ages, leads beneath Mt. Kidd, over rustic bridges, and through poplar and spruce forests to Wedge Pond. The route parallels Highway 40 but seems a world away.

Highlights

Begin at the Ribbon Creek recreation area (or at the Mount Kidd RV Park if camping there). From Ribbon Creek, the route gently undulates, passing over little bridges. The tour is best in early September, when the gold of the poplars contrasts with the deep green forests of the wide Kananaskis Valley. The Fisher Range is to the east and the Kananaskis Range to the west.

The path skirts the Kananaskis Golf Course and Mt. Kidd RV Park. Watch for sharp curves here. Continue over Highway 40 to Wedge Pond, ringed by a 1-km nature trail. Cyclists have the option of returning the same way or on Highway 40.

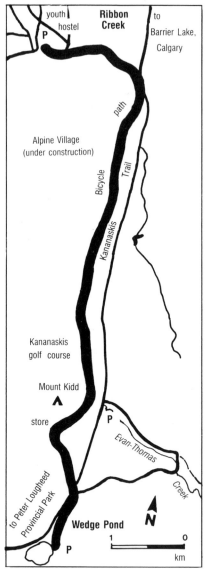

Barrier Lake information centre. Youth hostel, picnicking, hiking.

4 Kananaskis Country Golf Course. Licensed restaurant.

5.5 Mount Kidd RV Park. Camping, picnicking, grocery store, tennis, whirlpool, bicycle rentals. Reservations 403-591-7700.

8.5 Cross Hwy 40.

9.8 Wedge Pond.

Road Log Tour 29

0 km Parking lot at Ribbon Creek recreation area on Hwy 40, 17 km S of

KANANASKIS VISITOR CENTRE TO ELKWOOD(RETURN)

AN EASY RUN

Distance	9.4 km (6 miles) return
Time	1/2 hour to 1 hour
Rating	Easy, family cycle
Terrain	Fairly level, one steep portion
Road	Asphalt bicycle path
Traffic	No motorized traffic
Connections	Tours 28, 31, 32, 34

Highlights

A leisurely ride for those of all ages and fitness levels. An asphalt bike path, used as a ski trail in winter, makes an easy run through lodgepole pine forest.

The route can be linked to Tours 31 and 32 for an outing for several hours. Watch for one steep section near the junction with Sinclair Trail.

Cyclists may want to stop off at William Watson Lodge, a beautiful timber building overlooking Mt. Indefatigable, specially built for use by disabled persons.

Road Log Tour 30

0 km Parking lot at Kananaskis Visitor Centre, 4 km from Hwy 40 turnoff, Peter Lougheed Provincial Park.

4 Short trail leads to William Watson Lodge.

4.7 Elkwood Campground (130 sites, reservations accepted 403-591-7222, open June 19 to Sept. 2).

DISTANCE 9.4 km (6 miles)

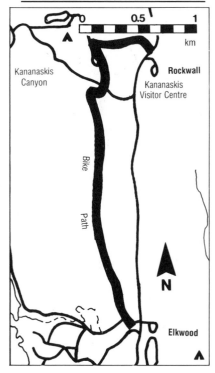

145

ELKWOOD TO BOULTON(RETURN)

BETWEEN TWO CAMPGROUNDS

Distance 9.4 km (6 miles) return

Time 1/2 hour to 1 hour

Rating Easy

Terrain One steep portion, otherwise fairly level

Roads Asphalt bicycle path

Traffic Closed to motorized traffic

Connections Tours 28, 30, 32, 34

This short cycle is the middle link in the Lower Kananaskis Lake bicycle system, and provides an hour or so of pleasant cycling through mixed terrain. If desired, cyclists can veer down at Boulton Trading Post to Lower Kananaskis Lake where there is picnicking.

Road Log Tour 31

0 km Elkwood Campground, 6 km S of Hwy 40 turnoff in Peter Lougheed Provincial Park (130 sites, reservations accepted, 403-591-7222). Follow signs to bicycle path.

4.7 Boulton Campground (118 sites, reservations accepted, above number). Return.

DISTANCE 9.4 km (6 miles)

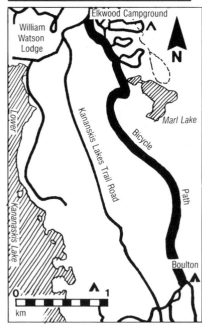

BOULTON TO
UPPER KANANASKIS LAKE (RETURN) 32

TO THE LAKES

Distance 10 km (6 miles) return
Time 1 hour
Rating Intermediate
Terrain Several steep pitches
Roads Asphalt bicycle path
Traffic Closed to motorized traffic
Connections Tours 27, 28, 30, 31, 34

Of the three sections which make up the Kananaskis Lakes bicycle path system, this is the most difficult—and the most interesting. There are several steep pitches as the trail undulates down to the lake, mostly through spruce and lodgepole pine forest. Keep a sharp watch for bicycle signs through campground areas.

The lake makes a pretty destination. Mt. Indefatigable dominates to the north and Mt. Sarrail to the south. To the west is Mt. Lyautey and the gleaming Lyautey Glacier.

There are a number of picnicking spots and trails here. Interlakes Campground has some excellent sites by the water.

Road Log Tour 32

0 km Boulton parking lot and trading post, 10 km S of Hwy 40 turnoff in Peter

Lougheed Provincial Park. Bicycle rentals.
1 Lower Lake Campground (95 regular sites, 9 walk-ins).
5 Upper Kananaskis Lake. Return same route.

DISTANCE 10 km (6 miles)

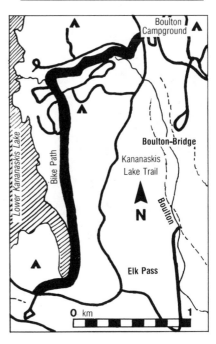

Upper Kananaskis Lake

8

Extended Tours in the Kananaskis and the Rockies' Eastern Slopes

Conquer Canada's highest paved road, explore the transition from the Great Plains to the foothills to the high peaks of the Rockies, traverse the boreal forest of black spruce wetlands and kettle holes, journey alongside wild rivers and up an historic and tragic pass. These are some of the challenges and joys of the longer tours on the sunny Alberta side of the Rocky Mountains.

Most of this territory is drier than typical Rocky Mountain habitat. The disadvantage is the wind speeds up in descending from the Continental Divide and Front Ranges to blast the open foothills and the plains behind them with all its fury. Generally, the further south you go along the edge of the mountains, the windier it gets. Tour 33 between Calgary and Banff is windier than Tour 39 from Hinton to Jasper. And Tour 36, Pincher Creek to Waterton is the windiest.

The outstanding alpine tour of this section is the smooth ascent up the Kananaskis River to Peter Lougheed Provincial Park (Tour 34).

From Highwood Pass above the provincial park, cyclists can coast into ranching country (Tour 35), loop north to Calgary and head back towards Banff and Kananaskis on a winding, relatively quiet highway along the Bow River (Tour 33).

To the north is one of the least travelled roads of the Rockies and something of a paradise for cyclists: the stunning David Thompson Highway

(Tour 38) which follows the North Saskatchewan River past a huge turquoise lake. There are no passes to climb and the route leads to the middle of the Icefields Parkway.

Further north, Hinton is the starting point for a leisurely and not difficult trip along the Athabasca River (Tour 39) into Jasper National Park. A side trip heads into boreal wilderness up to Grand Cache (Tour 40).

In southern Alberta, a distinctive route leads through plains and foothills into limestone mountains and past the tragic Frank Slide, coal mines and urban ticky-tacky up to Crowsnest Pass (Tour 37). A connecting route (Tour 36) leads south on the edge of the transition zone between prairie and mountains, ending at quiet Waterton National Park.

BANFF TO CALGARY

THE OLD BANFF COACH ROAD

Distance 140 km (87 miles)
Time 2 days. Strong cyclists can do it in one
Rating Intermediate
Terrain Rolling. One long grade
Elev. loss 334 metres (1095 feet) eastbound
Road Trans-Canada has excellent shoulder. 1A has small shoulder in places, none in others
Traffic Trans-Canada busy. 1A usually moderate, sometimes busy on Sunday
Connections Tour 14, 15, 17, 34

The Trans-Canada Highway from Banff to Calgary is busy and dangerous, so try the relaxing alternative. On the north side of the Bow River, follow a winding, relatively quiet highway called the Old Banff Coach Road as it makes a gradual transition from mountains to foothills to the Great Plains. The route passes two deep-blue lakes and has been newly-paved in many sections.

The government has painted markings on the shoulder of the Trans-Canada indicating it as a bicycle route between Banff and Calgary. But these are deceiving.

TOUR 33 BANFF TO CALGARY

DISTANCE 140 km (87 miles)

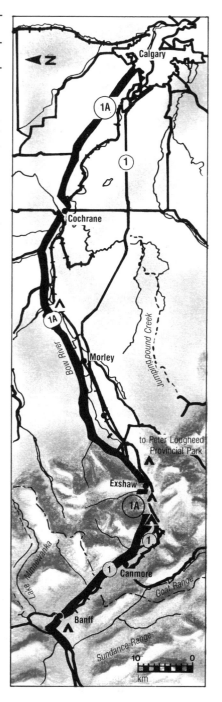

While the shoulder does provide good separation from traffic, Canada's principal east-west highway can be dangerous for cyclists. The Trans-Canada is hillier than Highway 1A, only slightly shorter and to us, at least, it is the antithesis of what bicycle touring is all about.

The cyclist coming from Banff will often be helped by the prevailing strong west winds, adding to the enjoyment. Conversely, the winds can be draining for cyclists heading from Calgary to Banff (who might prefer to take the train on really bad days).

The tour can be made into a round trip by taking the daily Banff-Calgary train back to the start. Bicycles travel free and need not be boxed. For reservations and times, phone toll free to Via Rail at 1-800-665-8630.

One drawback to this route can be the lack of campgrounds in convenient places. The newly-developed private campground at Ghost Lake helps fill the gap. Some cyclists will want to camp out on their own off the highway.

Highlights

From Banff, the Trans-Canada leads under the cliffs of Mt. Rundle on a divided highway, passing a couple of picnic grounds. Once past Canmore on 1A, you're in a different world, a low-key, away-from-it-all place. You make a gradual transition from spruce forests to the mixed aspen terrain to open prairie.

Stop for ice cream at MacKay's in Cochrane. Everybody does. You'll burn up the calories on the 3-km hill beyond town. Traffic is heavier after Cochrane but the paved shoulder is huge.

In Calgary, the direct route downtown is via the Crowchild Trail. We can't recommend it for cyclists, especially the super-busy stretch south of 16 Ave N.W. Our suggestion below is more complicated but avoids the worst of the fast traffic.

Road Log Tour 33

0 km Banff townsite. Pop. 6949, elev. 1383 m. All services. Follow signs N to Trans-Canada and turn E for Calgary.

17 Park gate.

23 Canmore. All services. Restwell Trailer Park and Campground. Turn right on Hwy 1A.

29 Picnic tables.

34 Picnic tables.

38 Picnic tables.

41 Exshaw. Store.

47 Turnoff R. for Bow Valley Provincial Park (camping).

56 Stoney Indian Park. Store.

69 McDougall historic church.

77 Ghost Lake Campground and store.

95 Cochrane historic ranch. Picnic tables.

96 Cochrane. Restaurants, stores.

97 Begin steep, 3-km ascent.

115 Calgary city limits. Pop 619,814, elev. 1049. Hostel at 520 - 7 Ave SE, 403-269-8239. Continue straight as 1A becomes Crowchild Trail.

126 Turn left (N) on Brisbois Dr.

135 Turn right (E) on Northmount Dr.

137 Turn right (S) on Cambrian Dr. which leads into 10 St. Continue S on 10 St. crossing Louise Bridge.

140 Downtown. Via Rail and bus stations.

GAIL HELGASON

BARRIER LAKE TO PETER LOUGHEED PROVINCIAL PARK (RETURN) **34**

THE KANANASKIS TRAIL

Distance 110 km (68 miles) return
Time 1 to 2 days
Rating Intermediate
Terrain Long well-graded ascent, some level stretches
Elev. gain 366 metres (1200 feet)
Roads Wide shoulders, excellent surface throughout
Traffic Busy summer weekends, otherwise moderate
Connections Tours 28, 29, 30, 31, 32

This tour is in many ways a cyclist's dream: a ride through a wild valley of peaks, forests, streams and lakes. Views are continual as you ascend to stunning Peter Lougheed Provincial Park (formerly called Kananaskis) on a wide, well-graded highway. There are ample picnic spots, a youth hostel, even a deluxe campground complete with sauna and whirlpool tubs. Five campgrounds are situated at Upper and Lower Kananaskis lakes. Although you backtrack to return, the views and the smooth descent make up for the repetition.

Campgrounds at Kananaskis Lakes often fill up by Thursday afternoon on summer weekends. If possible, reserve ahead. Smaller campgrounds, such as Eau Claire, reach capacity less quickly. Cyclists can usually squeeze in somewhere.

OPTION: Make Peter Lougheed Park a base for further forays up Highwood Pass and along the system of short bicycle trails in the park. (See Chapter Seven.)

Highlights

Cycling is fairly level as you leave the Barrier Lake Visitor Centre and pedal toward man-made Barrier Lake. If you have time, stop at the Kananaskis Forest Experimental Station, a living laboratory of more than 6,000 hectares run by the University of Calgary. Two short interpretive trails explain the basics of forest management, and there is a simulated forest fire lookout as well. The Colonel's Cabin, used by the officer in charge of German prisoners of war who were housed here during the Second World War, is at the same site.

A highway engineer who wanted to do something more imaginative than construct a simple culvert across a road is responsible for man-made O'Shaughnessy Falls. The public protested when frowning officials planned to tear down his

11,000 years ago. They probably didn't have much trouble finding a campsite.

Cyclists are much less likely to spot wildlife along the roads in Kananaskis than in other Rocky Mountain Parks — roadsides have been planted with a special blend of grasses designed to discourage animals from grazing near the road, hence preventing road kills.

Highway 40 undulates, climbing gradually. Mt. Lorette and the turbulent Kananaskis River are on the right; Mt. Allan, just south has been developed as the site of downhill skiing events for the 1988 Olympic Games.

The Ribbon Creek recreational area has a beautiful cedar-slabbed youth hostel and fine hiking and cycling paths. A hotel complex is planned.

OPTION: To get off the highway and enjoy a beautiful asphalt bike trail for a few kilometres, turn right into Ribbon Creek and take the Evan-Thomas bicycle trail to Wedge Pond. (See Tour 29.)

The Kananaskis Golf Course, one of the world's most scenic, is just ahead. The clubhouse has an attractive lounge with impressive views of Mt. Kidd and Mt. Allan, plus reasonable prices for food that ranges from nachos to reubens. Just the place to wait out a rain storm.

work. The falls stayed.

The Kananaskis Valley has been inhabited for thousands of years. Archaeologists have found traces of campsites used by early hunters

There's a dining room next door. The clubhouse originally imposed dress standards; the latest word is that any reasonable apparel is acceptable, so long as it's not "scruffy". Mt. Kidd campground is probably Canada's most deluxe; facilities include tennis courts, saunas, a lounge with a fireplace and a games arcade.

Continue on with Mt. Kidd — part of the Kananaskis Range — on the right and The Wedge — part of the Fisher Range — on the left. The Kananaskis Visitor Centre with its interpretive displays and information staff is worth a stop, especially on a cool day. No food is sold at the visitor centre although cyclists can bring their lunch into the lounge to enjoy the fine views and magnificent fireplace. Boulton Trading Post, further along, contains a well-stocked grocery store. A cafeteria serves light snacks.

Cyclists can take asphalt bicycle paths from either the Kananaskis Visitor Centre or Boulton to the campgrounds, or just continue on the road. All the campgrounds are attractive; perhaps the most sought-after are lakefront sites at Interlakes.

Peter Lougheed Provincial Park was originally called Kananaskis, but was renamed in 1986 to honor the former premier who spurred development of this park during his 14-year tenure. The multi-use recreational land surrounding the park retains the name Kananaskis Country.

Road Log Tour 34

0 km Barrier Lake Travel Information Centre, 6 km S of Trans-Canada on Hwy 40 (the Kananaskis Trail) in Kananaskis Country. Elev. 1371 m. Overnight parking on request, picnic area.

2 Kananaskis Forest Experimental Station. Self-guiding trails. Colonel's Cabin, exhibits, picnicking.

4 Barrier Lake. Turnoff right for boat launch, two picnic areas, interpretive trails.

6 O'Shaughnessy Falls.

10 Wasootch Creek. Picnicking.

11 Porcupine Campground (group use only).

12 Mt. Lorette fishing ponds, for wheelchair fishermen. Beaver often observed at dusk or dawn.

15 Beaver Pond. Picnicking, fishing.

16 Mt. Allan, site of downhill skiing, 1988 Calgary Winter Olympics.

17 Ribbon Creek recreational area. Picnicking, hiking, no camping. Ribbon Creek Youth Hostel, 403-591-7333, accommodates 40, family rooms available.

OPTION: Take Evan-Thomas bicycle path instead of Hwy 40 to Wedge Pond and rejoin route there. See Tour 29.

21 Kananaskis Country Golf Course (lounge, restaurant) under Mt. Kidd.

23 Mt. Kidd RV Park and picnicking area. Camping, including tents, 227 sites, grocery store, deli, tennis courts, wading pool, whirlpool, sauna, bicycle rentals, trails. Reservations 403-591-7700.

25 Wedge Pond and The Wedge. Picnicking, short hiking trails.

30 Eau Claire recreation area. 51 campsites, picnicking.

31 Opal picnicking area. Recommended. Views, screened from road.

37 Fortress Mtn. jctn. Service station. Groceries, camping supplies.

40 Enter Peter Lougheed Provincial Park.

46 King Creek picnic site. Elev. 1737 m. Picnicking, interpretive trail. Turnoff right 4 km for Kananaskis Visitor Centre (information, exhibits, no supplies). Five campgrounds:
Canyon Campground. 4 km, 52 sites, open May 16 to Sept. 9
Boulton Campground. 10 km, 118 sites, showers, open year-round, reservations 403-591-7222. Well-stocked grocery store at Boulton Trading Post. Cafeteria, bike rentals.
Elkwood Campground. 6 km, 130 sites, open June 19 to Sept. 2.
Lower Lake Campground. 11 km, 110 campsites, 9 walk-in sites, open May 16 to Sept. 9
Interlakes Campground. 13 km, open May 16 to Sept. 16, 44 tenting campsites, open June 8 to Sept. 16.

AXING A NAME

The name Kananaskis has a wild poetic sound long fascinating to visitors. Capt. John Palliser is credited with giving this beautiful name to the turbulent river which runs through this valley.

Palliser, who explored the area in 1861, had apparently heard the legend of Kananaskis, a brave Indian warrior. According to legend, the warrior was struck in the head by an axe blow during a battle between the Kootenay and Stoney tribes for control of the valley. He survived, and some say Kananaskis lived to a ripe old age with a piece of axe imbedded in his skull.

HIGHWOOD PASS TO LONGVIEW

A SENSE OF DISCOVERY

Distance 80 km (49 miles)

Time 1 day

Rating Easy descent southbound. Strenuous climb northbound

Terrain Well-graded drop from high pass. Second half mostly level along river.

Roads Excellent shoulder. Gravel portion of less than 17 km is rough and dusty but is gradually being paved

Traffic Light to non-existent in off season. Moderate in summer

Connection Tour 28

Few descents are more glorious than the swoosh down from Highwood Pass on Canada's highest paved road. From subalpine meadows, a beautifully-paved highway leads gradually down to the Highwood River through tranquil mountain terrain not often visited by cyclists. There's a sense of discovery in every kilometre and

the scenery, in its way, rivals the famed Icefields Parkway.

The highways over Highwood Pass and down to Longview were once a nightmare for cycling. The problem was a long, bone-shaking, dusty stretch of gravel road between Longview and Highwood Junction. Even cyclists on mountain bikes tended to shun this stretch. Well, highway paving has been proceeding steadily on this section. An unpaved gap still existed in 1986 but the gravel section was becoming short enough for cyclists to reconsider the route. A few hours of unpleasantness on rough gravel is small pain compared with the tour's many glories.

In the past, Highway 40 between the turnoff to Kananaskis Lakes and Highwood Junction has been closed December 1 to June 15 (although this may change). That shouldn't stop cyclists. Indeed, the closure has provided splendid carless cycling in the off-season, after the snow season.

Please note that the road is closed not because of snow but to protect wildlife, especially bighorn sheep. Don't disturb them.

Be sure to take adequate supplies as the only groceries along the way are at Highwood Junction and it is closed in the off-season. Bring

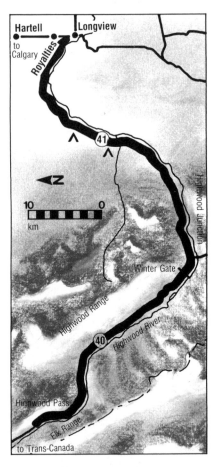

lots of good food; few roads anywhere in the world are so well supplied with pleasant picnic spots.

Highlights

From the larches and subalpine meadows of Highwood Pass, a stiff climb up from Kananaskis Lakes (Tour 28), Highway 40 begins a well-graded descent along Storm Creek with the Misty Range on the

east and the Elk Range to the west. Button up. The road soons passes the southern boundary of Peter Lougheed Provincial Park (formerly Kananaskis), crosses avalanche paths and traverses the partially re-forested devastation of a vast 1936 forest fire.

The valley widens and the countryside begins to look like the ranching country of Hollywood westerns. The high peaks are gradually replaced by more rounded foothills above the meadows and the Highwood River. The district resembles parts of Colorado. The road becomes more level after Highwood Junction, only place to get food and supplies along this wilderness stretch. The beautiful valley begins to widen and the rolling plains gradually replace the mountains. This can be a windy area.

The route passes two provincial campgrounds and enters the Savanna Creek natural gas field, complete with pumping stations, sour-gas plants and sometimes the distinctive odor that goes under the name of progress. But no smells can really distract from the beauty and variety of this route.

From Longview, cyclists can easily make their way north on Highway 22 to 22X and then west into Calgary, a distance of 66 km on a fairly busy road with narrow to adequate shoulders.

A more ambitious trip is to continue on Highway 22 through Bragg Creek and then north to either the Trans-Canada or Highway 1A just west of Cochrane. Distance from Longview to the Trans-Canada is 90 km and it's 103 km to Highway 1A.

The 1A route back to Kananaskis Country (Tour 33) is quieter and more scenic than the Trans-Canada although it's 20 km further.

From Highway 22, it's a total of 47 km back to Highway 40 main entry into Kananaskis Country. (See Tour 34.) From 1A, the distance is 54 km.

Road Log Tour 35

0 km Highwood Pass, 21 km S of Kananaskis Lakes in Peter Lougheed Provincial Park. Elev. 2253 metres, 7392 ft. Hiking trails. Begin descent.

4 Boundary Peter Lougheed Provincial Park, formerly Kananaskis.

6 Mt. Lipsett picnic area.

8 Storm Creek.

10 Road levels.

18 Picklejar picnic area.

19 Trout Ponds picnic area.

20 Lantern Creek picnic area.

25 Lineham Creek picnic area.

31 Cat Creek picnic area.

34 Fitzsimmons picnic area.

37 Highwood Jct. Store. Gravel road S. to Coleman. Turn onto Hwy 541 to Longview.

39 Ranger Station.

41 Eyrie Gap picnic area.

42 Sentinel Gap picnic area.

43 Fir Creek picnic area.

46 Etherington Creek Campground and picnic area. Hiking trails.

52 Cataract Creek Campground and picnic area.

57 Wilkinson Creek picnic area.

80 Longview. All services.

Bighorn sheep   TRAVEL ALBERTA

PINCHER CREEK TO WATERTON

COWBOY COUNTRY

Distance	57 km (35 miles)
Time	1/2 to 1 day
Rating	Intermediate
Terrain	Many short but steep hills
Roads	Well paved with shoulder
Traffic	Usually moderate
Connections	Tours 37, 41, 42, 45

Nowhere else in Alberta do the mountains rise so abruptly and dramatically from the plains. The transition from grassland, from rolling ranching country to high alpine (1,000 metres within a kilometre) without intervening foothills gives this land a magical feel. Here is the cowboy country of our dreams.

The tour from Pincher Creek to Waterton parallels the chain of the Rockies along this splendid transition zone. It connects the route over Crowsnest Pass with Waterton National Park and the fine tours south into Glacier (U.S.).

The disadvantage of this stretch is basic: the wind. Some days, especially in spring, it blows so strongly you have trouble standing upright, much less cycling. Even lesser winds can be disheartening, fatiguing and frustrating.

Of course, the wind direction is generally from the west and this route heads north-south. Crosswinds aren't nearly as bad as headwinds. Cyclists can often avoid the worst of them by travelling early in the morning or in late evening.

Highlights

The further south you go from Pincher Creek, the better the mountains get. There are many up and downs as the road descends to cross creeks and climbs the far bank. There's a campground, exposed to the winds at Yarrow Creek, just before Twin Butte, a community scarcely big enough for twins. Here a friendly gas station-cafe has homemade pies and a guest book for cyclists.

From there, it's a grand cycle south into Waterton, Mt. Dungarvan and Mt. Galwey dominating the horizon. There's a large campground just outside the park where everybody goes if Waterton is full. It's a windy location, however. Cyclists should be able to squeeze in somewhere inside the park.

From Highway 5, the tour turns right past the park gates and along the Waterton River, past lower Waterton Lake, numerous picnic tables and the turnoff for Red Rock Canyon. The wooded Crandell

Mountain Campground, less busy than the super-popular campground in the townsite, is 8.5 km up the road. The main route passes the park information centre before descending to the cozy townsite and its large open campground with showers, right on the lake.

Road Log Tour 36

0 km Pincher Creek. All services. Pop. 3,757. Municipal Campground in town. Turn S on Hwy. 6.

24 Yarrow Creek Campground.

28 Twin Butte. Store-cafe.

47 Waterton National Park.

48 Jct. Hwy 5. Turn right. Park entrance station.

56 Park information centre.

57 Waterton townsite and campground. All services. Pop. 176, elev. 1280 m. Hiking trails, boat rides, day cycles into mountains.

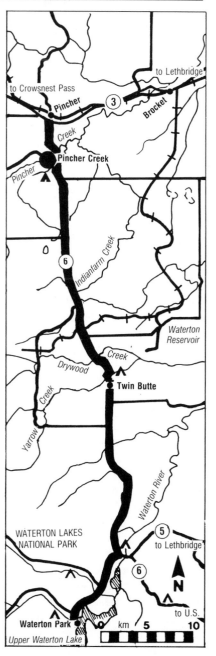

161

CROWSNEST PASS TO PINCHER CREEK

THE EARTH IS RESTLESS

Distance	63 km (39 miles)
Time	Half-day eastbound, longer westbound
Rating	Moderate eastbound, strenuous westbound
Terrain	Gradual descent from the pass, a few uphill stretches
Roads	Good shoulder
Traffic	Busy. Many trucks
Connections	Tours 36, 58

Here's a distinctive and unforgettable cycling tour. It has beautiful, craggy peaks, waterfalls, volcanic rock, limestone mountains, plains and foothills. There is natural beauty and urban ticky-tacky. There are gas plants, coal mines — and an enduring sense of history and tragedy. This route has ghosts indeed.

The descent from the pass is relatively gentle. Below the summit one community runs into the next. Highlight of the trip is the desolation of the Frank Slide where 90 million tons of limestone slipped off the side of Turtle Mountain at 4:10 a.m. on April 29, 1903 and swept two kilometres over the valley, burying a portion of the town of Frank and taking 70 lives. The highway goes right through the rubble.

Highlights

The top of the pass isn't nearly as scenic as most other crossings of the Continental Divide. The route has other joys.

The railway is part of the history, built through swamps and limestone by Slavic and Chinese workers in the late 1890s. Right from the summit, the settlement of the pass begins. The tiny town of Crowsnest lies just below the height of land and was once a thriving railway supply point with eight taverns.

Even wilder times came in 1916 after a majority of Albertans voted for prohibition. While the citizens of the Crowsnest Pass area voted to keep their booze, they were a minority in the province. Still the liquor came. Back in the hills, some turned to making moonshine. Others brought in liquor over the pass from British Columbia — until the police set up roadblocks. Then the liquor was brought over more obscure passes by mule train.

The highway runs between Sentry Mountain on the north and Sentinel Mountain on the south above picturesque Crowsnest Lake, a natural meeting place for traders from east and west.

The highway descends to the Crowsnest River and the non-stop development begins. Some of the land has been cleared and the countryside begins to look more like prairie than Rockies, despite the impressive peaks on both sides. Above Coleman, the road passes outcroppings of volcanic rock, the only major volcanic occurrences in Alberta. A sign indicates that the rock is formed from volcanic ash and cinders, rather than actual lava, suggesting a violent explosive eruption. The rocks are 100 million years old, more ancient than the Rockies.

Although the countryside is built-up, the views are fascinating. Below are the towns of Coleman, Blairmore, Bellevue and Frank, now incorporatated into a single municipality. Above the river, the homes and numerous mines and plants, hillsides bear the black bands of coal seams.

From Blairmore, main residential distict of the pass area, the road remains above the river, descending gradually to the tiny community of Frank. Across the bridge is the turnoff for the province's Frank Slide interpretive centre, a very steep 2-km ascent for cyclists. The climb is worth the effort. This is a first-class centre with lavish exhibits showing the history of the whole area and excellent viewpoints over the desolation of the Frank Slide. The centre is open every day from

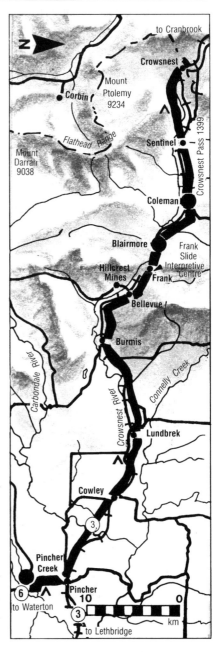

9 a.m. It closes at 9 p.m. in summer and 4 p.m. after Labor Day, although the viewpoints can be visited anytime. There are also picnic tables.

The main highway passes through the jumbled mass of boulders and the traveller can't help imagining how it must have sounded and felt when the great wedge of rock broke off the mountain above and roared down onto the valley floor.

The community of Hillcrest has a tragic history too. On the morning of June 19, 1914, a full shift of 228 men was working deep in the Hillcrest Mine. An explosion rocked the ground — and 189 were killed.

The highway passes abandoned mine buildings, a tiny wayside chapel and the remains of the Leitch Collieries, now a historic site.

The terrain begins to open up into grasslands and foothills. This area often experiences strong winds, normally from the west. The transition from mountain to prairie is sudden and startling.

Road Log Tour 37

- **0 km** Crowsnest Pass. Elev. 1396 m. Continental Divide. Alberta-B.C. boundary.
- **2** Turnoff Alberta provincial campground.
- **4** Crowsnest Lake.
- **6** Begin gradual descent.
- **7** Crowsnest River.
- **11** Historical point of interest. Volcanic rock outcroppings. Viewpoint.
- **15** Turnoff Coleman business centre. All services. Turnoff right for campground.
- **19** Blairmore turnoff. Services along highway. Turnoff for campground.
- **24** Turnoff Frank Slide interpretive centre 2 km on very steep paved road.
- **25** Frank Slide area.
- **27** Hillcrest turnoff. Old mine on hillside.
- **29** Campground turnoff. Wayside chapel.
- **33** Leitch Collieries historic site.
- **37** Turn off Hiawatha Campground.
- **43** Lundbreck Falls turnoff. Campground.
- **53** Cowley. Restaurant. Store. Castle River recreation area.
- **55** Turnoff Sleepy Hollow Campground
- **63** Pincher. Jct. Hwy 6. Turnoff for Pincher Creek and Waterton National Park. All services.

Kootenay Plains, David Thompson Highway
GAIL HELGASON

A DREAM TOUR

Distance 88 km (55 miles) one way
Time 1 day each way
Rating Intermediate
Terrain Rolling. A few long hills
Roads Wide, well-paved. Excellent shoulder
Traffic Moderate on summer weekends, light weekdays,
Connections Tours 14, 15

A journey through gorgeous mountains, along a wild river, past a huge turquoise lake with no steep passes to climb and only light to moderate tourist traffic: this is the sort of tour cyclists dream about. The route between Nordegg and Saskatchewan River Crossing is seldom travelled by cyclists because it lies just outside Banff National Park and off the Icefields Parkway. But it is equipped with first-rate Alberta Forestry campgrounds (free) which often provide more privacy and better facilities than the crowded national parks sites. Two well-stocked grocery stores along the route help reduce the load that the cyclist must carry.

Long-distance touring cyclists could connect with the Icefields Parkway route and even do an extended loop of mountains, foothills and plains for a week or more: Head west to the Icefields Parkway, south to Banff, east to Cochrane on 1A, then north to Sundre on 22, north again to Caroline and Rocky Mountain House (the last stretch partly on gravel), then west again to Nordegg.

Highlights

Nordegg, a once-thriving coal mining community and now the site of a detention centre, marks the transition from the wooded foothills to the mountains. Highway 11 is perhaps the least crowded entrance to the Rocky Mountains in Alberta. In the off-season, this road is almost deserted and the cyclist can feel intimately connected to this gorgeous country, a sense difficult to attain amid the roar of the Trans-Canada in Banff.

The road passes close to Abraham Lake, a widening of the North Saskatchewan River created by Big Horn Dam. Slate-grey Mt. Michener (2,545 metres), an impressive triangle, rises on the other side. The further you travel the more stunning the scenery becomes. Cline River Resort makes a good stop. From its funky cafeteria, cyclists can keep an eye on their bikes through the windows.

There's a good descent down to

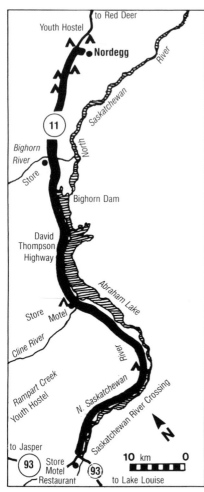

grounds are found here. The plains have witnessed human activity for 10,000 years from prehistoric hunters to the Indians who used it as a trading place in the late 1700s. A hiking trail leads to Siffleur Falls.

The road climbs again to Whirlpool Point where bighorn sheep can often be seen. A lookout offers vistas over the fast-moving river and the trail down to the water leads past a monument to "the original trailblazers who first drove between here and Rocky Mountain House in 1940.

"It was 118 miles and took 10 days!"

Cyclists returning to Nordegg the following day might wish to stay at Thompson Creek Campground (free) just before the national park boundary. Otherwise cyclists could head 11 km north from the junction with the Icefields Parkway to Rampart Creek Campground or the youth hostel. Waterfowl Lake Campground is 20 km south of the junction, a substantial climb up from the river.

Cline River and the road begins to traverse some longer hills before descending into historic Kootenay Plains and passing the well-designed Two O'Clock Creek campground.

These plains, bisected by the North Saskatchewan River, are a natural grasslands because of the microclimate created by the surrounding peaks. Indian ceremonial

Road Log Tour 38

0 km Nordegg, 168 km W of Red Deer. Groceries, motel. Turn W on Hwy 11. Shunda Creek Youth Hostel (403-721-2140) is 3 km N. Reservations through Edmonton office 439-3086.

<table>
<tr><td>3</td><td>Forestry Trunk Road.</td></tr>
<tr><td>5</td><td>Fish Lake recreation area. Campground.</td></tr>
<tr><td>9</td><td>Goldeye Lake Campground.</td></tr>
<tr><td>12</td><td>Haven Creek Campground.</td></tr>
<tr><td>13</td><td>Shaw Creek group campground.</td></tr>
<tr><td>18</td><td>Big Horn cafe, store, gas station. Display of native handicrafts.</td></tr>
<tr><td>21</td><td>Big Horn River.</td></tr>
<tr><td>33</td><td>Picnic area.</td></tr>
<tr><td>47</td><td>Cline River Resort. Store, cafe, motel (721-2203).</td></tr>
</table>

48 Cline River bridge.
61 Two O'Clock Creek Campground.
80 Thompson Creek Campground.
83 Banff National Park boundary.
88 Jct. Icefields Parkway Hwy 93. Store (limited supplies), cafeteria, motel (403-721-3920). Rampart Creek Campground and youth hostel 11 km N on Icefields Parkway. For hostel reservations, phone 283-5551.

HINTON TO JASPER TOWNSITE

TOUR **39**

TASTE OF THE YELLOWHEAD

Distance	81 km (50 miles) one way
Time	1 day
Rating	Intermediate
Terrain	Rolling to national park. Remainder mostly level
Elev. gain	70 metres (230 feet)
Roads	Good condition, good shoulders
Traffic	Busy in summer, especially weekends. Otherwise mostly moderate

Connections Tours 14, 15, 20, 40 and Jasper townsite tours

From Hinton, the wide, smooth Yellowhead Highway rolls to viewpoints over the Athabasca River, then descends into Jasper National Park, to unfold a panorama of peaks, lakes, forests and wildlife.

You can cycle the Yellowhead Highway from Edmonton all the way to Jasper National Park. We don't recommend it, however. Traffic is swift and dangerous and there are many long, flat stretches. The most scenic — and safest — portion is

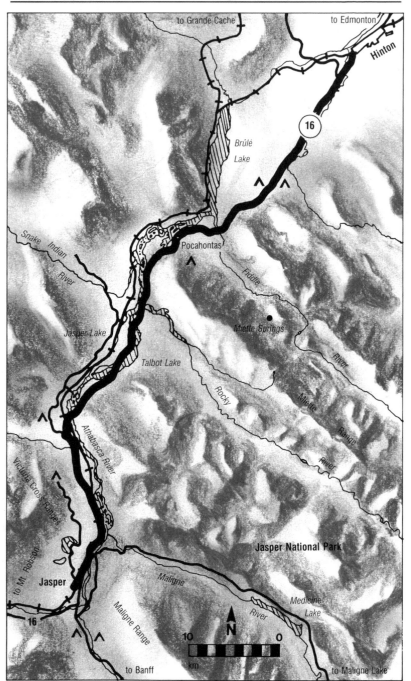

the Hinton-to-Jasper route described here.

This tour makes a challenging day-trip, a leisurely two-day trip and a fine warm-up for cycling the Icefields Parkway or onwards to Mt. Robson. Cyclists starting in Edmonton can ride VIA Rail to Hinton and wheel their bikes up to the baggage compartment. Call VIA Rail at 1-800-665-8630 for schedules. Note that no tenting is allowed at the Hinton campground. The nearest campground is 21 km west.

OPTIONS: Cyclists can make this a leisurely two-or three-day trip, perhaps stopping one night at Overlander Lodge (km 28) or Pocahontas Campground (km 38).

Highlights

The tour begins at Hinton, a lumber town set in view of the Front Ranges of the Rockies. Hungry cyclists can find plain but stick-to-your ribs food at the Athabasca Valley Hotel (the one with the odd roof) near the east end of town.

The town's History of Forestry Museum, on the grounds of the Alberta Forest Technology School, has displays of the work of the early forest rangers. The museum is open from 8:30 a.m. to 4:30 p.m. Monday to Friday. Inquire at the school's general office.

Cycling is fairly easy out of Hinton. The shoulder is good and fine views of Folding Mountain open to the left. Distinctive Roche Miette is behind it. The scenery becomes

steadily more glorious and the feel of the wilderness more pronounced. It is not uncommon to spot black bears along this road.

An enjoyable descent leads down to the Athabasca River, past Folding Mountain Campground and scenically-set Overlander Lodge. The road levels off at the Jasper park gates, crossing the Fiddle River under the cliffs of Roche Miette. The Miette Range is to the south and the Bosche Range to the north.

The national park campground at Pocahontas is pleasantly wooded and a number of walk-in sites at the south end are particularly well-suited to cyclists. There is, however, a steep 2-km climb to the campground on the road to Miette Hot Springs. Punchbowl Falls, 0.5 km up, is worth a stop. The newly-refurbished Miette Hot Springs, 17.5 km from the highway, opened in 1986. The road to the springs is extremely steep and not recommended for cyclists.

Back on the Yellowhead, superb views open across the Athabasca to the Colin Range. The roadside at Disaster Point is frequented by bighorn sheep. The triangular peak to the right is, not unexpectedly, called Pyramid Peak.

The road passes Talbot Lake to the south and Jasper Lake to the north, a shallow widening of the Athabasca River. Sheep are often seen at the Athabasca River Crossing at the 57-km mark. The cliffs of Morro Peak on the left side of the road are a popular practice area for mountain climbers. To the north is the imposing Palisade.

The grassy meadows beyond Snaring River Campground are a good place to spot elk, especially in the early morning. The forested mass of Signal Mountain is to the south, with more rocky Mt. Tekarra, named after Sir James Hector's guide, behind. The white face of Mt. Edith Cavell appears to the southwest.

The road is mostly level into Jasper townsite. Whistlers Campground, the park's largest, is 13 km south of the townsite on Highway 93A and Wapiti is opposite. Low-key Wabasso Campground, 20 km south on the same highway, is nicely situated along the Athabasca River.

Road Log Tour 34

0 km Hinton, 282 km W of Edmonton on the Yellowhead, Hwy 16. Pop. 8,819, elev. 990 m. Via Rail and Greyhound Bus access. Accommodation, groceries, no tent camping. History of Forestry Museum, 1176 Switzer Dr. Head W on Hwy 16.

3 Turnoff for Forestry Trunk Road (gravel).

9 Jct Hwy 40 to Cadomin. Views of Folding Mountain, Roche Miette.

11 Turnoff Hwy 40 N to Grande Cache. 19 km to William Switzer Provincial Park (camping).

18 Picnic area.

21 Private campground.

26 Folding Mountain Campground, 110 sites, store.

28 Overlander Lodge. Bungalows, riding, hiking. 403-866-3790.

31 Jasper Park East Gate. No fee for cyclists.

33 Fiddle River.

38 Pocahontas Bungalows. Groceries, 1-403-866-3732. For camping, continue 2 km E to Pocahontas Campground up Miette Hot Springs Road (60 sites, including several walk-in sites).

42 Disaster Point. Bighorn sheep.

44 Rocky River.

46 Picnic tables.

50 Talbot Lake.

53 Jasper Lake.

60 Picnic tables. Sheep frequently sighted.

61 Athabasca River crossing.

69 Turnoff right for Snaring Campground, 60 sites.

71 Picnic tables left.

72 Views of Edith Cavell.

74 Picnic table by river.

76 Maligne Lake Road right.

79 Turnoff right for Jasper townsite.

81 Jasper townsite. Pop. 3970, elev. 1060 m, all services. Information Centre on Connaught Dr., the main street.

HINTON TO GRANDE CACHE

INTO THE NORTHERN FOREST

Distance	144 km (90 miles) one way
Time	1 to 2 days each way
Rating	Strenuous
Terrain	Long, steep hills
Elev. gain	108 metres (354 feet)
Roads	Well-paved, small shoulder
Traffic	Usually light to moderate
Connections	Tour 39

This is a pure wilderness cycle over steep, pine-topped ridges and down into black-spruce wetlands and kettle holes left by the retreating glaciers. Highway 40 to Grande Cache forces its way across the grain of the landscape, a fascinating area in transition from the Rockies to the foothills to the northern boreal forest. A difficult trip that usually seems to be uphill or downhill, it probably offers as splendid a feeling of wilderness as any paved route in the West and has largely been undiscovered by cyclists.

The highway passes through the middle of large William A. Switzer Provincial Park, which offers five campgrounds, picnicking, hiking trails, swimming, showers, groceries, laundry facilities, boating and interpretive programs.

Highlights

The Rockies loom ahead as you leave busy Hinton on a good shoulder of busy Highway 16. The Grande Cache turnoff brings a smaller shoulder and peace from the drone of trucks, motorhomes and high-speed tourists. Here you'll find horses running free.

The price is hard work and the occasional logging truck. The road climbs immediately to good views over the wooded Athabasca Valley and west to peaks such as the striking Roche Miette in Jasper. The highway descends steeply to cross the Athabasca River and begins a long uphill grade, the mountains on the left, the countryside easing out into low rolling hills on the right. The roadside in summer is bright with fireweed.

The highway descends to William A. Switzer Provincial Park, an area formerly known as Fish Lakes Valley. A fee is charged at campgrounds here, unlike others along the highway. On the other hand, park facilities are lavish, especially at Gregg Lake Campground, the most easily-reached of the five in the park. The lake has a day-use area and the nearby campground contains hot showers,

DISTANCE 144 km (90 miles)

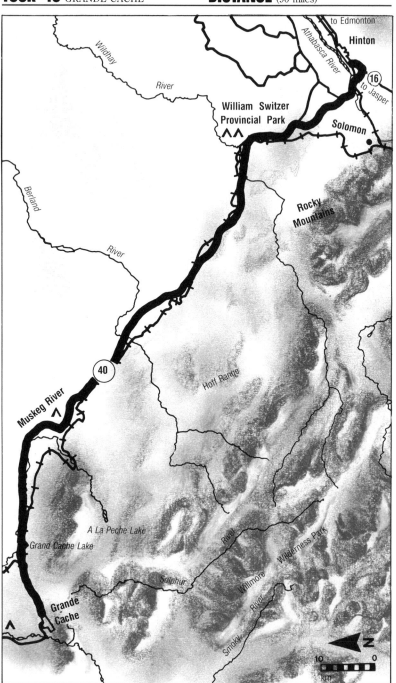

an information centre and offers naturalist programs.

The highway passes the entrance to the renowned Blue Lake Centre, a provincial facility offering low-cost instruction in wilderness skills including canoeing, kayaking, native plant recognition, bird watching, photography, fly fishing, orienteering, bush survival and others. The courses fill up fast and must usually be applied for weeks in advance. For a program, write to Blue Lake Centre, Box 850, Hinton, Alta., T0E 1B0.

The road passes numerous ponds, many of them with beaver or muskrat lodges. The shoulder narrows and the road climbs out of the valley, leaving the park. The forest of spruce and pine begins to open up after the Rock Lake turn-off, partly the result of forest fires, and the road does a roller coaster imitation up and down the good-sized hills. Unofficial camping is common at the Little Berland River. Cyclists should carry water purification tablets as there is no well.

The open areas are excellent places to spot wildlife, including mule deer and caribou. The Berland River Campground is well-situated for those taking two days for the trip. Those doing the trip in one day each way might prefer to stay at the well-designed Pierre Grey's Lakes campground, rather than pushing on into Grande Cache itself.

Grande Cache has a free Alberta forestry campground two km north of town by the Smoky River. However, the campground is down a long and very steep descent from the community. It had been seriously vandalized, last time we visited.

The Grande Cache area is interesting, nonetheless, and might make a good day trip from a base at Pierre Grey's Lakes. Grande Cache Lake, just before the town, has picnic tables and a beach for swimming (no camping). The climb from the lake to the town centre is steep. Views west to the mountains of the Willmore Wilderness are impressive.

This area was used by trappers through the 1800s. Some of them would each year make a cache of their furs near the Smoky River in preparation for spring trading downriver. Pierre Grey, one of the trappers, eventually established a trading post nearby. The area remained remote until high grade coking coal was discovered nearby in the 1950s. In 1969, McIntyre-Porcupine Mines started a coal mine and the town sprung up in a few years.

Although the descent beyond the town is steep down to the wildly-rushing Smoky River, it's interesting to follow the paved road a few kilometres north along the river to the mine site.

Road Log Tour 40

0 km Hinton, pop. 9,000. Elev. 990 m. Rail and bus connections to Edmonton or Jasper and Vancouver. Turn W on Hwy 16.

4 Jct Hwy 40 S to Cadomin.

6 Turn right Hwy 40 N to Grande Cache.

9 Jct Entrance road.

11 Athabasca River.

20 Beginning of William A. Switzer Provincial Park.

21 Jarvis Lake turnoff. Campground.

27 Entrance Blue Lake Centre. Reservations only. No camping.

30 Turnoff to Cache Lake and Graveyard Lake campgrounds on gravel road.

32 Turnoff to Gregg Lake Campground 1 km on pavement and Gregg Lake day use area, 3 km on gravel.

34 Leaving provincial park.

39 Wildhay River.

46 Rock Lake turnoff, 32 km on gravel.

69 Little Berland River. Unofficial camping.

73 Fox Creek.

82 Berland River. Campground 1 km.

108 Pierre Grey's Lakes Campground.

111 Muskeg River community. No services.

123 Picnic area. Day use only.

138 Grande Cache Lake and picnic area. Day use only.

144 Town centre for Grande Cache, population 5,000. Elev. 1098 m. All services. Daily bus service to Hinton.

9

Day Tours in Waterton Lakes National Park

Waterton Lakes National Park is Canada's tiny perfect park. The Rocky Mountains rise abruptly from the prairies, creating a rich landscape of peaks, deep lakes, hanging valleys, grassland and forest. The range in elevation produces a quasi-Pacific climate and some of the best wildflower displays in North America.

The good news for day cyclists is that the park, situated in Alberta's southwest corner (264 kilometres southwest of Calgary, adjoining Glacier National Park in the United States) is much quieter than its better-known counterparts, Banff or Jasper. No main road traverses it, so there is almost no truck traffic and most vehicles are slow-moving. Wildlife is easy to spot from the road. And there is a mellow ambience to the tiny village, delightfully set on Upper Waterton Lake under the stately Prince of Wales Hotel.

Perhaps the best way to enjoy the park is to combine biking and hiking. Tours to both Red Rock Canyon and Cameron Lake are ideally suited for this.

The bad news is that Waterton winds can be brutal, and that all the short trips from Waterton townsite involve an initial steep climb. Cyclists who want a leisurely pedal can simply start above the townsite (if they have vehicles to get there), as described in Tours 43 and 44.

Pat's Texaco just behind the marina rents 18-speed mountain bikes, scooters and surreys but no 10-speed touring bikes. (Call 403-859-2266 to reserve.)

Buses serve the park in summer from Pincher Creek, Alberta and from Great Falls and Kalispell in Montana.

WATERTON TOWNSITE TO RED ROCK CANYON (RETURN)

ASCENT TO A RUBY CANYON

Distance	31 km (19 miles) return
Time	1/2 to 1 day
Rating	Intermediate
Terrain	Steep climb out of townsite, then undulating
Elev. gain	213 metres (698 feet)
Roads	Narrow, good condition, no shoulder
Traffic	Busy but slow-moving on summer weekends, otherwise moderate
Connections	Tours 36, 42, 43, 45

Grassy meadows, great peaks, wildflowers, wildlife and a red rock canyon: this tour through Waterton's Blakiston Valley has much to recommend it.

Many cyclists are put off by the initial steep pitch out of the townsite. They shouldn't be. After the first grind, the uphill grade is gradual. The twisting road offers constantly changing vistas of prairie and peaks. Moreover, Red Rock Canyon is one of the surest places in Waterton to see bighorn sheep and deer. And the short hike along the canyon is unusual.

Brisk westerly winds can be a problem, especially at first. Further into the valley, the road is more protected. No services are provided along the way, so take ample supplies for the day.

OPTION: Cyclists may want to stay overnight at Crandell Lake campground, which is quieter than the townsite campground. Deer frequently roam the wooded campsites.

Highlights

Leave the stately Prince of Wales Hotel behind as you climb out of the townsite. The warm-up really begins at the turn-off to Red Rock Canyon Road. After a steep initial pitch, you find yourself in a transition zone between prairie and mountains.

Fescue grassland covers the rolling hills which are the remains of glacial moraines. Crandell Mountain is on the left, Bellevue Hill on the right, and the reddish rock of aptly-named Ruby Mountain soon comes into view ahead to the west. Brown-eyed susans and purple asters fringe the roadsides.

Some steep, small hills in the next portion provide an exhilarating roller-coaster ride. The road then descends to Crandell Lake campground.

The Kootenay Indians inhabited

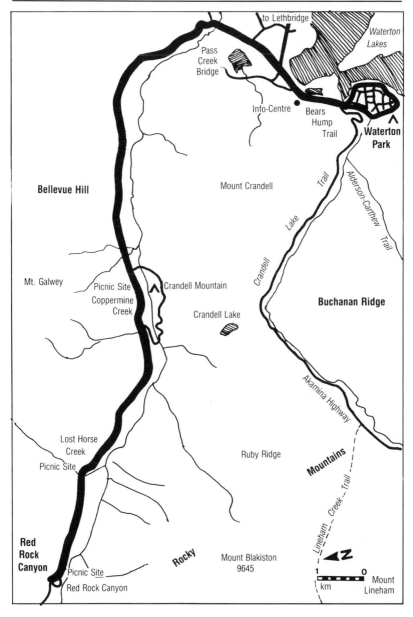

to Lethbridge

Waterton Lakes

Pass Creek Bridge

Info-Centre

Bears Hump Trail

Waterton Park

Bellevue Hill

Mount Crandell

Lake Trail

Alderson-Carthew Trail

Mt. Galwey

Picnic Site
Coppermine Creek

Crandell Mountain

Crandell Lake

Crandell Lake Trail

Buchanan Ridge

Akamina Highway

Lost Horse Creek

Picnic Site

Ruby Ridge

Mountains

Lineham Creek Trail

Red Rock Canyon

Picnic Site

Red Rock Canyon

Rocky

Mount Blakiston
9645

N

1   0
km

Mount Lineham

the Blakiston Valley for 2,000 years. Archaeologists digging here have found evidence of ancient bison kills and bison processing areas.

177

Around 1800, a major change in settlement occurred and there is little evidence of their presence in the early 19th century.

Lt. Thomas Blakiston explored this area as part of the Palliser Expedition between 1857 and 1860. He crossed the South Kootenay Pass on September 6, 1858 and continued on to Waterton Lakes.

The beautiful red, green and purple tones of the bedrock along the road are the result of iron reacting with different kinds of minerals. The oldest exposed sedimentary rock in the Canadian Rockies is found in Waterton.

Blakiston Creek below the road has carved through the glacial debris on the valley floor for thousands of years. Mount Blakiston, Waterton's highest peak, dominates to the left, at 2940 metres. The horn of Anderson Peak at 2683 metres was formed as ice sculpted opposite sides of the rock.

The route ends at a parking lot beside Red Rock Canyon, a fine place for a picnic. A short nature walk loops around the canyon and another leads to Blakiston Falls.

Road Log Tour 41

0 km Information Centre, N end of Waterton townsite. Pop. 136, elev. 1280, all services late June to Labor Day. Go NE on on Hwy 5.

0.5 Picnic tables and stables.

1.5 Turn left on Red Rock Canyon Road. Bridge and picnic area by Blakiston Creek. Steep initial climb.

3 Views into Blakiston Valley.

8 Sign commemorating Lt. Thomas Blakiston.

8.5 Turnoff left for Crandell Lake campground (129 campsites).

9.5 Coppermine Creek picnicking.

13.5 Lost Horse Creek, picnicking.

15.5 Red Rock Canyon (nature trails, picnicking). Return to Waterton same way.

RED ROCK CANYON

Who would have thought that old mud could be transformed into something as striking as Red Rock Canyon?

Yes, this water-carved gorge had its beginnings as mud deposited in an ancient, shallow sea. Parts of the sea dried up, and exposure oxidized the iron, forming a red mineral called hematite. Unexposed layers formed white and green bands, causing a layer-cake effect in parts of the canyon.

The canyon is the result of 7,000 to 10,000 years of carving by the forces of water. Erosion continues to wear it down by the thickness of a nickel or two a year.

A 20-minute self-guided walk displays canyon highlights, including mud cracks and ripple marks formed by the ancient sea.

WATERTON TOWNSITE TO CAMERON LAKE (RETURN)

VALLEY OF GLACIERS AND TARNS

Distance 31 km (19 miles) return
Time 1/2 day or more
Rating Strenuous
Terrain Steep ascent at first, then more gradual
Elev. gain 380 metres (1246 feet)
Road Narrow, good condition, no shoulder
Traffic Busy but slow-moving on summer weekends, otherwise moderate
Connections Tours 36, 41, 45

The Akamina Parkway leads through the historic Cameron Valley to offer plentiful views of peaks, waterfalls, wildlife and forests — plus more protection from Waterton's often-brutal winds than other tours hereabouts. You can explore the site of Oil City along the way and rent a canoe or hike at Cameron Lake, sanctuary for subalpine plants usually found further west.

The most difficult part is the gruelling climb out of Waterton townsite before the grade becomes manageable. Take lots of food. There are no stores or campgrounds along the way.

Highlights

A blood-warming beginning. The road winds beneath the rocky outcrops of Bear's Hump on the right. Then it's up, up, up. Views over the town and Upper Waterton Lake compensate somewhat for the steep grade.

Sylvan views into the wide, forested Cameron Valley begin around km 2.5. The parkway is bounded by the Buchanan Ridge on the left and Ruby Ridge on the right. Cameron Creek flows below.

During the Little Ice Age, which began about 4,000 years ago, ice reformed in many cirques and glaciers at the head of Cameron and Blakiston valleys. Numerous tarns along the valley are their legacy.

The ascent mercifully eases as the parkway enters a mixed forest of pine and aspen. It is not uncommon to see deer and bighorn sheep along the roadside, especially in early morning or evening. The road becomes level as it follows Cameron Creek. Picnic tables at km 6.5 make a pleasant rest stop. A plaque at km 8.5 commemorates the spot where oil was discovered in 1901, the first strike in Western Canada.

The road climbs gradually from here on, with lots of little trails leading down to the creek where

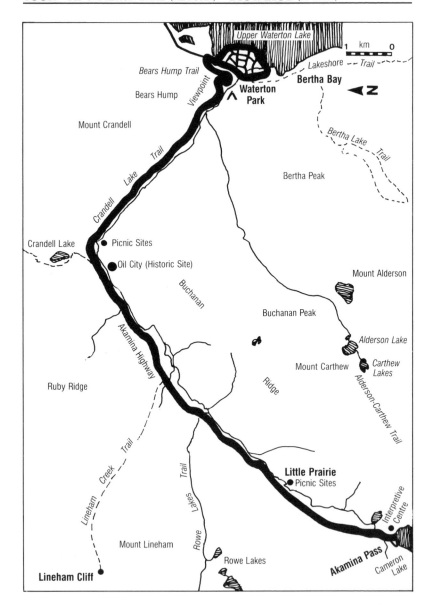

fishing is reported to be good. Mt. Carthew at 2623 metres is the dominant peak.

Most cyclists will want to linger at Cameron Lake. Canada and the United States meet here — the international boundary bisects the lake near the foot of imposing Mt. Custer.

The weather at the lake is moderated by pockets of moist air from nearby mountains, making it a sanctuary for subalpine plants and animals usually found further west. It is home to Steller's jay and the varied thrush, birds rarely seen any other place in the park. Huge 500-year-old spruce also survive in this special rain-ridden area.

Fishing tackle and canoes can be rented. An easy 1.5-km trail edges the north shore — note that meadows near the end of the trail are a prime grizzly habitat.

Road Log Tour 42

0 km Information Centre at N entrance to Waterton townsite, pop. 176, elev. 1280, all services late June to Labor Day. Head toward town on Hwy 5.

0.5 Right turn for Akamina Parkway (Cameron Lake Road). Steep ascent.

2.5 More gradual climb.

6.5 Picnic tables and shelter. Fairly level.

7.5 Trailhead for 2-km hike to Crandell Lake.

8.5 Oil City. Historic monument.

10.5 Trailhead for Rowe Lakes.

12.5 Picnic area.

15.5 Cameron Lake, elev. 1660 m. Interpretive centre. Canoe rentals. Hiking trails.

Cameron Lake, Waterton Lakes National Park   TRAVEL ALBERTA

CRANDELL MOUNTAIN TO RED ROCK CANYON (RETURN)

CAMPGROUND TO CANYON

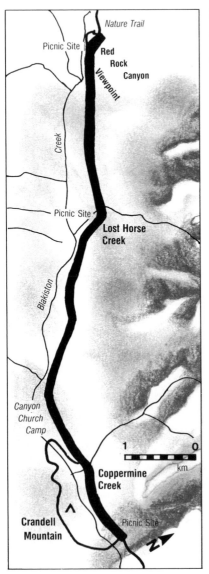

TOUR 43	CRANDELL MT. TO RED ROCK CANYON
DISTANCE	14 km (9 miles)

Distance	14 km (9 miles) return
Time	1 1/2 to 2 hours return
Rating	Intermediate
Terrain	Rolling ascent
Elev. gain	121 metres (400 feet)
Roads	Narrow, good condition, no shoulder
Traffic	Moderately busy but slow-moving on summer weekends
Connections	Tours 36, 41, 42

The Red Rock Canyon Road is a delight to bicycle. The easiest way to enjoy its sweeping views is to start at Crandell Mountain campground, although a more strenuous tour from the townsite is described in Tour 41. A pleasant half-day or more can be enjoyed by packing a picnic lunch and exploring one or two of the short trails which begin at Red Rock Canyon. There are no services on this route.

Take your camera — the canyon parking lot is one of the surest places in Waterton to come nose-to-nose with bighorn sheep and deer. Morning is the best time.

Highlights

The starting point, Crandell Mountain campground, is a quieter and more low-key place to stay than the townsite campground. Begin the ride with excellent views of sharp-toothed Mt. Blakiston to the left, highest peak in Waterton at 2940 metres. Ruby Ridge is just south. Like many mountains in this park, it contains iron which has oxidized, accounting for its reddish tones.

The mountains gradually seem to close in around you, with Galwey on the right and the prominent horn of Anderson straight ahead. In certain light, this peak glows a golden hue, earning it the name "Millionaire's Peak." The tour follows high above Blakiston Creek which for thousands of years has carved out a place out for itself in the valley.

In the 19th century, this valley was used as a route to the South Kootenay Pass into British Columbia.

The route passes an inviting picnic stop at Lost Horse Creek before ending at Red Rock Canyon. A nature trail loops around the canyon and another short trail leads to Blakiston Falls.

Road Log Tour 43

0 km Crandell Mtn. campground, elev. 1371 m, 129 campsites. Campground is 8.5 km N of Hwy 5 on Red Rock Canyon Rd. Turn left from campground.

1 Coppermine Creek picnic area.

5 Lost Horse Creek. Picnic tables and shelter.

7 Red Rock Canyon, elev. 1493. Nature trails. Picnicking.

Mountain Pine Beetle

Puzzled by Waterton's ruddy forests? The coloring is the mark of the mountain pine beetle, a voracious insect which has attacked forests throughout the park, including those at Crandell Lake campground. It was first noticed in Waterton in 1977 and has since destroyed thousands of trees, mostly mature and over-mature lodgepole and whitebark pine. Biologists now believe the infestation may have been caused by the park policy of controlling forest fires, thus prolonging the life of older, more vulnerable trees which would normally have burnt.

Infestations generally last four to 15 years. By now it seems that most mature stands in Waterton have succumbed, and are being replaced by younger trees — a healing process that will take decades.

OIL CITY
TO CAMERON LAKE (RETURN)

EASIEST RIDE TO THE SUBALPINE

Distance	14 km (8.5 miles) return
Time	1 to 2 hours return
Rating	Intermediate
Terrain	Gradual ascent
Elev. gain	106 metres (347 feet)
Road	Narrow, good condition
Traffic	Moderately busy but slow-moving on summer weekends, otherwise moderate
Connection	Tour 42

The historic Cameron Valley has much to offer day cyclists. The valley is fairly protected from Waterton's sometimes fierce winds. The road is scenic and Cameron Lake makes for a lush subalpine destination where wildlife can often be seen.

The ride from the townsite (Tour 42) is recommended for strong cyclists. This tour is more leisurely.

Make a day of it by renting a canoe or fishing tackle at the lake, or take one of the hikes which begins there.

Highlights

Begin at Oil City where a white derrick marks the site of Western Canada's first oil well, drilled in 1901.

Initial hopes of an oil boom led to a frenzy of construction, with 20 blocks of buildings hammered up in haste not far from the derrick. Today, the foundations of the Oil City Hotel are among the few remains left.

Cycling is fairly level and easy. The road is fringed with wildflowers in summer. Mt. Carthew dominates to the left and the grey tower of Mt. Lineham to the right.

After the picnic area at km 4, the road begins an enjoyable series of roller-coaster ascents and descents.

Cameron Lake supports an unusual variety of plants and animals. The interpretive centre provides a detailed explanation of the lake's micro-climate.

A 1.5-km trail leads along the north shore, and a two-to-three hour hike goes up to Summit Lake, passing 500-year-old spruce along the way.

Perhaps the most pleasant activity is to rent a canoe and spend a lazy hour or two on the lake.

Road Log Tour 44

0 km Oil City parking lot, 8 km N of Waterton townsite on Akamina Parkway, elev. 1554 m, pop. 0. (Turnoff for parkway is just W of Information Centre on N side of the townsite). Historic display. Turn right.

2 Trailhead for Rowe Lakes.

4 Little Prairie picnic area.

7 Cameron Lake, elev. 1660 m. Interpretive Centre. Canoe and fishing tackle rentals. Hiking trails. No camping. Return same route.

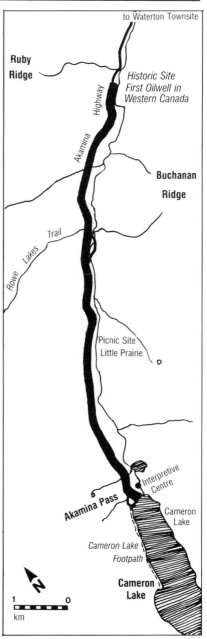

Waterton Lakes National Park   TRAVEL ALBERTA

10

Extended Tours in Waterton, Glacier and Northern Montana

We couldn't write about the Rockies and neglect the splendid cycling routes that lie just south of the Canadian border, a natural continuation of tours through Waterton and southeastern British Columbia.

Logan Pass in Montana's Glacier National Park (Tour 46) is perhaps the most exciting cycling route over the northern Rockies, rivalled only by the road through Rocky Mountain National Park in Colorado. The highways on the eastern side of Glacier (Tours 45 and 48) traverse high ridges and moraines through the fascinating transition zone between prairie grassland and high mountains.

On the west side, Tours 49, 50 and 51 head deep into quiet back-country and then into British Columbia through logging and ranching country with friendly people and good camping. Tours 46, 47 and 48 may even be combined for a first-class loop over Logan Pass and back over the easier Marias Pass.

These tours all connect with Bikecentennial routes that head south to Missoula, Mont. and then east and west all over the United States. See appendix for information on these tours.

Cyclists may bring their bikes by Amtrak to stations at East Glacier or West Glacier (the stations are called Glacier Park and Belton respectively) or to Whitefish. Phone Amtrak at 1-800-872-7245. There is bus service to most of the towns along these routes in Canada and the U.S.

WATERTON TO
St. MARY, MONTANA

BETWEEN TWO PARKS

Distance	74 km (46 miles)
Time	1 day
Rating	Strenuous
Terrain	Several long climbs and descents
Elev. gain	410 m (1345 ft.)
Roads	Good with small shoulder in Canada. Sometimes rough paving with no shoulder in U.S.
Traffic	Moderate
Connections	Tours 36, 41, 42, 46

Travel between two national parks and two countries on a scenic tour bridging two distinct types of terrain—prairie and mountain. The beautiful stretch of Chief Mountain Highway between Waterton National Park and the entrance to Glacier National Park at St. Mary, Montana, climbs past splendid viewpoints. It traverses glacial debris at the very point where the prairie grasslands end and sculpted glacial peaks suddenly rise 1,000 metres or more.

With such variation in terrain and flora — from grasslands to aspen groves, lodgepole pine, spruce and fir and from high viewpoints to lakeside and riverside, this is a first-class bicycle tour.

Note that the road between Waterton and Chief Mountain usually closes from mid-September to mid-May.

Highlights

Only a few hills slow the ride from Waterton townsite to the park entrance as the road heads past Middle and Lower Waterton lakes and down the river. Near the lower lake, the route passes near the grave of Kootenai Brown and his Indian wives. Brown was an early settler who became the park's first warden and superintendent.

Once across the Waterton River, the road climbs from about 1,275 metres to a splendid viewpoint at 1,585 metres. The panorama takes in Lower Waterton Lake and the sculpted mountains beyond from Vimy Peak on the left to Crandell behind the townsite to the far prospects of Galwey and Dungarvan peaks on the park's northeastern edge. Note how the rock layers are twisted and folded, especially Crandell whose sides bear a distinctive S-shaped fold.

At the top of the hill, the route passes under the crumbling sides of Sofa Mountain where great blocks of stone have rolled down the hillside. Moose are sometimes seen in the bogs and ponds alongside the

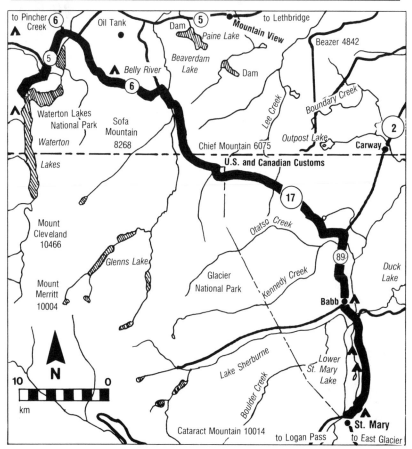

highway. After passing a picnic area between Sofa Mountain and low Lookout Butte, the road descends again, entering the Blood Indian Reserve and crossing Belly River. The route re-enters the park and passes the paved, 1-km road to quiet Belly River Campground. Another climb brings cyclists to the U.S. and Canadian customs and the border where the road narrows. Cyclists should carry identification such as a birth certificate.

On the left the terrain descends abruptly to rolling grassland. To the right are the massive cliffs of Chief Mountain (2,763 metres), a peak of Precambrian limestone once joined to a great rock mass. Today erosion has left it isolated among the softer rock of the plains.

The descent is glorious through glacial debris to the St. Mary River and Chief Mountain store that offers "buffalo sausage" among more conventional groceries.

While Highway 89 south is busier than the park road, the cycling is easier through farmland following the river. The open ranchland contrasts with the deep woods behind.

OPTION: At Babb is a paved, 19-km sidetrip deep into Glacier National Park along Sherburne Lake and a valley frequented by bighorn sheep. The road ends at the huge Many Glacier Hotel. Close by is a campground and a network of hiking trails.

After crossing the St. Mary River, the main road follows a lateral moraine along the east shore of beautiful Lower St. Mary Lake. It remains mostly on the level through the Blackfoot Indian Reservation before reaching the tourist hordes of St. Mary, at the entrance to Glacier National Park.

Road Log Tour 45

0 km Waterton townsite. Pop. 176, elev. 1280 m., all services late June to Labor Day. National Park campground, showers. Turn E on Hwy 5 towards park entrance, passing information centre.

1 Picnic tables beside lake

1.5 Small picnic area. Entering prairie grasslands. Route mostly flat.

3 Picnic area by Waterton River. Turnoff left for Red Rock Canyon.

7 Picnic tables.

8 Park gates. Turn right to cross Waterton River

9 Junction Hwys 5 and 6 (17). Keep right on 6 (17) for Chief Mtn. Ascent begins.

15 Waterton Valley Viewpoint.

16 Top of hill.

17 Terrain opens up.

19 Pump for drinking water.

22 Begin gradual descent.

24 Bottom of hill. Gas station, gift shop. Blood Indian Campground.

25 Belly River bridge. Re-entering Waterton Park. Gradual ascent.

27 Turnoff 1 km for Belly River Campground (national park). Cook shelters.

29 Steep climb.

30 Viewpoint over Waterton Valley.

31 Border crossing. Customs opens 7 a.m. - 10 p.m. Closed mid-September to mid-May. Road narrows. shoulder ends. Still ascending.

43 Steep hill.

46 Scenic overlook. Right is Chief Mountain 2768 metres. Steep descent.

51 Terrain opens. Excellent views. Descent continues.

53 Chief Mountain Motel, store, campground, buffalo sausage. Turn

right on Hwy 89 for St.
Mary. Road busier. No
shoulder. Terrain level.

60 Babb. Store, cafe, motel.
Turnoff for Many
Glacier.

62 St. Mary River and
lake.

65 Chewing Bones Campground by lake. Marina,
swimming pool, laundro-
mat and picnic area.

66 Cafe. Lakeview Campground. Small shoulder.

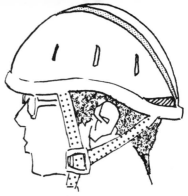

74 Turnoff KOA Kamp-
ground. Entering St.
Mary. Stores, cafes.
Accommodation. Park
entrance.

St. MARY TO WEST GLACIER, MONTANA (LOGAN PASS) TOUR **46**

GOING TO THE SUN

Distance	82 km (50 miles)
Time	1 to 2 days
Rating	Super-strenuous
Terrain	Steep climb to high pass. Dangerous descent
Elev. gain	656 metres (2,152 feet) westbound) 1066 metres (3497 feet) eastbound
Roads	Narrow with sharp, blind curves. No shoulder. Loose rocks or pebbles at the edge
Traffic	Moderately heavy to heavy. No trucks or large trailers
Connections	Tours 45, 47, 48, 49

The Going-to-the-Sun Road may simply be the most gorgeous mountain cycle in the United States. From St. Mary Lake on the east or Lake McDonald on the west, the road does seems to climb to the sun and edges along the rock face of the Garden Wall, an engineering triumph. It traverses alpine tundra around Logan Pass on the Continental Divide with craggy Clements Mountain towering above the Hanging Gardens.

And yet there are many reasons for cyclists to stay away. The Going-to-the-Sun Road is, simply put, a dangerous route for cyclists. The road is narrow and usually choked

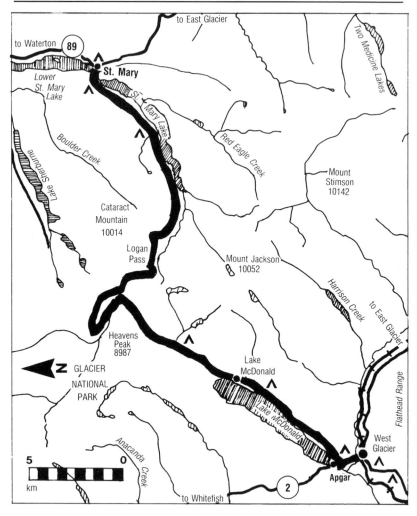

with cars. Numerous blind curves obscure the cyclist from a motorist's vision until the last minute, as the road edges around the rock face. There's no shoulder and the side of the road is frequently littered with small stones that have avalanched down the slope. The roadway is often wet with either rain or melting snow that reduces traction. Visibility is often poor near the top. What's more, cyclists are banned from two stretches of the road during the prime hours of 11 a.m. to 4 p.m., June 15 to Labor Day. And, of course, the ascent, from either east or west, is relentlessly long and steep.

So consider carefully before setting out. Marias Pass on Highway 2 to the south makes for a much easier, safer crossing of the Divide, although it lacks the stunning beauty — and the challenge.

Wind can also be a significant factor, especially in the crossing from east to west. The wind often sweeps down St. Mary Valley with impressive force, adding to the cyclist's battle against the steep grade.

Highlights

Most cyclists try for a really early start to reach the top of the pass by 10 a.m. or so and thus avoid the 11 a.m. to 4 p.m. ban on bicycles from Logan Pass to Logan Creek far beneath the Garden Wall on the other side. Some plan to wait out the afternoon at the Logan Pass visitor centre or go for short hikes in the alpine grandeur until 4 p.m. Note that while the visitor centre does provide a refuge from the often frigid conditions on top, it is usually crowded and isn't a terribly restful place. There are only a few chairs, usually occupied, and no food concession or other services.

An overnight stay at Rising Sun Campground makes it easier to clear the pass in time. While the thrilling 19-km descent from the top can be done in less than an hour, that doesn't leave much time for sightseeing on this amazing stretch down the rock face. And high speeds can be dangerous.

The 11 a.m. to 4 p.m. road ban for cyclists between Sprague Creek Campground and Apgar Village at the end of Lake McDonald also requires planning. Many westbound cyclists pass the early afternoon at Lake McDonald Lodge or on the lakeside beaches until 4 p.m. Others call it a day and camp at Sprague Creek, nicely located overlooking the lake. (This campground fills up fast.)

Eastbound cyclists also need an early start to reach the top by 11 a.m. since it's a harder push from that side. Many start from Sprague Creek.

From the east, the going is easy at first as the road curves through beautiful prairie grass, wildflowers and aspen groves above St. Mary Lake, which reaches depths of 88 metres and a length of almost 18 kilometres. The transition from prairie to mountain is remarkable and the peaks seem to draw the visitor in. Across the water, Divide Mountain and Triple Divide Mountain to its right come into view. The latter is the apex of three watersheds: to Hudson Bay via the St. Mary, Saskatchewan and Churchill rivers; to the Gulf of Mexico via the Cut Bank, Missouri and Mississippi rivers and to the Pacific via the Flathead and Columbia rivers.

From Rising Sun campground, cafe and store, the road leads past one of the best viewpoints on St. Mary Lake where all the peaks of the upper valley are exposed down the water. The impressive peak to the right is the famous Going-to-the-Sun Mountain, a brown monolith with crumbling towers. The road leads under sheer cliffs curtained by white waterfalls. Further down the lake, don't neglect to stop at the Sun Point viewpoint and nature trail 0.5 km off the main route on a paved road. A short trail leads in a few minutes to a promontory overlooking the lake and craggy peaks beyond. A 1.2-km trail leads along the edge of the lakeside cliffs to Baring Falls. It's a beautiful walk through juniper and lodgepole pine twisted by the strong winds that blow down this valley.

The climb is gradual beneath Going-to-the-Sun and the trees gradually change to spruce and fir from lodgepole pine, Douglas fir and mountain alder. Jackson Glacier is visible across the valley. Soon the road turns to the right to cross Siyea Creek on a sharp, unmistakable horseshoe bend. Abruptly, it begins to climb the side of Piegan Mountain very steeply above the St. Mary Valley towards the turret of Mt. Clements. It passes through a short tunnel, beside waterfalls and a deep snowdrift that continues to melt for most of the summer.

The trees begin to drop away, leaving only scattered islands of fir and spruce, huddled for protection against the bitter conditions. Above, Clements Mountain rises over a glacial moraine, a bare, distinctive rock tower of greys and reds, contrasted with the snowfields below that linger into the summer.

Around a bend, the visitor centre finally comes into sight, a welcome refuge from the cold, wind and, all-too-frequently, the rain. This is Logan Pass, the Continental Divide. In reasonable weather, the 3-km Hidden Lake Overlook Trail is a worthwhile trip, climbing gradually through alpine flowers to a point high above the startling blue of the lake.

Bundle up well for the 19-km descent from the pass. This is the most impressive — some might say forbidding — part of the journey. The road leads from an alpine meadow filled with glacier lilies around a corner and onto a narrow ledge cut out from the cliffs of the Garden Wall: a rock face to the right and a sharp drop to the left. On the downgrade, cyclists can't be expected to keep far enough to the right for vehicles to pass easily on this narrow road. So stop and pull off frequently for cars behind or whenever four or more vehicles stack up behind you. You really have to pull over to take in the scenery — the McDonald Valley, 1,000 metres below, and the peaks beyond.

You soon whiz past the famous Weeping Wall where snowmelt pours down on the roadside all summer. The road begins to re-enter the trees, although it continues to be steep. An exhibit marks a large burned area and fireweed dots the steep hillside below.

Cyclists need to take special care in the west-side tunnel, whose gloom is relieved by two openings in the rock, an excellent place to photograph Heavens Peak. The road then widens and soon reaches

Logan Creek and the bottom of the valley. The descent, which has averaged 5.6 per cent, grade, becomes relatively gentle.

While the scenery on the valley floor isn't as spectacular as above, the cyclist has time to view the deep pools and cascades along the creek before the road passes the short turnoff for Lake McDonald Lodge.

The road leads down the lake past Sprague Creek Campground, nicely situated on the edge of the lake. It fills up fast. This marks the beginning of another 11 a.m. to 4 p.m. road restriction for poor cyclists.

The going is mostly level to the turnoff for Apgar Village and the large campground. It's only a couple of kilometres to the park gates and all the roadside tourist services of West Glacier — which come as a shock to some and a reassurance to others after the purity and the wildness of the park.

OPTION: Cyclists staying in the Apgar Village area or just seeking relief from traffic can take a paved bicycle path through a generally level, pleasant forest. The trail extends from Apgar Village to the park headquarters, crossing the main road just inside the park gate.

Road Log Tour 46

0 km St. Mary. Elev. 1370 metres. All services. Camping at KOA, 1.5 km N on Hwy 89: Cafe, 406-732-5311. Johnson's Campground 0.3 km N on 89, cafe, 732-4621.

St. Mary Campground (national park), 2 km W inside park.
Turn right
on Going-to-Sun Hwy.
1 Park gate. Information Centre. Cross St. Mary River.
2 Turnoff St. Mary Campground. Mostly level along St. Mary Lake.
10 Rising Sun Campground, cafe, groceries, boat tours. Begin climb. Sharp turns.
14 Viewpoint. Picnic tables. Interpretive hiking trail. Road levels.
19 St. Mary Falls trail.
22 Road climbs gradually away from lake.
23 Jackson Glacier viewpoint.
26 Siyea Creek curve. Ascent becomes very steep.
29 Short tunnel.
31 Summit Logan Pass, 2026 m. Visitor Centre. Hiking trails, guided walks. No food, accommodation or camping. No bicycles allowed next 19 km between pass and Logan Creek 11 a.m.- 4 p.m., June 15 to Labor Day. Road narrows, begin steep descent.
35 Weeping Wall.
36 Re-enter trees.
43 Trail for Granite Park

Chalet. Road widens.

44 Short tunnel.

48 Logan Creek. Road mostly level along creek. End of cycling restriction westbound.

55 Avalanche Creek picnic area and trails.

61 Sacred Dancing cascade

63 Lake McDonald Lodge. Cafe, beach.

66 Sprague Creek Campground. No bicycles allowed next 11 km between campground and end of lake at Apgar 11 a.m.-4 p.m., June 15 to Labor Day.

77 Turnoff for Apgar Village. Picnic tables by lake. Turn right for campground, services.

78 Campground.

79 Apgar Village. Cafe, groceries. Bicycle trail. Left for West Glacier.

81 Stop sign. Right for West Glacier. Road widens.

81 Park gates. Bicycle trail.

82 West Glacier, elev. 960. All services. Campgrounds: Glacier, laundromat, 406-387-5689. KOA (4 km SW on Hwy 2, 1.5 km E on Hwy 60) Laundromat. Winnakee (1.5 km W on U.S. 2).

CYCLING RULES FOR GLACIER

Special cycling rules apply in Glacier National Park because of traffic congestion on the narrow roads built in the 1930s. The rules tend to be strictly enforced.

— Cyclists must pull off the road and allow traffic to pass whenever four or more vehicles stack up behind them.

— Bicycles are allowed only on established roads and bike trails.

— At night or in periods of low visibility, bicycles must have a white light on the front and a red light or reflector on the rear.

— Bicycles must ride single file, well over to the side of the road.

— From June 15 through Labor Day, bicycle travel is prohibited between 11 a.m. and 4 p.m. from Logan Creek to Logan Pass and from the Apgar Campground turnoff at the south end of Lake McDonald to Sprague Creek Campground.

WEST GLACIER TO EAST GLACIER, MONTANA

AN EASIER ALTERNATIVE

Distance 88 km (55 miles)
Time 1 day
Rating Strenuous
Terrain Well-graded ascent to Continental Divide. Remainder is hilly
Elev. gain 686 metres (2,250 feet)
Roads Good with small shoulder most of way
Traffic Light to moderate
Connections Tours 46, 48, 49

The well-paved highway connecting West Glacier with the rustic village of East Glacier across the Continental Divide is not as scenic or interesting as the almost-parallel Logan Pass route just to the north.

Yet the route does traverse redrock wilderness on the southern edge of Glacier National Park and has several major advantages over the famous Going-to-the-Sun road. First of all, it's easier. Grades are relatively gentle as the road closely follows the Middle Fork of the Flathead River most of the way. And it's certainly safer. The highway is wide, fairly quiet and even has a decent paved shoulder part of the way, in contrast to the narrow, tourist-clogged splendor of the Logan Pass highway in summer.

What's more, it is a year-round highway, whereas the Logan Pass road is usually closed from about September 15 to June 1. And unlike the Logan Pass route, there are no riding restrictions.

For those interested in a circle route, the trip over Logan Pass and back via East Glacier and the easier Marias Pass makes an excellent loop of three or more days.

Highlights

The route is known as the Theodore Roosevelt Highway and follows the tracks of the Burlington Northern Railroad all the way. When a road stays close to railway tracks, cyclists can usually be assured that the grades won't be too bad, (Kicking Horse Pass in B.C. being a notable exception).

From the tourist congestion of West Glacier, the highway turns southeast, following the major bends in the Middle Fork of the Flathead River. The countryside is mostly wooded. The rounded Flathead Range rises to the right while the higher peaks of Glacier National Park can sometimes be seen up the long valleys on the left. The river marks the southern boundary of the park.

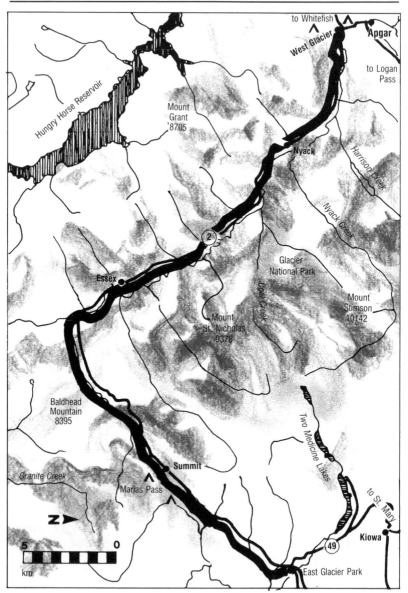

The highway appears red in many stretches, its color matching the dominant hue of the rocks hereabouts. The rocks are part of the Grinnell Formation of sediments containing much iron. The tour passes a few isolated bar-cafes and private campgrounds, although there isn't much development at all along this highway.

While several long hills keep the cyclist working, steady climbing doesn't really begin until the highway leaves the Middle Fork beyond Essex and starts ascending Bear Creek, passing a goat lick and entering Flathead National Forest. The views begin to open to more impressive peaks on the left such as Elk and Summit mountains, the latter above Marias Pass.

The pass itself isn't much of a thrill, although there's a monument to Theodore Roosevelt and a statue of John Stevens. He developed a route through here, the most northerly year-round crossing of the Continental Divide in the U.S.

From the pass, you enter Lewis and Clark National Forest. Surprisingly, the road remains on a high plateau which opens up to reveal grey, ragged peaks on either side. The descent begins about 10 km beyond the pass and you quickly leave the big mountains behind and enter a fascinating transition zone of foothills where prairie grass mixes with aspen groves and lodgepole pines.

East Glacier is a rustic town, home of the famous Glacier Park Lodge. At the Amtrak railway station, service is available east or west once a day on the Empire Builder.

Road Log Tour 47

0 km West Glacier. All services. Elev. 960. Campgrounds: Aspar in

national park, 5 km N; Glacier (406-387-5690); KOA 4 km SW on Hwy 2 and 1.5 km E on Hwy 60; Winnakee, 1.5 km W on U.S. 2.
From West Glacier, turn left (E) on Hwy 2. Small shoulder.

27 Stanton Creek Lodge and campground.

33 Motel. Cafe and bar.

42 Essex store.

58 Devil's Creek Campground (National Forest).

59 Bar, cafe.

60 Three Forks Campground. Bear Creek guest ranch.

69 Marias Pass. Continental Divide. Elev. 1646 m (5400 feet). Summit Campground (National Forest).

81 Begin descent.

83 Leaving national forest.

88 East Glacier Park. All services. Elev. 1460 m. Amtrak Station. Camping at Y Lazy R camper park 1 block E of Hwy 2.

EAST GLACIER TO St. MARY, MONTANA

OVER THE HIGH MORAINES

Distance 50 km (31 miles)
Time 1/2 to 1 day
Rating Highly strenuous
Terrain Frequent and very steep ascents, exhilarating descents
Elev. gain 835 metres (2,743 feet)
Roads Mostly narrow, no shoulder and some blind curves.
Traffic Moderate to moderately busy
Connections Tours 45, 46, 47

Unlike the highway over Marias Pass, the roads between East Glacier and St. Mary are spectacular, often leading along high ridges and moraines overlooking the glacial lakes and great peaks to the west. Few places are as fascinating as this transition zone between prairie grassland and the Rockies.

The price for this beauty is hard work. Many of the roads are steep and narrow. The hills are long and the tourist traffic can be very busy in the summer.

This route combined with the easier highway between East Glacier and West Glacier and the steep, stunning Going-to-the-Sun Road over Logan Pass can be used for a gorgeous and demanding circle of Glacier National Park.

Highlights

From the rustic main street of East Glacier, the Blackfeet Highway climbs to the Amtrack station. Across from it is the imposing East Glacier Park Lodge, built of huge Douglas fir logs and surrounded by landscaped gardens that contrast with the wildness of Squaw Peak behind them.

The scenery becomes even more splendid as you climb steeply over glacial moraines from the lodge. This truly looks like the wild west of legend, the dry cowboy country where mountains meet the plains. Beyond Two Medicine River, the road climbs steeply again to a viewpoint overlooking Lower and Upper Two Medicine lakes, the latter notched deeply into the high mountains. The most prominent peak beyond them is Rising Wolf Mountain.

The road winds high above the lower lake. This region is especially breathtaking in fall when the aspens below turn red and yellow. In spring, the meadows along the roadway are lush with wildflowers. A rich and often windy spot, anytime.

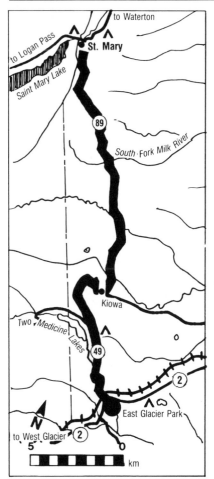

From the top of Looking Glass Hill, the road descends very steeply through deeply-eroded terrain down to the prairie again and the tiny community of Kiowa.

Northwards, the road climbs and descends over huge moraines and finally ascends a ridge that marks the divide between the drainage basins of Hudson Bay and the Gulf of Mexico. Behind, water flows into

the Milk River which runs north into Canada, then curves south again into the Missouri and then to the Mississippi. North of the ridge, water flows into the St. Mary, Saskatchewan and Nelson rivers to Hudson Bay.

The descent from the ridge into St. Mary is long and glorious. The smooth highway is steep but straight, enabling cyclists to build up an exhilarating speed. Cyclists who have traversed the long and tiring ridges behind deserve this great descent.

Road Log Tour 48

0 km East Glacier Park. All services. Elev. 1460 m. Amtrack Station. Camping at Y Lazy R camper park 1 block E of Hwy 2. In the middle of town, turn left on Hwy 49, passing railway station and Glacier Park Lodge.

2 Steep ascent. No shoulder. Sharp curves.

5 Descend to Two Medicine River.

6 Steep ascent. Red Eagle Campground. Paved, 12-km side road into mountains to Two Medicine Campground (national park) and hiking trails.

14 End of steep ascent. Steep descent. Very sharp curves.

20 Kiowa. Store, cafe. Jct.

Hwy 89. Turn left for St. Mary. (Sidetrip 12 km to Browning and Museum of the North American Indian.) Several long hills and descents.

28 Cutbank River.

38 Top of hill. Elev. 1852 m. Divide between drainage of Hudson Bay and Gulf of Mexico.

39 Major descent, runaway lane. Road widens. Good shoulder.

50 St. Mary. Bottom of hill. Elev. 1370 m. All services. Camping at KOA, 1.5 km N on Hwy 89, cafe (406-732-5311); Johnson's 0.3 km N on Hwy 89, cafe (732-4621); St. Mary (national park), 2 km W inside park.

WEST GLACIER TO WHITEFISH, MONTANA
TOUR **49**

SALOONS AND GO-KARTS

Distance 41 km (25 miles)

Time A few hours

Rating Easy connecting section

Terrain Gradual descent westbound. Level after Columbia Falls

Roads Some new paving with good shoulder. Other sections narrow

Traffic Busy

Connections Tours 46, 47, 50

The route between Glacier National Park and the pleasant community of Whitefish is not especially scenic. The road, which follows the Flathead (out of sight of the river), is usually very busy, although a brand-new highway offers a reasonable shoulder part of the way.

And the route passes some of the worst developments in American tourism, such contrast with the purity of the national park and the relatively undeveloped highways beyond.

There are T-shirt stores, a chain-saw circus, also known as "Courage College," go-karts, a house of mystery, gift shoppes, the Dew Drop Inn and all kinds of roadside joints that style themselves after western saloons.

On the plus side, the national park campgrounds in Glacier do fill up fast and this strip is loaded with private campgrounds, many of them with elaborate facilities such as saunas and swimming pools (and higher camping fees).

For all the route's drawbacks, many cyclists do pass this way. Everyone heading into Glacier Park

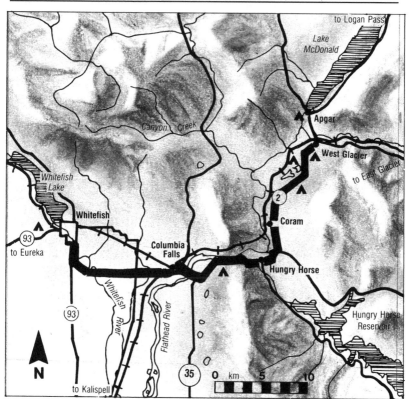

or Waterton from the West takes this route. It connects with the major population centres of western Montana, plus the route to Eureka and up into British Columbia.

Road Log Tour 49

0 km West Glacier. Elev 960. All services. Campgrounds: Apgar in national park, 5 km N; Glacier (406-387-5690); KOA 4 km SW on Hwy 2 and 1.5 km E on Hwy 60; Winnakee, 1.5 km W on U.S. 2.

Turn right on Hwy 2 to Columbia Falls. New highway. Good shoulder.

5 Lake Eden Campground.

10 Sundance Campground.

11 Coram. Cafe, store, inn, saloon.

16 Hungry Horse. All services. Crooked Tree Motel and campground. Flathead River Ranch and campground.

22 Bad Rock Canyon Campground.

24 Jct. Turn right on Hwy 40 to Columbia Falls. Busy 5-lane road, huge

shoulder. Cross Flathead
River.

27 Columbia Falls. All services. Keep straight.

31 Jct. Hwys 2 and 89.
Turn right for Whitefish.
Good shoulder. Logging
trucks.

39 Jct. Hwy 93. Turn right
on 93 for Whitefish.

41 Whitefish. All services.
Amtrak station, bike
store. Campground at
Whitefish Lake recrea-
tion area, 1 km W of
town on Hwy 93,
milepost 129, then 1.5
km N.

WHITEFISH TO EUREKA, MONTANA

TOUR **50**

INTO THE BACKWOODS

Distance 82 km (51 miles)
Time 1 day
Rating Moderate
Terrain Mostly level
Roads Rough and nar-
row, except for
new paving near
Whitefish. No
shoulder
Traffic Moderate. Watch
for logging
trucks
Connections Tours 49, 51

This is a low-key, backroads route
that is mostly level, travelling
through deep woods and past small,
clear lakes following the Rocky
Mountain Trench. The towns are
tiny, the people friendly and camping facilities good.

The major hazards are a steady
flow of high-speed logging and chip
trucks on a fairly narrow highway.
Initial sections of Highway 93 near
Whitefish have been improved while
the remainder is often very rough
for a paved road.

Highlights

From Whitefish, a pleasant town
with a number of sporting goods
stores and a bike store, the road
heads into the great northern forest
with rounded, wooded peaks on
both sides. The road is relatively
level, leading past several pretty
lakes and an excellent state forest
campground above green Dickey
Lake.

After Fortine, the countryside
gradually opens up for cattle grazing and small farms in what has
historically been called the Tobacco
Plains named after largely unsuccessful tobacco-growing experi-
ments by the early missionaries.

Eureka is a funky town on a
hillside with a western-style main
street.

Road Log Tour 50

0 km Whitefish. All services.
Bike store. Amtrak sta-

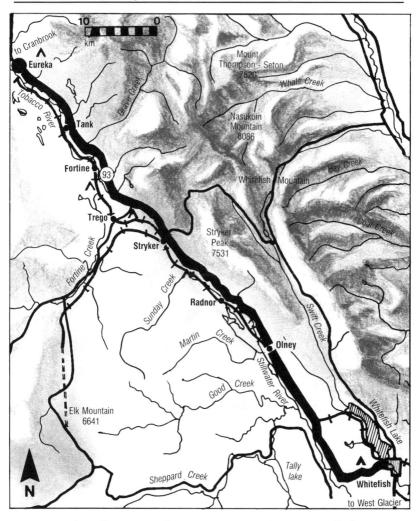

tion. Campground at Whitefish Lake recreation area, 1 km W town on Hwy 93, milepost 129, then 1.5 km N. From Whitefish, turn N on Hwy 93.

24 Lower Stillwater Lake. Hotel.

28 Olney turnoff. Store.

33 Dog Creek Campground.

41 Dog Lake State Forest Campground.

48 Stryker. No store.

56 Turnoff N. Dickey Lake state forest campground.

63 Sawmill.

65	Fortine turnoff. Store, cafe.
82	Eureka. All services. Camping at KOA, 2 km

N and 3 km W (steep climb) and at Wildrose restaurant and campground N of town.

EUREKA, MONTANA TO ELKO, BRITISH COLUMBIA

INTO DRY RANCHLAND

Distance	51 km (32 miles)
Time	1/2 to 1 day
Rating	Intermediate
Terrain	A few short hills
Roads	Extremely narrow with no shoulder in U.S. Wider with small shoulder in Canada
Traffic	Moderate
Connections	Tours 50, 58, 59

This is a fascinating route, traversing dry, open ranchland north of Eureka, the rounded, treeless hills littered with boulders. Then the cyclist crosses the international boundary into Canada and travels through mixed open woods and cattle country, up the Rocky Mountain Trench, here part of the Kootenay River Valley.

Highlights

Just north of Eureka, the terrain changes abruptly to dry ranchland with scarcely a tree in sight. Distinctive hills called drumlins were formed here from the debris dropped by glaciers. The road to the border is extremely narrow although traffic is usually moderate.

Cyclists should have some form of identification at the border, such as a birth certificate. U.S. and Canadian citizens don't need passports or visas. Cyclists under 18 travelling on their own may be asked for a letter signed by parent or guardian giving them permission to visit Canada (or the United States).

Across the border, the road widens and follows the broad Kootenay Valley with the fairly low, wooded Galton Range on the east and the McGillivray Range in the distance on the west across wide Lake Koocanusa, a name that appears to be Indian. On closer examination, it becomes clear the name is derived from the words Kootenay-Canada-U.S.A. The big lake, which straddles the border, has been created by a dam in Montana, one of many on the Kootenay River.

At the junction of Highways 93 and 3 near Elko, cyclists have the choice of continuing north towards Fort Steele or turning west to head up Crowsnest Pass. The closest campground is at Kikomum Creek Provincial Park, located about 2 km north of the junction and 8 km west on a gravel road.

Road Log Tour 51

0 km Eureka. All services. Camping at KOA, 2 km N and 3 km W (steep climb) and at Wildrose restaurant and campground N of town. In Eureka, turn N on Hwy 93.

2 Jct. Hwy 37. Keep straight. Right for KOA 3 km W (steep climb). Enter open rangeland. Narrow road.

10 North Fork restaurant and RV park. Homemade pies.

14 International border. U.S. and Canadians customs. Duty free store. Road widens. Small shoulder.

26 Grasmere. Store.

37 Steep descent and ascent at Elk River crossing.

51 Jct. Hwy 3 and 93. Elko is 2 km to E. All services.

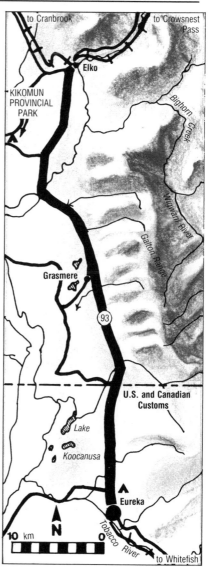

GAIL HELGASON

11

Extended Tours in Southeastern British Columbia

These nine tours are natural continuations of longer routes in the Rockies. They offer cyclists exciting opportunities to link extended tours between the Rockies, the Monashees, the Selkirks and the Kootenays, splendid country indeed.

These tours are, in our minds, as enjoyable as most through the Rockies, although their appeal is different. The Rockies awe the visitor with their sweeping lines and grandeur; the Columbias enfold him with their deep, narrow valleys, more hospitable climate and lusher vegetation.

There is, as well, a human dimension to these tours lacking in pristine national parks. Many take the cyclist through remote and isolated terrain, yet there are frequent reminders here of the lively days of sternwheelers, saloons and silver strikes. Small towns are quaintly tumbledown.

We recommend the beautiful Nelson-New Denver-Kaslo Loop as perhaps the perfect three-day weekend tour for strong cyclists. It could easily be drawn out to a week if you stop to enjoy sandy beaches along the way. The Kimberley Loop, although not as varied, is also scenic and can be done in a weekend.

The ideal way to explore this region, however, is to plan an extended tour.

The most ambitious could begin in Banff, Lake Louise or Golden (or take the train to Revelstoke), then head down through the remote beauty of the Columbia Valley to Nakusp, New Denver and Nelson.

From there, follow along Kootenay Lake, cross it by ferry and continue on to Creston, Cranbrook and Radium, ending in Banff. The entire trip would take one to two weeks.

If you begin in Jasper townsite and link these tours with the Icefields Parkway, you will have a two- or three-week holiday combining the best of the Canadian West.

Via Rail stops at Revelstoke and Golden. Most communities are served by bus. Pacific Western Airlines flies to Cranbrook and Castlegar, near Nelson.

REVELSTOKE TO NAKUSP

A TASTE OF THE FJORDS

Distance 103 km (64 miles)
Time 1 day
Rating Intermediate
Terrain Some long hills and steep climbs, level stretches
Elev. gain 6 metres (20 feet)
Road No shoulder, fairly good condition
Traffic Light
Connections Tours 19, 53

A cyclist's dream — a remote, remarkably quiet highway winds along the Columbia Valley between the attractive communities of Revelstoke and Nakusp, offering changing vistas of the Selkirk and Monashee ranges and beautiful Upper Arrow Lake. You cross the lake on a free ferry between Shelter Bay and Galena Bay and for the look of it, this could be Norway.

Hot springs near Nakusp are an added attraction. Cyclists, however, should be prepared for the isolation of this tour, strenuous climbing and frequent strong winds off the lake. Carry food and water. Water purification tablets are worth taking so you can drink safely from roadside streams.

Highlights

Revelstoke, the starting point, is an historic railroad town established in 1880 as Farwell. It was renamed after Lord Revelstoke, who headed a London banking firm which backed the completion of the Canadian Pacific Railway. Revelstoke became a mountain divisional centre for the CPR in 1899 and is still an important rail centre.

Stock up for the long miles ahead. You'll find a deli and health-food store on the main street, and a bike store at 120 Mackenzie Avenue for last-minute adjustments or supplies. The Revelstoke

Museum, 315 West 1st Street, has displays of local railroading, logging and riverboating. An art gallery is housed above.

Ride over the Columbia River on a suspension bridge. A sign just beyond gives ferry times. (Ferries left Shelter Bay hourly at time of writing.)

The remote flavour of the tour is apparent as the cyclist climbs out of town through the lonely forest. Although British Columbia is Canada's third largest province in area and population, most people live in the southwestern corner.

The northwest arm of Upper Arrow Lake, which is really a widening of the Columbia River, can be seen ahead. The Columbia is the longest river on the Pacific seaboard. It stretches 1,954 km and drains almost 100,000 square km. The Columbia is harnessed by 13 dams, two in Canada and the rest in the United States, making it the greatest hydroelectric producer in the world.

The jagged Selkirks to the east and the Monashees to the west are mostly made up of ancient metamorphic rock of the Jurassic, Triassic and Cambrian ages.

Enjoy the long descents before the road levels off close to Shelter Bay. It takes 20 minutes to cross the lake on a small ferry. There's a pretty picnic site right above Galena Bay.

The climb out of the bay, beneath Mt. Murray, is fairly steep. It leads

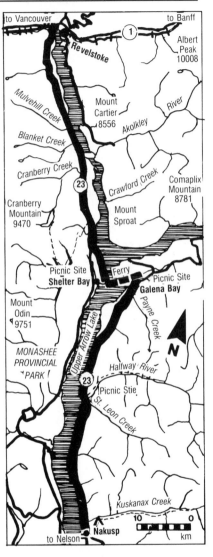

into semi-open wilderness that has been extensively logged. In the mining days of the late 1800s, steamers plied Upper Arrow Lake, bringing in loggers, rich tourists and merchants.

211

You may catch a whiff of sulphur from Halcyon Hot Springs, three undeveloped hot springs with average temperature about 48 degrees C. The springs are privately owned.

The remaining stretch into Nakusp is challenging and wildly beautiful. Nakusp Hot Springs is 10 km up an asphalt road. Cyclists who don't mind a long climb may want to spend the night at the cottages or campground.

Overlooking the lake, Nakusp thrived at the turn of the century as a transportation stop for stern-wheelers. Now it's a stop for 16-wheelers. Nature's Way Health Food Store carries trail mix and dried food and makes fresh peanut butter. Nakusp Meat and Deli is also worth checking. Green Door Sports on the main street does bike repairs (604-245-4013).

Road Log Tour 52

0 km Revelstoke, 144 km W of Golden. Pop. 9,682, elev. 457 m, all services. Head W out of town on Hwy 1, cross Columbia River on suspension bridge.

2 Turn L on Hwy 23 S. (Lamplighter campground on L, 60 sites, (604-837-3385). Sign for ferry schedule.

7 View over NW arm of Upper Arrow Lake. Gradual climb between Monashee Mountains on W and Selkirks to E.

11 Road levels.

16 Views open to higher peaks.

18 Gradual descent to lake.

24 Blanket Creek campground and gorge. Climb.

29 Beginning of long descent.

33 End descent.

39 Steep downhill.

43 Road levels off close to lake.

51 Shelter Bay. Picnic area, ferry to Galena Bay (free, hourly, check times).

51 Galena Bay. Picnicking overlooking bay. Steep climb up from ferry on narrow road.

52 Jct. Hwy 31 & 23. Keep right. Some steep climbing.

65 Easy cycling with views of Upper Arrow Lake on right Halcyon Hot Springs (private).

74 Steep hill, wonderful views of lake.

81 Rest area by waterfall. Picnic tables.

87 Steep downhill.

94 Route close to lake again.

99 Turnoff left for Nakusp Hot Springs (10 km up asphalt road, campground, chalet, fishing, Nakusp Hot Springs cedar Chalets, Radio Phone N695800.)

99 Royal Coachman campsite, 265-4212.)

101 Nakusp. Pop. 1416, elev. 451 m, all services. Camping, bike repairs, Green Door Sports, health food store, deli.

THE COLUMBIAS, NOT THE ROCKIES

Many believe Canada's Rocky Mountains extend from the Pacific Ocean to the Prairies. In fact, the Rockies are bounded on the west by the Rocky Mountain Trench, the gear-grinder cyclists have to climb out of to travel west or east of Golden. The trench, the continent's largest valley, extends more than 1500 km from Yukon to Montana.

Between the Pacific Coast and the Rockies are the sharp-toothed Columbia Mountains, made up of the Purcell ranges on the southeast, the Monashees on the west, the Selkirks in the centre and the Cariboo in the north. These mountain ranges, seldom called by their collective name, are split by deep, narrow valleys, covered with thick forests and composed of hard rock. This landscape creates a closed-in feeling very different from the relative openness of the Rockies, which have well-defined peaks and sweeping lines. Both have unique beauty.

The Rockies are characterized by softer sedimentary rocks such as limestone, mudstone, sandstone and shales.

The Columbias are older, although they were also originally formed from soft sedimentary rock deposited in shallow seas covering Western North America millions of years ago. The rock was compressed, melted and transformed into harder metamorphic rock, such as gneiss, quartzite, slate and granite.

The forests of the Columbias and the B.C. coast are similar. Both experience heavy rainfall and occupy mountainous terrain. Watch for Western red cedar, Western hemlock, Douglas fir and Western white pine.

NAKUSP TO NEW DENVER

TOUR **53**

PARADISE'S ONLY RIVAL

Distance	47 km (29 miles)	**Road**	Narrow and winding in places
Time	1/2 day		
Rating	Intermediate	**Traffic**	Mostly moderate
Terrain	Some hilly stretches, mostly level along lakes	**Connections**	Tours 52, 54
Elev. gain	86 metres (282 feet)		

New Denver, the destination of this tour, calls itself Canada's Lucerne. A pioneer newspaperman of the

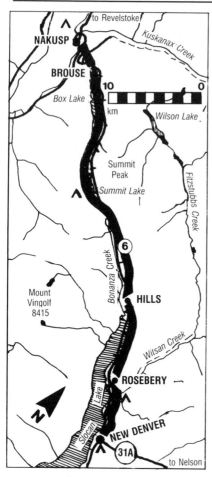

wilderness park, rise to the west. To the east are the Selkirks.

The few rustic settlements seem a throwback to a more tranquil era. Yet the region's history, dominated by the silver mining boom of the 1890s, was anything but tranquil.

Scenery, history, light traffic, a moderate grade: here is a rich strike indeed.

Highlights

Stock up on provisions at Nakusp. The ride begins with a steep climb and descends to marginal farmland. Only about five per cent of British Columbia's land base, mostly on deltas and flood plains, is suitable for farming.

Cycling is fairly level most of the way. Summit Lake, cupped between Summit Peak to the east and Silvery Mountain on the west, is an appealing rest stop. Views emerge of Slocan Lake and the Slocan Valley which extends between the Valhallas to the west and the Kokanee Range to the east. Valhalla Wilderness Park comprises 500 square kilometres of pristine landscape, left untouched by the Silvery Slocan boom and raised to park status in 1983.

Rosebery has a tumbledown appeal. The Wild Rose Restaurant features Mexican food. Rosebery Provincial Park (on the banks of Wilson Creek) is a pleasant spot to camp and perhaps swim. There's a chamber of commerce campground nearby if sites are full.

1890s waxed even more poetic — he maintained Paradise was Lucerne's only rival. Ninety years later, the wild, peak-sliced scenery of New Denver and its surroundings still warrant hyperbole.

You climb out of Nakusp into a picturesque valley, then cycle by fjord-like Summit and Slocan lakes. The stunning Valhallas, recently established as a provincial

The ride into New Denver is easy and scenic. The Denver Glacier gleams across the lake and Idaho Peak rises immediately above the town. New Denver, first named Eldorado, was once the bustling centre for recording claims during the short-lived silver boom of the 1890s.

The Silvery Slocan Museum in the former Bank of Montreal building features an extensive photographic exhibit of the social-economic impact of mining in the region, as well as collections of domestic equipment and logging tools used in nearby Sandon during the boom.

Slocan Lake cyclist   TOURISM BRITISH COLUMBIA

Road Log Tour 52

0 km Nakusp. Pop. 1416, elev. 451. All services, camping, bike repair.

1 Steeply climb out of town on Hwy 6 to Nelson.

4 Top of hill, views of Box Lake.

16 Summit Lake Park. Picnicking, campground.

19 Scenic rest area, picnic tables by lake.

20 Nakusp Ski Club. Road narrow and winding.

30 Hills. One snack store, no groceries. Slocan Lake.

41 Rosebery. Licensed restaurant.

42 Rosebery Provincial Park. Camping, 23 sites.

42.5 Chamber of Commerce Campground.

47 New Denver. Pop. 600, elev. 537 m. Municipal campground S. side of village, 30 sites, showers, beach adjacent, 604-358-2316. Lucerne Hotel, 358-2228.

HOT SPRINGS OF THE KOOTENAYS

Almost all of Canada's natural hot springs are found in the mountainous regions of Western Canada. Fortunately for the cyclist exploring the Kootenays, some of the finest hot springs in the world are along tours described in this book.

Legend has it that wounded animals, including grizzlies, were the first to discover the refreshing properties of these hot mineral waters. Native Indians in turn learned their therapeutic value, and occasionally fought over ownership rights.

When mining, logging and the railroad began to open up these mountains, word spread among visitors of the fabulous spas of Western Canada.

The heyday of the hot springs peaked in the last century however; only recently has redevelopment been occurring.

Perhaps the most unusual hot springs are at Ainsworth, 50 km north-east of Nelson. Bathers creep into a horseshoe-shaped cave which was originally a mineshaft. Drillers abandoned it when they found more hot water than ore. You can enjoy pool temperatures of around 45 degrees C plus vistas of Kootenay Lake and the Purcells. The mineral waters contain salts of calcium, magnesium, sodium, potassium and lithium. Unlike most hot springs in this area, they do not contain sulphur, a pleasant change for the nostrils. Ainsworth recently underwent a facelift; today there are four pools including an invigorating cold-plunge pool.

Halcyon Hot Springs are situated about 16 km south of Revelstoke along Upper Arrow Lake. According to Joan Thompson in Hot Springs of Canada, native Indians first called them "Great Medicine Waters": "The tribes often camped beside the springs and many a battle was fought over the possession of these healing waters," she writes.

In the late 1800s, a sanitarium was erected at Halcyon for tuberculosis patients, as well as for tourists who arrived on steamers plying the Arrow Lakes. The hotel was later destroyed by fire.

Nakusp Hot Springs, about 109 km northeast of Nelson, also dates back to the steamer era. The water temperature lingers around 42 degrees C. Self-contained cottages are available for rent near the springs and there is a campground on the banks of the Kuskanax Creek.

NELSON TO KASLO
TO NEW DENVER (LOOP)

TOUR **54**

THE SILVERY SLOCAN

Distance 212 km (132 miles)
Time 1 to 3 days
Rating Strenuous
Terrain Several long, steep climbs
Roads Mostly good condition, narrow
Traffic Light to moderate
Connections Tours 53, 55

If the Golden Triangle is cyclists' gold, here is cyclists' silver. The tour begins in the gracious city of Nelson, skirts beautiful Kootenay and Slocan lakes. Magnificently set against the backdrop of the Valhallas and Selkirks, the area surrounds visitors with the romance of silver mining days.

Few kilometres are without interest. You'll see an old paddle-wheeler in the harbor at Kaslo, soak

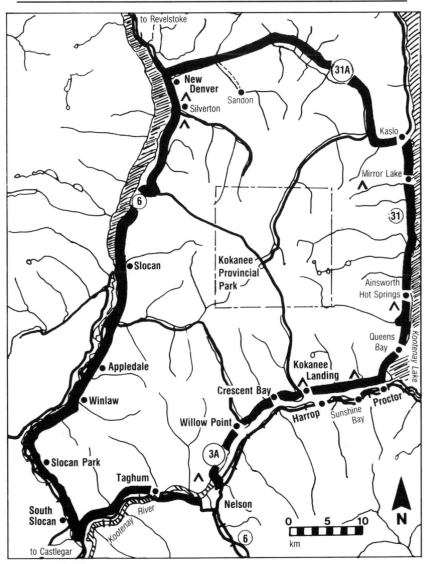

in a mist-filled cave at historic Ainsworth Hot Springs, catch a glimpse of abandoned silver mines, pass several inviting beaches, perhaps even visit the ruins of an old mining town.

All this, plus deliciously quiet roads (except on the stretches in and out of Nelson). Perhaps the perfect long weekend tour for strong cyclists.

Highlights

Nelson, "Queen City of the Kootenays," had its beginnings in 1887 with the discovery of the Silver King Mine on Toad Mountain. More than 150 fine heritage buildings are preserved in this small city. Of particular interest is the Nelson courthouse constructed of Kootenay marble and embedded with bits of gold.

Lakeside Park on the way out of town has a sandy beach. Cross the west arm of Kootenay Lake and follow its pretty cottage-lined shore for a good portion of the stretch to Kaslo. The 145-km lake is one of British Columbia's most important freshwater fisheries and is home to the world's largest kokanee, land-locked salmon which spawn in the Kokanee Creek. They begin moving upstream in late August and September.

Recently The Globe and Mail called this stretch of road "one of the most beautiful scenic routes in Canada."

Small Redfish campground makes a pleasant woodland stop. If the day is hot, stop at the busier Kokanee Creek Provincial Park which has broad beaches along the lakefront. The West Kootenay Visitor Centre contains exhibits of flora and fauna of the region and has an extensive interpretive program.

Balfour is departure point for the Kootenay Lake ferry, longest free ferry ride in North America. Those with time could ride across the bay and back (about 40 minutes each way); views of the Purcells are lovely and there is a cafeteria aboard.

Continue north to Ainsworth Hot Springs, discovered by the Indians around 1800. They noticed hot water flowing from the caves (and, the story goes, animals bathing their wounds,) and crawled on all fours to the back of the tiny caves to join them. Later zinc and lead were found nearby and six hotels were built.

The next section veers away from the lake for several kilometres before reaching Kaslo, another historic mining town. Vintage storefronts and a beautifully preserved city hall hint of Kaslo's booming past. Don't miss the S.S. Moyie by the harbor. Launched in 1898, the paddlewheeler plied Kootenay Lake for 59 years before being turned into a landlocked tourist information centre.

The ascent from Kaslo is a grind, although traffic is usually moderate. The reward is a thrilling, 19-km ride down into New Denver. Take supplies through this lonely stretch of cliffs and forest. The route follows the Kaslo River with Mt. Carlyle on the left and Mt. Jardine on the right.

Cyclists have the option of cycling 7 km off Highway 31A to view the ruins of Sandon, a boom town which served more than 100 nearby mines by 1895. Only traces remain.

During the feverish silver boom of the late 1800s, New Denver served as centre for recording mine claims for all the Slocan. Artifacts from these days are preserved in

Kootenay Lake, B.C.　　　　　　　TOURISM BRITISH COLUMBIA

the Silvery Slocan Museum.

The road between New Denver and Slocan follows the shoreline of Slocan Lake. The Valhallas rise abruptly on the other side. Silverton is a picturesque village with a refurbished hotel and civic park overlooking the water. Pilings where sternwheelers loaded ore are reminders of the silver boom.

The steep climb out of Silverton leads to a spectacular vista high above the water with views of abandoned silver mines in the nearby mountains. The landscape, with its ochre cliffs and dark forests, is wildly beautiful.

The road to Slocan is narrow, hilly and winding. At km 140 the road shrinks to one lane for a precarious one kilometre ride under cliffs above the lake. Pull over for approaching traffic.

Slocan, once a city of 6,000, is now home to only 600 and calls itself the smallest incorporated city in the world.

Beyond this point, small farms appear beside the Slocan River and the terrain is pleasantly rolling. Cycling is not as relaxed after the turn onto Highway 3A East because of heavier traffic and an uncertain shoulder. You follow the Kootenay River past a dam. The road narrows and the shoulder returns after a few kilometres. Fruit stands line the way.

Road Log Tour 54

0 km Nelson. Pop. 9,031, elev. 543 m. City of Nelson Museum, Centennial Building. Chamber of Mines Museum, 215 Hall St., 604-352-5242. Camping: City Tourist Park, corner of High and Willow, overlooking lake, 604-354-4944. Start at tourist information booth, 501 Front St., near city centre.

Head NE along Front St., which turns into Anderson and then Nelson Ave.

5 Pass Lakeside Park on left before crossing bridge over W arm of Kootenay Lake, following Hwy 3A to Balfour.

6 Follow along N shore of Kootenay Lake.

22 Redfish Campground left. Redfish day use area right. Picnicking, beach.

24 Main entrance, Kokanee Creek Provincial Park. Camping, 112 sites. Includes wilderness walk-in sites, interpretive centre, nature trails, beach, excellent picnicking.

25 Store.

33 Birch Grove Campground, 229-4275.

34 Laird Camping Park, 229-4742.

35 Kokanee Campground, 229-4974. Store.

37 Balfour. Pop. 1,000, elev. 1740 m. Kootenay Lake ferry, Balfour Beach Inn and motel, 229-4235. Keep straight on Hwy 31 to Kaslo.

45 Steep hill, seven-percent gradient, narrow and twisting.

50 Ainsworth Hot Springs. Cafe, camping. 19th century Mermaid Lodge, 100 metres from springs, housekeeping rooms, 229-4248.

55 Woodbury Resort and Marina. Mining museum, beach, store, pub, accommodation, 353-7717.

56 Long climb starts.

66 Mirror Lake.

67 Mirror Lake Campground. Private lake, swimming, boat rental, 353-7102.

70 Kaslo. Pop. 950, elev. 546 m. All services. Historic mining community. Leave Kaslo on Hwy 31A for New Denver. Long climb.

99 Climb ends. Long descent into New Denver.

117 New Denver. Pop. 600, elev. 537 m. Municipal campground S. side of village, beach adjacent, 30 sites. Lucerne Motel, 358-2228. Turn left (S) on Hwy 6.

121 Silverton. Pop. 500. Store, art gallery. Camping, public beach. Silverton Hotel, 358-7929.

122 Start climb. Historic marker for Slocan mines.

128 Viewpoint over Slocan Lake and Valhallas. Picnic tables.

129 Long descent.

134 Bottom of hill. Steep bends and hairpin curves.

140 Extremely narrow, scenic stretch under cliffs above lake. Stop for approaching vehicles.

141 Road improves.

147 Down to Slocan, six-per-cent gradient.

148 Turn-off for Slocan down steep road.

155 Lemon Creek Campground 1.6 km right on dirt road. Hot tubs, 26 sites. Lodge, sauna, bed and breakfast, dining by reservation, 355-2403.

155.5 Rest area.

156 Steep hill.

165 Winlaw. Restaurant, store, motel.

169 Robert's restaurant.

183 Slocan Valley country store and restaurant, groceries.

193 Crescent Valley. Store.

195 Turn left for Nelson at Jct. with 3A East. Narrow shoulder.

204 Shoulder widens. Fruit stands.

207 Cross Kootenay River.

209 Grohman Narrows Provincial Park.

212 Return Nelson.

VALLEY OF GHOSTS

Long before white man appeared in British Columbia's Slocan Valley, natives of the area made bullets out of lead and silver galena deposits.

A surge of silver prices in the late 1800s transformed the tranquil valley into a feverish district of prospectors, rascals and dance-hall girls. Almost overnight, communities such as Lardeau, Ymir, Sandon, Ainsworth, Slocan, New Denver, Kaslo and Three Forks sprang up to service the boom.

Near Kaslo, an ore boulder worth $20,000 was discovered in 1892. Kaslo soon had more than 20 hotels, two newspapers, 14 barbershops, a sawmill, brick and tile yard, brewing company and the notorious "Theatre Cominque" with 80 dancing girls. A fire in 1894 devastated the town. It was quickly rebuilt and survived the fall in the price of silver by diversifying.

More than 10,000 persons crowded into Sandon, site of a huge silver strike which pumped enough money into the town to sustain 24 hotels — a saloon in each. The town did not, however, survive a disastrous plunge in silver prices in the 1930s. The community took on a disturbing role in the Second World War, when more than 4,000 Japanese persons were interred there from the West Coast for alleged security reasons. That story has been dramaticized in a recent play, Enemy Graces, by B.C. playwright Sharon Stearns.

Sandon was virtually abandoned after the war. Only recently have attempts been made to preserve what is left.

Nelson thrived with the discovery of the Silver King Mine on Toad Mountain in 1887. Gold, silver and coal discoveries provided the impetus for development in Kimberley, Cranbrook, Fort Steele and other East Kootenay communities.

The Kootenays of the 90s weren't only characterized by toil — the Metropolitan Opera Company sent a touring section to Cranbrook in 1899 and Pauline Johnson gave poetry readings there.

Today, many of these towns are only names on a map. Some, like Cranbrook, still prosper. Others, like Nakusp, New Denver and Silverton, look for their silver in tourist dollars now that the Valhallas have become B.C.'s newest provincial park.

NELSON TO CRESTON

THE LEISURELY LAKESIDE

Distance	116 km (72 miles)
Time	1 to 2 days
Rating	Intermediate
Terrain	Fairly level
Elev. gain	68 metres (223 feet)
Roads	Narrow, mostly good condition
Traffic	Moderate weekdays. Moderately heavy on summer weekends
Connections	Tours 54, 56

This outstanding tour of peaks, forests, orchards and a huge lake is tailor-made for cycling. The road is rarely out of sight of Kootenay Lake as it follows the west arm. The route then crosses to Kootenay Bay on a ferry and follows the southern arm of the lake into the fertile Creston Valley.

Numerous rustic stores, campgrounds, beaches and one youth hostel add to cycling convenience. Traffic is mostly private automobiles, although there are some logging trucks.

While the trip can be done in one day, cyclists who rush through miss too much.

Highlights

Begin the tour in Nelson, "Queen City of the Kootenays." This city of 9,000 had its beginnings in 1887 with the discovery of the Silver King Mine on Toad Mountain. More than 150 fine heritage buildings have been preserved.

Cross the west arm of 145-km Kootenay Lake and follow its pretty cottage-lined shore all the way to Balfour through cottonwood, alder and spruce woods.

Forested Redfish campground is a good place to stop. If the day is hot, turn into adjacent Kokanee

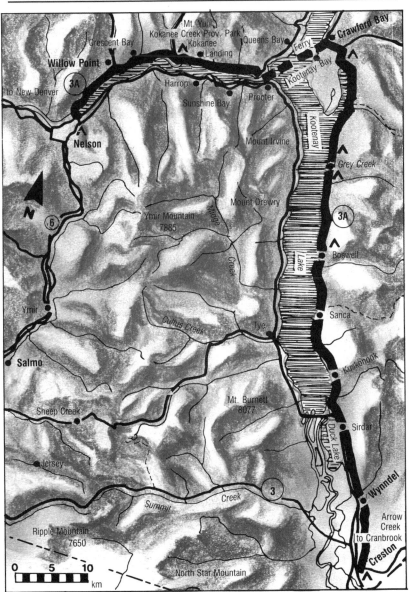

Creek Provincial Park which has broad beaches along the lakefront. The West Kootenay Visitor Centre contains interpretive exhibits of the flora and fauna of the region.

Balfour is departure point for the crossing to Kootenay Bay, the longest free ferry ride in North

America. The ride takes about 40 minutes and offers excellent vistas of the eastern fringe of the Purcells. There's a snack bar aboard. Ferries leave frequently. Phone 604-352-2211 for ferry schedules. Remember that B.C. is on a different time zone from Alberta.

The road climbs steeply from the ferry landing. Cycling is fairly level thereafter although winds coming off the lake can be troublesome. The south arm of the Kootenay Lake soon comes into view with Mt. Drewry predominant to the west. There are numerous beaches.

Black Bear Park at the 56-km mark has a collection of giant wood carvings. Even more unusual is the Glass House at 78 km which is open to the public in summer for an admission fee.

Lockhart Beach Provincial Park is our recommended camping spot. The park is on a small lakefront site, with campsites situated amongst ponderosa pine and douglas fir. There's a beach and trail along Lockhart Creek.

The gradient remains relatively easy. Eventually the road leaves the lake and enters the wide, flat Creston Valley. W.A. Baillie-Grohman, a British sportsman, envisioned reclaiming this land from the lake for agriculture by building canals to drain off the water. His first venture at Canal Flats across the mountains to the west had proven unsuccessful but he succeeded here in 1893. Today more than 25,000 acres have been reclaimed, using 53 miles of dykes.

The last section into Creston is surrounded by dry hills and leads past the Creston Valley Museum as you approach the town. Exhibits include the unique Kutenai canoe and an early fruit sprayer.

Fruit stands on the east side of town are a good place to fill your panniers. Apricots and apples are at their best in early August, and peaches and plums by mid-August. Cyclists seeking a splurge meal will find Greek food at Dionisos, 1403 Canyon Street, 604-428-4011.

Road Log Tour 55

0 km Nelson, pop 9,031, elev 543 m. City of Nelson Museum, Centennial Building. Chamber of Mines Museum, 215 Hall St, 604-352-5242. Camping: City Tourist Park, downtown, corner of High and Willow, overlooking lake. Reservations 354-4944. Start at tourist information booth, 501 Front St, near city centre. Head NE along Front St, which turns into Anderson and then Nelson Ave

5 Pass Lakeside Park before crossing bridge over W arm of Kootenay Lake

6 Follow N shore of Kootenay Lake.

22 Redfish Campground (left). Redfish Day Use area (right) picnicking, beach.

24 Main entrance, Kokanee Creek Provincial Park. Camping, 112 sites. Includes wilderness walk-in sites, interpretive centre, nature trails, beach, excellent picnicking.

25 Store.

33 Birch Grove Campground, private, reservations 229-4275.

34 Laird camping park, private, (229-4742).

35 Kokanee Campground, private, store, (229-4974).

37 Balfour, pop 1,000, elev 1740 m. Balfour Beach Inn and motel, (229-4235). Take free 40-minute ferry to Kootenay Bay. Phone 604-352-2211, local 239 for ferry schedules.

37 Kootenay Bay. Rest area, accommodation. Last Chance Motel, near private beach, (227-9331.)

39 Turn-off for private campground. Keep right on Hwy 3A.

41 Downhill.

43 Kokanee Springs Resort. Licensed restaurant, attractive chalets, campground, beach access, 227-9226. Road follows S Arm of Kootenay Lake.

50 Grey Creek. Store, boat rentals, sandy beach.

Old Crow campground, reservations 227-9495.

53 The Lakeview natural food store and groceries.

56 Black Bear Park. Large wood carvings.

63 Mountain Shores resort.

65 Lockhart Beach Provincial Park. 12 camping sites, picnicking, swimming. Bayshore Resort also has good camping, 223-8270.

67 Heidelberg Inn. Licensed restaurant, Wednesday seafood buffets from 4 pm in July and August, 223-8263.

74 Destiny Bay. Deluxe cottages, sauna, swimming. Licensed restaurant and coffee shop, 223-8234.

78 Glass House, open to public, admission fee, gift shop.)

87 Lake Falls Resort. Motel, campground, 223-8201. Descend toward end of lake.

92 Rest area. Picnic tables on lake, art gallery.

99 Sidar. Pub, old country store. Steep climb out of town.

103 Opening onto wide flat plain at end of lake.

108 Wynndel. Groceries, cafe, fresh fruit, picnicking. Wynndel mini-hostel 11 km from Creston on Hwy 3A, 866-5482.

111 Big climb out of town.

113 Viewpoint. Historic marker, picnic tables.
116 Jct. Hwy 3. Entering Creston. Pop. 4,190, elev. 611 m, all services. Swimming pool, Creston Valley Museum. Candle factory tours. Tourist Information in town centre, 1711 Canyon St, 428-4341.

THE GLASS HOUSE

Funeral director David H. Brown hated waste. For years he watched as funeral homes discarded thousands of glass bottles used for embalming fluid. Could the bottles be given a second life, he wondered?

When Brown retired, he decided "to indulge a whim of a peculiar nature." He checked with building contractors, and ascertained that a house could be constructed of glass "bricks."

Brown travelled all over Western Canada collecting 500,000 embalming bottles. He began construction in 1952 along the shore of Kootenay Lake. The result? A 1,200-square-foot home that, with its rock-walled terraces, thousands of flowers, winding pathways and lake vistas, seems a combination of Disneyland and medieval England.

Brown died in 1970, but his family still lives in the house. It is open to visitors between May 1 and Thanksgiving weekend.

CRESTON TO CRANBROOK

TOUR 56

FOREST AND SKY

Distance	106 km (66 miles)
Time	1 day
Rating	Intermediate
Terrain	Some long hills, frequent level stretches
Elev. gain	309 metres (1013 feet)
Roads	Good surface, good shoulders
Traffic	Light to moderate
Connections	Tours 55, 57, 60

This tour, though less dramatic than others in the region, offers the best southern connecting route between the Rockies and the Kootenays. You ride through wide forested valleys and a few tiny villages. Long climbs are interspersed with several flat, easy sections along the Goat and Moyie rivers. Winds can be gusty in places.

Be prepared for the remoteness of this stretch. Cyclists should fill their water bottles and carry water purification tablets.

Highlights

The Creston Valley is the beginning of a dry belt, dramatic change from the interior wetbelt forest. Fruit stands are abundant on the outskirts of Creston, providing a good chance to stock up for the isolated kilometres ahead.

The road is fairly busy and narrow at first. It soon widens and traffic drops off. Follow the Goat River with the low forested mountains of the Moyie Range ahead and to the right. Farmhouses appear now and then; little else except forest and sky fills this lonely landscape.

Idaho is just 11 km south of the junctions of Highways 3 and 95. In Prohibition days whiskey runners made Yahk a favorite rendezvous. The settlement was a major supplier of railway ties for the Canadian Pacific Railway. The Yahk hotel is now a heritage building.

Both wet and dry belts combine in an interesting micro-climate by long Moyie Lake, which once had its own steamship line. The southeastern pocket of British Columbia contains the richest variety of flora and fauna anywhere in this lush province. An interpretive program is provided in summer at the provincial campground at the north end of Moyie Lake, our recommended camping spot. Both Moyie Lake and Jimsmith Lake are fine for swimming.

The once-booming mining in-

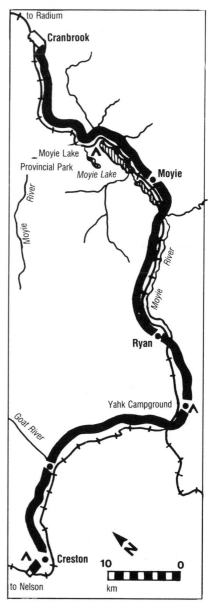

dustry of this region began in 1893 when a a Kootenay Indian named Pierre discovered a rich galena silver outcrop in nearby hills.

Cranbrook is the major supply centre of the East Kootenays. It was named after the English birthplace of James Baker, an early settler.

The city owes its prosperity to the decision of the Canadian Pacific Railway in 1898 to build its line through the community. Railroad buffs would enjoy a look at the ambitious Railway Museum and Gallery at 1 VanHorne St. It contains a complete collection of CPR luxury cars of the 1920s, including the dining car Argyle, complete with inlaid black walnut panelling, and a wooden caboose.

Hungry cyclists might stop at the Casa Dela Pasta for Italian food or the City Cafe on main street which has a salad bar.

Road Log Tour 56

0 km Creston. Pop. 4,190, elev. 611 m. All services. Creston Valley Museum. Tourist Information Centre, 1711 Canyon St., 604-428-4342. Head E on Hwy 3.

5 Erickson. Fruit stands, camping.

12 Road cuts through valley, with Moyie Range on right.

16 Bridge over Goat River.

26 Kidd Creek.

28 Begin climbing.

40 Moyie River. Turn left on Hwy 95. Tourism information. Ambleside Park, cabins, licensed restaurant, camping, swimming, some riverside sites, groceries, 424-5559. Fairly level cycling.

44 Yahk. Pop. 300, elev. 860 m. General store. Provincial campground on banks of Moyie River. Yahk Hotel, food served in pub, 424-5583.

47 Hay U Ranch. Store, motel, campground, 424-5556.

53 Begin climbing again. Moyie Range on left and Yahk Range of Purcells on right.

65 Descend.

75 Moyie Lake. Historic marker.

77 Moyie. Groceries, pub.

80 Climb begins.

87 Open grasslands.

89 Moyie Lake Provincial Park. Camping, 104 sites, picnicking, swimming, store 1 km left.

91 Moyie River Campground, private, store, reservations 489-3047. Dramatic views of Rockies to E.
Turnoff for Jimsmith Lake Provincial Park 4 km further, swimming, 59 campsites.

106 Cranbrook. Pop. 17,500, elev. 920 m. All services. Tourist information 489-5261. Railway Museum, 1 VanHorne St., 489-3918.

KIMBERLEY TO CRANBROOK TO FORT STEELE (LOOP)

LITTLE BAVARIA LOOP

Distance 92 km (57 miles)
Time 1 day
Rating Strenuous
Terrain Several long climbs and descents
Elev. change 351 metres (1151 feet)
Road Mostly good shoulders, narrow on 95A South
Traffic Mostly moderate or quiet
Connections Tours 56, 59, 60

You begin in Canada's highest city, recently transformed into Little Bavaria, descend to the St. Mary River and cross to Cranbrook. Then drop into the Rocky Mountain Trench for a visit to historic Fort Steele. The tour provides good views of the Rockies, the Purcells and extensive drybelt grasslands. It's a long but scenic climb back up to Kimberley.

The tour could easily take two days if you spend time at Fort Steele and Wasa Lake. Because of all the climbing, it is best tackled by strong cyclists.

Highlights

Begin with a look around the Bavarian Platzl in the centre of Kimberley. Residents energetically redid this unique shopping area in a Bavarian theme, right down to construction of the world's largest cuckoo clock.

Cycling is easy out of town. Stop to see Marysville Falls, 150 metres downstream from the highway bridge over Mary Creek. A footpath leads to a natural waterfall and canyon.

The countryside opens up ahead. The road threads through uplands of dry meadows and lodgepole and ponderosa pine, with views across the river to the Purcells.

The route traverses the edges of Cranbrook. Cyclists may enjoy seeing the railway museum in town. The high peaks of the Rockies rise to the west on the hilly descent into Fort Steele. Mt. Fisher is the most prominent peak at 9336 metres and The Steeples are to its right.

The turn-of-the-century East Kootenay town of Fort Steele has been recreated with painstaking care. You can shop on a restored frontier main street, enjoy live stage at the Wildhorse Theatre and home baking in the tea shop at the museum modelled after the Wasa Hotel.

Campbell Lake Recreational Area a few kilometres beyond, set

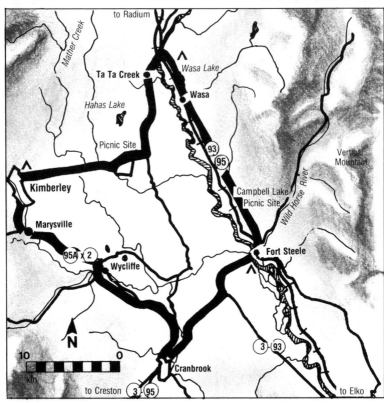

beside a small lake, makes a particularly pleasant picnic stop. Cycling is relatively easy as you enter the dry belt of the Skookumchuck Prairie. Wasa Lake Provincial Park, at the north end of the lake has one of the best recreational lakes in the East Kootenay. It has beaches, nature trails and interpretive programs, as well as camping.

The road narrows at the junction with Highway 95A South. Here the work really begins. It's up and down — but mostly up — all the way back to Kimberley.

Road Log Tour 57

0 km Kimberley city centre, 29 km N of Cranbrook on Hwy 95A. Pop. 7,700, elev. 1113 m, all services. Museum, Bavarian Platzl. Happy Hans Kampground, 1.6 km N on ski hill road. Follow signs S for Hwy 95A to Cranbrook.

6 Marysville. Falls, stores.

15 Big climb. Views over St. Mary River.

19 Descend to river.

20 Bridge.

27 Cranbrook. Pop. 17,500, elev. 920, all services. Skirt town and head W following signs for Radium. Long descent into Kootenay Valley.

30 Bottom of hill. Ascend.

31 Down again.

32 Turn left on on Hwy 93 N.

37 Steep descent.

38 Turn off 1 km for Fort Steele Campground. Private, 55 sites, 604-426-5117.

39 Kootenay River.

40 Fort Steele Provincial Historic Park.

41 Wildhorse Campground. Private, 115 sites, store, pool, laundromat, 489-4268. Begin easy, level cycling.

44 Campbell Lake Recreational Area. Picnic tables. Descent.

50 Entering flats of Skookumchuck prairie.

56 Wasa Wildlife Sanctuary.

60 Wasa. Cafe, accommodation.

62 Turnoff 1 km for Wasa Lake Provincial Park. Camping, swimming, hiking.

65 Kootenay River. Jct. with Hwys 95 & 93. Turn left on 95A South for Kimberley.

66 Begin climb.

68 Ta Ta Creek. Store, pub.

81 Rest area. Picnic tables.

92 Return Kimberley.

THE BAVARIAN CITY OF THE ROCKIES

Imagine a Canadian city where fire hydrants are painted to resemble little men in lederhosen, the world's largest cuckoo clock ticks away in the town square and most stores, even automobile showrooms, display timbered fronts.

Welcome to the Bavarianization of Kimberley. In the early 70s, merchants and residents of the mining city, disheartened at its decline, got the idea of transforming their community into a Bavarian-style burg so as to attract the tourist dollar.

The idea caught on rapidly. The city core became a pedestrian square and merchants of all sorts got out the Bavarian decorations.

Kimberley hosts an annual Julyfest the third weekend in July, complete with a beerfest. The International Old Time Accordion Championships are held the second weekend in July.

Places of interest include the Heritage Museum in the Platzl, Cominco Gardens by the hospital, and the terminal of the Bavarian City Mining Railway. In July and August the railway offers a 2.5-km trip with views over the city and the entrance to the famous Sullivan Mine. The ride begins at the end of the Happy Hans Kampground one km from the city centre on the road to the ski and summer resort.

ELKO TO CROWSNEST PASS

COAL SEAMS AND TRAGEDY

Distance	81 km (50 miles)
Time	1 day
Rating	Strenuous climb
Terrain	Gradual ascent along river for first portion. Moderately steep climb for last portion
Elev. gain	482 metres (1580 feet)
Roads	Good shoulder most of the way
Traffic	Fairly heavy. Many trucks
Connections	Tours 37, 51, 59

Ascend historic and tragic Crowsnest Pass, on a reasonable grade, most of the way. The tour passes through rugged mountains, past mining towns and the ruins of old mines. While the Crowsnest Pass tour is not as spectacular as the Banff-Windermere Highway or the Kicking Horse, it probably has more variety and history than any other route through the Canadian Rockies.

The highway, while busy, has a good, paved shoulder most of the way. The grades are generally easier compared with the Sinclair Canyon climb above Radium or the ascent of the Kicking Horse from Field.

Highlights

From Elko, the tour leaves the northern end of the Tobacco Plains and heads deep into the Rockies, following the Elk River. The CPR and Trans Mountain pipeline also follow this natural route, assurance of reasonable grades ahead. A short tunnel marks the entrance to the long valley. Big horn sheep are often found along the road, cut out from the side of the cliff above the river. For a few kilometres, the shoulder is frequently littered with small rocks that have fallen from the cliffs, forcing the cyclist out onto the main portion of the highway.

The tour passes between the Lizard Range to the north and Mt. Broadwood to the south and the valley soon widens although the road stays close to the river.

Fernie, established near a major coal seam after the railway was built through the valley in 1890, has a tragic history. In 1902, an explosion in the mine killed 128 men. In 1904, a fire which began in the general store destroyed the main portion of the town. Four years later, an explosion in the Coal Creek Mine trapped 23 miners. The very next day, strong winds fanned a fire west of Fernie and the sparks ignited the wooden buildings on the outskirts of town. It spread rapidly through

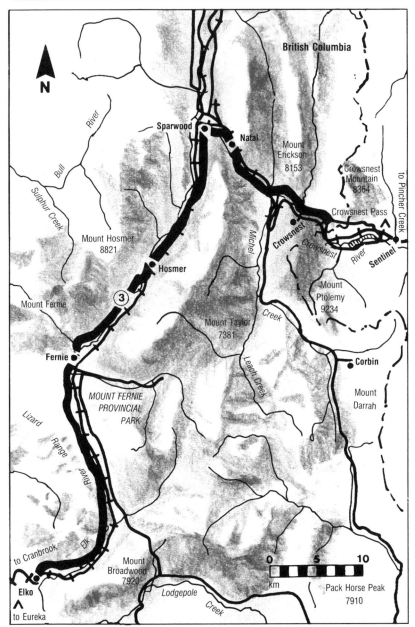

Fernie, destroying almost everything. The townspeople had no time to save their belongings; they could only grab the children and run for their lives. Most of the town of 6,000 was destroyed and the fire continued up the valley through Sparwood.

Fernie rebuilt — and still the earth rumbled. In 1917, another explosion at the Coal Creek Mine killed 34.

From Fernie, the highway runs through flat bottomland ringed by dramatic peaks. A few steep hills and much meandering lead to Sparwood and Natal where deserted mine buildings near the highway give evidence of this district's dramatic past. Here too is a story of fires and mine disasters, beginning in 1902 when a blaze swept a major portion of town. Then in 1904, seven miners were killed in an explosion. Another in 1916, killed 12 more. And once again, in 1938, an explosion killed three.

Beyond Sparwood, the road leaves the Elk River and the climbing becomes steeper up fire-scarred slopes, the road passing through narrow cuts. The railway makes a wide loop along Michel Creek to gain elevation gradually while the highway goes more or less directly up. Ahead is craggy Crowsnest Mountain to the left of the highway and Mt. Ptolemy to the right.

The 1,396-metre pass marks the Continental Divide and the boundary between Alberta and British Columbia. The pass may have been named after the Crow Indians who lived east of here. More likely the name simply came from an actual crowsnest that an early traveller noticed hereabouts.

This relatively easy passage through the southern Rockies had long been used by Indians. The Palliser Expedition of 1860 indicated it on their maps but only from what they had heard about it from the Indians. The first recorded crossing by white men was in 1873 by Michael Phillips who had a ranch near Elko, the first homesteader in the East Kootenay. Prospecting for gold, he turned east up the Elk River and topped the pass, thereby becoming the first white man to cross these mountains from west to east through an unexplored pass. But there was no gold. Phillips was disgusted to find nothing but coal.

Road Log Tour 58

0 km Jct. Hwy 3 and 93. Elev. 914 m. Elko is 2 km to E. Kilomum Creek Provincial Park is 9 km ahead: N on 93 for 1 km, then W on paved side road. For Crowsnest Pass, turn E on Hwy 3. Climbing.

2 Elko. All services. Continue on wide shoulder.

17 Morrissey Regional Park. No camping.

28 Turnoff Mt. Fernie Provincial Park.

31 Elk River bridge. Entering Fernie, pop. 7,500, elev. 1009 m. All services. Historical museum at 5th St and 5th Ave.

33 Bridge. Leaving Fernie.

42 Motel/campground.
Climbing.
49 Picnic area.
56 End of climb.
59 Industrial development.
61 Sparwood. Mine tours
(July and August),
undeveloped mineral

springs. All services.
76 Steep climb.
81 Crowsnest Pass. Elev.
1396. Alberta-B.C.
boundary and Continen-
tal Divide. Provincial
campground 2 km E.

ELKO TO
FORT STEELE

THE DEWDNEY TRAIL

Distance	60 km (37 miles)
Time	1/2 to 1 day, allowing time for Fort Steele
Rating	Moderate
Terrain	Several long hills, remainder mostly level
Roads	Busy section has adequate shoulder. None for quiet section
Traffic	Usually quiet, except Elko to Kootenay River which is busier
Connections	Tours 51, 57, 58, 60

From Elko, cyclists follow a portion of the historic Dewdney Trail on which thousands of prospectors came north in the late 1860s after gold was discovered on Wild Horse Creek near Fort Steele. The trail leads up the Rocky Mountain Trench with the Lizard Range of the Rockies on the right and the McGillivray Range of the Purcell Mountains to the left. From the Kootenay River, the route climbs to good viewpoints overlooking the wide valley, passes an excellent provincial park campground at Norbury Lake and ends at Fort Steele, a ghost town tranformed into a first-rate heritage village representing lifestyles of the 1890s.

Highlights

From the junction of Highways 93 and 3, the route is mostly level up the broad Kootenay Valley, though still far from the river. Just past the junction, a paved road leads left for 8 km to the large, well-appointed Kilomun Creek Provincial Park, a good spot for swimming, camping and picnicking. Cyclists can use the paved back road between the park and Jaffrey as a quieter alternative to Highways 3-93.

The main highway leads past the turnoff to Jaffrey and finally descends to the Kootenay River at the top of long Lake Koocanusa.

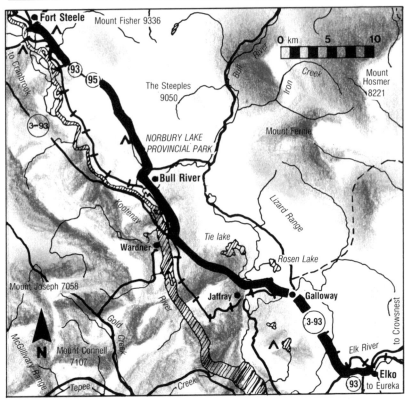

Unless heading for Cranbrook and points west, don't neglect to take the side road right before the bridge. The route past Norbury Lake is much more interesting than the main road and is usually quiet. It reflects what cycling is all about.

The road heads through open rangeland and begins to climb from the river, passing a trout hatchery, leading towards the striking peaks of The Steeples. Norbury Lake Provincial Park just off the road to the left has a good campground and a separate picnic area on another lake across the highway.

From the junction with Highway 93, it's only 1 km south to Fort Steele Historic Park, which shouldn't be missed.

This turn-of-the-century East Kootenay town has been recreated with exceptional care. You can almost visualize Supt. Sam Steele of the North West Mounted Police riding down the dirt streets to quell a dispute between settlers and the Indians in 1887.

You can shop on a restored frontier main street, enjoy live stage at the Wildhorse Theatre, or sample delicious home baking in the tea shop at the Wasa Hotel.

Road Log Tour 59

0 km Jct. Hwy 3 and 93. Elko is 2 km to E. All services. For Fort Steele, turn N on Hwy 3-93. Small shoulder.

2 Turnoff 8 km (paved) to Kilomum Creek Provincial Park.

6 Rock Lake Campground. Rest area, picnic tables.

12 Galloway. Cafe, store, motel.

16 Jaffrey turnoff. Cafe, store, motel.

27 Kootenay River. Before bridge, turn right onto paved road leading to fish hatchery and Norbury Lake Provincial Park. No shoulder.

35 Fish hatchery. Steep ascent.

37 Top of hill.

43 Norbury Lake Provincial Park Campground.

44 Norbury lake picnic area.

52 Begin descent.

58 End descent.

59 Wildhorse Campground and store (604-489-4268).

59 Jct. Hwy 93. Turn left for Fort Steele. Turn right for Invermere-Radium.

60 Fort Steele Historic Park. Free admission. Fort Steele Campground (426-5117) 2 km S acrosss river and 700 metres on hwy. Cook shelter.

CRANBROOK TO RADIUM

ROCKIES HO

Distance	138 km (88 miles)
Time	1 to 2 days
Rating	Intermediate
Terrain	Some long climbs interspersed with level stretches
Elev. gain	112 metres (367 feet)
Roads	Good condition, good shoulders
Traffic	Light to moderate
Connections	Tours 16, 56, 57, 59

You cycle from Cranbrook on an undulating road into the Canadian Rockies. The tour passes historic Fort Steele, heads into the dry grasslands and then the logging country of the Columbia River Valley.

Bicycle wheels seem almost to whisper by the beautiful Columbia and Windermere lakes and the pretty town of Invermere. There are few towns along the way; the ride has a rich backwoods flavour.

Take your choice of two hot springs, at Fairmont and Radium.

Highlights

Begin at Cranbrook, hub of the East Kootenays. The Railway Museum here is situated in restored CPR passenger cars from the 1929 "Trans-Canada Ltd.", one of the most luxurious trains of that era. Inlaid walnut and mahogany panelling, original china, silver, glassware and furniture are featured. Open 9 a.m. to 8 p.m. daily, June to August, 1 Van Horne St. North.

The Rockies rise ahead as you leave the city. There are a number of long hills between here and Fort Steele. The fort stands on a bluff overlooking the Kootenay River with Mt. Fisher prominent to the east.

The fort is a fine reconstruction of a turn-of-the century East Kootenay town. You can easily spend half a day at this provincial historic park (admission free), perhaps taking in a performance at the Wildhorse Theatre. Had the CPR not bypassed Fort Steele at the turn of the century in favour of Cranbrook, it would likely have become the pre-eminent city of the East Kootenays instead of a ghost town.

Cycling is mostly level and easy north of Fort Steele, and traffic is usually quiet. Tiny Campbell Lake, backdropped by snow-capped mountains, makes a lovely rest stop.

Enjoy an inspiring descent onto the Kootenay River flats, a grassland drybelt dotted with sagebrush. Wasa Lake Provincial Park is one of the best recreational parks in the East Kootenays. Look for some of the tastiest honey in Canada at the rustic grocery store and restaurant in Skookumchuck. The honey comes from nearby Sheep Creek Farm Apiaries, winners of the highest honors at a recent Royal Winter Fair in Toronto.

The cyclist will encounter a few climbs and long descents into Canal Flats, a small logging community nearly devastated by forest fires in 1985.

This is the beginning of Columbia Lake, crossed by early geographer David Thompson in 1808. Thunderhill Provincial Park, with views over the lake, makes a pleasant camping spot.

The going from here to Invermere is easy. Note the option of following the quieter, more scenic West Side Road to Invermere above Lake Windermere, although generally out of sight of it. The main route passes the luxurious resort community of Fairmont Hot Springs, up a steep hill from the highway. The next 16 kilometres are fairly flat and uneventful with few views of Lake Windermere, as the road passes through the Columbia Indian Reserve.

Invermere, a couple of kilometres off the main highway, has an interesting museum housed in pioneer log cabins and a log CPR station. Cyclists wanting a splurge meal might head to The Strand Restaurant, in a gracious old house just up from the main drag on 12th Street. Or find picnic fixin's at the Alpen Meats and Delicatessen.

Those heading on to Lake Louise or Banff on the Banff-Windermere Highway should consider making their overnight stop hereabouts, as campgrounds by Radium either do not accept tents or else demand a steep climb. The long, difficult climb from Radium to Sinclair Pass should probably be tackled early in the day when the cyclist is fresh.

The last few kilometres into Radium involve a long descent, often in busy traffic. This is the last major supply point for more than 100 kilometres north.

Cyclists who choose to camp at Redstreak, a national park campground, will face a stiff grind up. There is a compensation — from the campground you can walk along an almost level trail to the hot springs. Cyclists heading up Sinclair Pass can use this trail from the campground as a shortcut (you're supposed to walk your bike), saving considerable climbing from the main highway.

Otherwise, the climb from the town of Radium to the Aquacourt

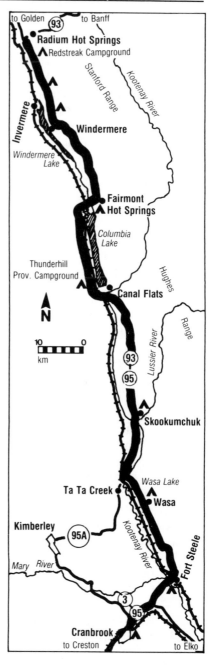

just inside Kootenay National Park is steep and narrow. Here you can soak in waters ranging in temperature from 35 degrees C (95 F) to 47 degrees C (117 F). You might even see mountain sheep grazing close to the pool.

Road Log Tour 60

0 km Cranbrook. Pop. 17,500, elev. 920 m. All services. Tourist information, 604-489-5261. Railway Museum, 1 Van Horne St., 489-3918. Head NE on Hwy 95 N (3 E). Long descent into Kootenay Valley.

3 Bottom of hill. Ascend.

4 Down again.

5 Turn right on Hwy 93 N.

10 Steep descent.

11 Turnoff 1 km for Fort Steele Campground, 55 sites, 426-5117.

12 Kootenay River.

13 Fort Steele Provincial Historic Park. Free admission.

14 Wildhorse Campground, 115 sites, groceries, pool, laundromat, 489-4268. Begin easy, level cycling.

17 Campbell Lake Recreational Area. Picnic tables.
Descent.

23 Entering flats of Skookumchuck Prairie.

29 Wasa Wildlife Sanctuary.

33 Wasa. Cafe, accommodation.

35 Turnoff 1 km for Wasa Lake Provincial Park. Camping, swimming, hiking.

38 Kootenay River. Jct with Hwys 95 & 93. Keep straight.

42 Rest area.

44 Echo Inn, restaurant.

53 Skookumchuck. Accommodation, restaurant, camping.

54 Start ascent, levels.

69 Long downhill.

72 Canal Flats. Accommodation, groceries, picnicking.

75 S end of Columbia Lake, headwaters of Columbia River.

78 Thunderhill Provincial Park. Camping, 23 sites, views of lake.

81 Mountain Village licensed restaurant.

84 Viewpoint. Rest area and picnic tables.

87 Long downhill.

90 Dutch Creek.

91 Hoodoos Mountain Resort. Cabins, campsites, store, 345-6631.

92 OPTION: Turnoff left on West Side Road for quiet alternate route to Invermere.

93 Spruce Grove Resort. Motel, campground, store, 345-6561.

94 Long hill.

95 Fairmont Hot Springs Resort. No tenting, hot springs 2 km up, stores, lodge, saunas for hotel guests only, 345-6311.

96 Fairmount Bungalows. 345-6365. Level cycling along Columbia Indian Reserve.

112 Twin Range Campground.

113 Turnoff 3 km for Athalmer Beach on N end of Windermere Lake. Sandy beach, picnicking, groceries, restaurant, no camping.

123 Visitor Information and turnoff left for Town of Invermere. Pop. 1969, all services, museum.

129 Dry Gulch. Camping.

130 Groceries.

133 Viewpoint, picnic tables.

135 Radium. Pop. 1,000, elev. 808, all services. Campers turn right at sign for Redstreak Campground. Otherwise turn right at Jct. with Hwy 93. Steep climb.

137 Kootenay National Park information centre. Entering Sinclair Canyon.

138 Radium Hot Springs Aquacourt. Hot springs, cool pool, cafeteria.

Fort Steele

The Kootenay Gold Rush of 1864, sparked by rich placer diggings on Wildhorse Creek, lured thousands of fortune seekers into this quiet valley. John Galbraith, an Irishman, saw that they needed an easy way to cross the Kootenay River — and Galbraith's Ferry was born.

Within a year, the gold became too expensive to retrieve and the miners moved on. Settlers gradually appeared after the Canadian Pacific Railway reached Golden.

In 1887, Superintendent Sam Steele and 75 North West Mounted Police were called in to Galbraith's Ferry to quell hostilities between the settlers and Kootenay Indians over land ownership. Steele restored equanimity without firing a bullet, and the force departed in 1888. Galbraith's Ferry changed its name to Fort Steele in his honor.

During the next decade, Fort Steele boomed on the crest of huge silver-lead discoveries in the East Kootenays. But bust followed boom. When the railway bypassed Fort Steele for Cranbrook at the turn of the century, the fort soon became a forgotten settlement.

Then in 1961, the British Columbia government established Fort Steele as a provincial heritage park. The restoration and renovation of Fort Steele into a typical turn-of-the-century East Kootenay town, with more than 40 buildings, has been meticulous and imaginative.

You can watch a pioneer paper being printed on an old press, visit a pioneer woman's home to watch quilting, baking or spinning, or take in a production at the Wildhorse Theatre, B.C.'s largest indoor summer theatre, to name only a few of the attractions.

The museum, modelled after the Wasa Hotel, has a Tea Room featuring home-baking and light lunches.

Tiger Lily   TRAVEL ALBERTA

Appendix

TRAVEL INFORMATION ALBERTA

Travel Alberta
Box 2500
Edmonton, Alta. T5J 2Z4
Toll-free information on travel conditions, campgrounds, accommodation, attractions and special events. Within Alberta: 1-800-222-6501. In Edmonton only: 427-4321. From across Canada: 1-800-661-8888; from British Columbia and rural Saskatchewan: 112-800-661-8888.

An Alberta accommodation guide, touring guide and adventure guide are available free.

Kananaskis Country

Suite 412
1011 Glenmore Trail S.W.
Calgary, Alta. T2V 4R6
403-297-3362
Information, maps and brochures.

BRITISH COLUMBIA

Tourism British Columbia
1117 Wharf Street
Victoria, B.C. V8W 2Z2
604-387-1642

Seasonal Information Centres

Golden B.C.
(Highway 1, 0.8 km East)
604-344-5666

Mt. Robson Provincial Park
(No phone)

Banff, Alberta
224 Banff Ave. (Parks information centre)
403-762-5656

Other Tourist Information

Kootenay Boundary Visitors'
Association
P.O. Box 172
Nelson, B.C. V1L 5P9
604-365-8461

British Columbia Rocky Mountain Visitors' Association
Box 10, Kimberley, B.C. V1A 2Y5
604-427-7469

MONTANA

Glacier National Park
West Glacier, Mt. 59936
406-888-5441

Apgar Visitor Centre (Glacier)
Apgar Village, 3 km from West
Glacier
406-888-5512

St. Mary Visitor Centre (Glacier)
East entrance to park
406-732-4424

Travel Montana
Department of Commerce
1429 9th Avenue
Helena, Mt. 59620
1-800-5483390

United States Forest Service
Northern Region
P.O. Box 7669
Missoula, Mt. 59807

Campground Owners Association
of Montana
c/o KOA of Harve
Rt 36, Box KOA
Harve, Mt. 59501
406-265-50120

PARKS CANADA

Information Service
Parks Canada
220-4th Ave. S.E.
Calgary, Alta. T2P 3H8
Information on Canada's Rocky
Mountain national parks.

Banff National Park

The Superintendent
Banff National Park
Box 900
Banff, Alta. T0L 0C0
403-762-3324

Banff/Lake Louise Chamber of
Commerce
Box 1298
Banff, Alta. T0L 0C0
403-762-4646/762-3777

Banff Information Centre
224 Banff Ave.
403-762-4256.

Banff Warden Office
403-762-4506
Situated between townsite and
highway interchange, open 24 hours

Lake Louise Warden Office
403-522-3866
Visitor Centre, Lake Louise

JASPER NATIONAL PARK

The Superintendent
Jasper National Park
Box 10
Jasper, Alta. T0E 1E0
403-852-6161

Jasper Park Chamber of
Commerce
Box 98
Jasper, Alta. T0E 1E0
403-852-3858

Jasper Information Centre
Connaught Drive, Jasper townsite
403-852-6176

Warden Office
Off the Maligne Road
8 km east of Jasper townsite
Near Sixth Bridge
403-852-6156

KOOTENAY
NATIONAL PARK

The Superintendent
Kootenay National Park
Box 220
Radium Hot Springs, B.C.
V0A IM0
604-347-9615

YOHO NATIONAL
PARK

The Superintendent
Yoho National Park
Box 99,
Field, B.C. V0A IG0
604-343-6324

MOUNT
REVELSTOKE
AND GLACIER
NATIONAL PARKS

The Superintendent
Mount Revelstoke and Glacier
national parks

Box 350
Revelstoke, B.C. V0E 2S0
604-837-5155

WATERTON
LAKES NATIONAL
PARK

The Superintendent
Waterton Lakes National Park
Waterton Park, Alberta
T0K 2M0
403-859-2262

Waterton Information Bureau
In Waterton Townsite
403-859-2445

RAIL SERVICE

VIA Rail (Canada)
1-800-665-8630
Service from Montreal, Toronto
and Vancouver to Banff, Lake
Louise, Field and Revelstoke on
CPR line and to Edmonton, Hinton
and Jasper on CNR line

Amtrak (U.S.)
1-800-872-7245
Service from Chicago and Seattle
to Whitefish, Belton (West Glacier)
and Glacier Park (East Glacier),
Montana

MAPS
Topographical and
Access Maps

Alberta-Bureau of Surveys
2nd Floor
Petroleum Plaza
9945-108th St.
Edmonton, Alta. T5K 2G6
403-427-3520

British Columbia — Map and Air
Photo Sales
Ministry of the Environment
Parliament Buildings
Victoria, B.C. V8V 1X5

Canada Map Office
615 Booth St.
Ottawa, Ont. K1A 0E9

Free Highway Map

Travel Alberta
Box 2500
Edmonton, Alta. T5J 2Z4

BICYCLE DEALERS, REPAIRS AND RENTALS

Banff

Park 'N' Pedal
229 Wolf Street
403-762-3191
(includes rentals)

Spoke 'N' Edge
315 Banff Ave.
403-762-2854
(includes rentals, also one-way
rentals to Jasper for Icefields
cyclists)

Canmore

Inside Lane Sporting Goods
Ste. 5 1000 - 7 Avenue
403-678-2553

Outdoor Adventure Centre
Highway 1 West
403-678-2000
(includes mountain bike rentals)

Cranbrook

Kade Cycle and Sports
1107 Baker
604-426-4641

Sun 'N' Powder Sports
230-1500 Cranbrook N.
(Tamarack Mall)
604-489-4701

Kootenay Cycle and Sports Ltd.
1817 Cranbrook St.
604-426-2525

Creston

Creston Cycle and Ski
219-10th Avenue N.
604-428-2511
(includes rentals)

Golden

Selkirk Sports
523 East 9th Ave.
604-344-2966

Invermere

BJ's Sports Emporium
1313-7th Ave.
604-342-3239

West Side Cycle
1756-7th Ave.
604-342-6488

Jasper

Freewheel Cycle
600 Patricia St.
403-852-5380

Jasper Mountain Bikes
Box 1365
403-852-5252

Mountain Air Sports
622 Connaught Dr.
403-852-3760
(includes rentals, one-way rentals
to Banff for Icefields cyclists)

Sandy's Rentals
Jasper Park Lodge
(By swimming pool)
403-852-5708
(Rentals only, includes tandems)

Kananaskis

Mt. Kidd RV Campground
Kananaksis Country
(Rentals only)
403-591-7700

Boulton Trading Post
Peter Lougheed Provincial Park
(mountain bike rentals only)
403-591-7577

Kimberley

Bavarian Sports and Hardware
Ltd.
235 Spokane
604-427-2667

Rocky Mountain Sports
185 Deer Park Ave.
604-427-3877

Lethbridge

Alpenland Ski and Sports
1289 - 3 Ave.
403-329-6099

Bridge Cycle
210- 12A St. N
403-329-6622

Gotschna Ski Haus Ltd.
80 - 2 Ave. S
403-329-6655

Nakusp

Green Door Sport
Corner, Broadway and 3rd Ave.
W.
604-265-4013
(includes rentals)

Nelson

Tu-Dor Sports
737 Baker
604-352-3677 (main)
604-352-3245 (repairs)

Revelstoke

Revelstoke Cycle Shop
120 Mackenzie Ave.
(In alley between Regent Inn
and Revelstoke Review)
Bus:604-837-2648
Res.604-837-2588
(includes rentals)

Waterton

Pat's Texaco
(just behind marina)
(mountain bike rentals)
604-859-2266

BICYCLE CLUBS AND BICYCLE TOURING INFORMATION

Alberta Bicycling Association
Ste. 302, 1711 - 26 Ave SW
Calgary, Alta. T2T 1C9
(bike club information, ride
  schedules)

Bicycle Association of British
Columbia
1200 Hornby St.
Vancouver, B.C. V6Z 2E2
604-669-BIKE
Bicycle hotline, specific inquiries
or requests for individual routing
will be answered as time allows;
send $3 or three international reply
coupons and allow 2 to 4 weeks for
reply.

Bikecentennial
P.O. Box 8308
Missoula, Montana 59807
406-721-1776
Touring information for U.S. and
parts of Canada, including routes
into Canadian Rockies. Mail-order
book service, magazine.

Canadian Cycling Association
333 River Road
Tower A, 11th Floor
Vanier, Ont. K1L 8H9
613-746-0060
(touring information)
(Note: Tourism British Columbia
publishes a free information sheet
on cycling in that province, available
on request. Address in travel information section.)

Creston Cycling Club
P.O. Box 2595 VOB 1GO

Edmonton Bicycle and Touring
Club
Box 5295, Postal Station S
Edmonton, Alta. T6E 4T3
403-473-2645
(group tours, newsletter)

Elbow Valley Cycle Club
225 - 10 St. NW
Calgary, Alta. T2V 1V5
(group tours, newsletter)

GUIDED TOURS

Alberta Hostelling Association
c/o Western Canadian Travel
Consultants
Box 96
Red Deer, Alta.
403-340-0292

Bikecentennial
Box 8308
Missoula, Montana
U.S.A. 59807
406-721-1776

Kootenay Mountain Bike Tours
Box 867
Nelson, B.C. V1L 6A5
604-354-4371

Rocky Mountain Cycle Tours
Box 895
Banff, Alta. T0L 0C0
403-762-3477

LUXURY ACCOMMODATION

Banff Springs Hotel
Spray Ave.
Box 860
Banff, Alta. T0L 0C0
403-762-2211

Chateau Lake Louise
Lake Louise, Alta. 0L 1E0
403-522-3511

Jasper Park Lodge
Jasper, Alta. T0E 1E0
403-852-3301

Prince of Wales Hotel
Waterton Park T0K 2M0
406-226-5551l

Glacier Park Lodge
Greyhound Tower
Station 5510
Phoenix, Ariz. 85077
602-248-6000
(Mid-September to mid-May)
or
East Glacier Park, Mt. 59434
406-226-5551
(Mid-May to mid-September)

Emerald Lake Lodge
Emerald Lake, Yoho
Reservations 1-800-661-1367

BED AND BREAKFAST ACCOMMODATION

Alberta Bed and Breakfast
4327-86th St.
Edmonton, Alta. 6K 1A9
403-462-8885
Locations at Calgary, Cochrane, Bragg Creek, Canmore, Hinton, Edmonton

Bed and Breakfast Bureau
Box 7094, Station E.
Calgary, Alta. T3C 3L8
403-242-5555

Banff-Canmore-Lake Louise
Box 369
Banff, Alta.T0L 0C0
403-762-5070

HOSTELS

The Alberta Hostelling Association operates a chain of youth hostels along the Icefields Parkway between Banff and Jasper. Open to all; reduced overnight fees available through annual membership. Reservations advised in summer and holiday weekends; essential for groups.

Southern Alberta Hostelling
Association
1414 Kensington Road. N.W.
Calgary, Alta. T2N 3P9
403-283-5551
Reservations for southern district hostels. Administration office, hostel shop, memberships, reservations, hostel information brochure available

Northern Alberta District
10926-88th Ave.
Edmonton, Alta. T6E 0Z1
403-439-3089
Reservations for northern district hostels. Administration office, hostel shop, memberships, hostel information brochure available

Ribbon Creek Hostel
403-591-7333
24 km S. of Hwy 1 along Kananaskis Rd. (Hwy 40). Accommodates 40, family rooms available. Closed Tues. in winter

Calgary International Hostel
520 - 7 Ave S.E.
Calgary, Alta. T2G 0J6
403-269-8239
Accommodates 114. Snack bar, laundry facilities, meeting room, cycle workshop

Banff International Hostel
403-762-4122
3 km from Banff townsite on Tunnel Mountain Rd., new building, accommodates 150 persons, family rooms available, cafeteria, cooking and laundry, accessible to handicapped

Spray River Hostel
3.5 km S. of Banff Springs Hotel on Spray River Fire Rd. Accommodates 47 persons, meals, groceries, outdoor shower, bicycle and cross-country ski rentals. Closed Thursday nights. Reservations through Calgary.

Castle Mountain Hostel
403-762-2367
On Hwy 1A, 1.5 km E. of Junction of Hwys 1 and 93. Accommodates 40 persons, meals, groceries available. Closed Wednesday nights. Reservations through Calgary.

Corral Creek Hostel
6.6 km E. of Lake Louise on Hwy 93. Accommodates 50 persons, closed Monday nights. Reservations through Calgary.

Whiskey Jack Hostel
Near end of Takakkaw Falls Road, Yoho National Park. Open mid-June to mid-September. Reservations through Calgary.

Mosquito Creek Hostel
26 km N. of Lake Louise on Hwy 93. Accommodates 30 people, wood-heated sauna available. Closed Tuesday nights. Reservations through Calgary

Rampart Creek Hostel
On Hwy 93, 20 km N. of Jct. with Hwy 11. Accommodates 30 persons, wood-heated sauna available. Closed Wednesday nights in winter. Reservations through Calgary

Hilda Creek Hostel
8.5 km S. of Columbia Icefields Centre on Hwy 93. Accommodates 19 persons, meals and limited groceries. Closed Thurday nights.

Beauty Creek Hostel
86.5 km S. of Jasper townsite on Hwy 93A. Accommodates 20. Closed Thursday nights in summer. Key system from mid-Sept. to April 30. Reservations through Edmonton.

Athabasca Falls Hostel
32 km S. of Jasper townsite on Hwy 93A. Accommodates 40. Closed Tuesday nights. Reservations through Edmonton.

Mt. Edith Cavell Hostel
13 km off Hwy 93A along steep Mt. Edith Cavell Rd. Accommodates 30. Winter access by cross-country skiing.
Closed Wednesday nights. Reservations through Edmonton.

Whistlers Mountain Hostel
7 km S. of Jasper townsite on Whistler Mtn. Rd. Accommodates 50. Reservations through Edmonton.

Maligne Canyon Hostel
15 km E. of Jasper townsite on Maligne Lake Rd. Accommodates 24, family rooms available. Closed Wednesday nights. Reservations through Edmonton.

Shunda Creek Hostel
Near Nordegg, 3 km N of Highway 11. Accommodates 44, family rooms available. Reservations through Edmonton.

METRIC CONVERSION

Canada is on the metric system. To convert kilometres to miles, multiply by 0.6. To convert metres to feet, multiply by 3.3

ABOUT THE AUTHORS

John Dodd and Gail Helgason have been cycling in the Canadian Rockies for more than a decade, sometimes combining those trips with canoeing, kayaking or hiking. They have also cycle-toured extensively in Britain, Ireland, Continental Europe, Eastern Canada, New England and the southwestern United States.

Both former outdoor columnists, they are the authors of Bicycle Alberta, the first book about bicycle touring in the province and The Canadian Rockies Access Guide which describes 103 day hikes and opportunities for a variety of other outdoor activities. Both books are published by Lone Pine. They have also written for numerous outdoor publications, including Outside, Bicycling and Nature Canada.

They are married and live in Edmonton, beside a bicycle path. Both write for The Edmonton Journal.

Index